Vision of Advaita Vedānta
in Taittirīya Upaniṣad

Vision of Advaita Vedānta in Taittirīya Upaniṣad

With Special Reference to Śāṅkarabhāṣya

Swamini Atmaprajnananda Saraswati

DK PRINTWORLD
Publishers of Indian Traditions

Cataloging in Publication Data — DK
[Courtesy: D.K. Agencies (P) Ltd. <docinfo@dkagencies.com>]

Atmaprajnananda Saraswati, 1955-, **author.**
Vision of Advaita Vedānta in Taittirīya Upaniṣad : with special reference to Śāṅkarabhāṣya / Swamini Atmaprajnananda Saraswati.
pages cm
Includes selected text of Taittirīyopaniṣad and Taittirīyopaniṣadbhāṣya in Sanskrit (roman).
Includes bibliographical references (pages).
ISBN 9788124608531

1. Advaita. 2. Vedanta. 3. Upanishads. Taittirīyopaniṣad – Criticism, interpretation, etc. 4. Śaṅkarācārya. Taittirīyopaniṣadbhāsya. I. Śaṅkarācārya. Taittirīyopaniṣadbhāsya. Selections. II. Upanishads. Taittirīyopaniṣad. Selections. III. Title.

DDC 294.59218 23

ISBN 978-81-246-0853-1
First published in India, 2016

Printed and published by:
D.K. Printworld (P) Ltd.
Regd. Office: Vedaśrī, F-395, Sudarshan Park
(Metro Station: Ramesh Nagar), New Delhi – 110 015
Phones: (011) 2545 3975, 2546 6019; Fax: (011) 2546 5926
e-mail: indology@dkprintworld.com
Website: www.dkprintworld.com

SWAMI DAYANANDA SARASWATI

Foreword

Swāmini Ātmaprajnānada Saraswati is my disciple, bright and very highly committed to *śāstra*. She has been studying with me and other Ācāryas since 1996. She understands the intricate methodologies employed in the unfoldment of Vedanta well. I am sure her book, "Vision of Advaita Vedanta as reflected in Taittirīyopaniṣad with special reference to Śāṅkarabhāṣya" will be of great help to all those who are studying Advaita, whether in the Gurukulams or Universities, or in other settings.

Arsha Vidya Gurukulam, Anaikatti (P.O), Coimbatore 641 108 INDIA Tel : +91 422 265 7001 / 265 7007
Swami Dayananda Ashram, Purani Jhari, Rishikesh 249 201 INDIA Tel : +91 135 243 0769 / 243 6769
Arsha Vidya Gurukulam, P.O Box 1059, Saylorsburg, PA 18353 USA Tel : +1 570 992 2339 Email : sakshat49@gmail.com

Preface

īśvara anugrahāt eva puṁsām advaita-vāsanā ।

My interest in Advaita Vedānta is a personal one, and this book is the outcome of my study over a number of years in traditional *gurukulam*. I began studying Advaita Vedānta twenty years ago in 1996, when I had the good fortune to sit at the feet of my Spiritual Guru His Holiness Swami Dayananda Saraswati.

Since Upaniṣads are *śabda-pramāṇa*, I have retained certain words without translating such as *ānanda* and *mithyā*. I have also refrained from using the popular translations, i.e. illusion, realization, bliss and supreme, since they do not convey the same meaning to everyone.

In the translation and commentary, the words/sentences in Sanskrit are given in italics in the main body or in the footnotes. These are followed by English equivalents. Citations are given in the footnotes, and informative explanatory notes have been added as endnotes especially for the Chapters 5. Śīkṣāvallī, 6. Brahmānandavallī, and 7. Bhṛguvallī. These three chapters (5-7) are the bulk of the book where free translations of the Upaniṣad are given. My acknowledgement and profuse gratitude to Swami Swahanada's *Taittirīyopaniṣad*, whose explanations I have used as endnotes in these three *vallīs*.

I consider Chapters 2, 4, 8 and 9 as the significant chapters of this book. Chapter 2 gives adequate details of the six *pramāṇas*, which are very important to understand the significance of *śabda-pramāṇa*. Chapter 4 is the crux of the whole book, where I have analysed Śaṅkara's commentary on *Taittirīya*. The *Bhāṣyam*

I feel requires more than one time studying, since there are layers of understanding. A cursory study of this Upaniṣad may skip the depth of the commentary. Chapter 8, Vision of Advaita Vedānta, is the most important chapter where I have given my understanding of the triangle of the *jīva*, *jagat* and *Īśvara*. Chapter 9 explains the method of deciphering the *mahāvākyas*.

One may go through the thesis in the order of the chapters. Alternatively, one may go through Chapter 8 "Vision of Advaita Vedānta", Chapter 4 on *Taittirīya-Bhāṣyam*, which will be beneficial in understanding the deep layers of Advaita Vedānta in detail. These chapters should prove sufficient, and I look upon these as forming the principal chapters of the book. This approach will give the reader a good background on Advaita Vedānta.

I have closely used the source literature to the maximum. I do not pretend to have addressed and clarified all the terminological and other difficulties that stand in the way of a student in clearly comprehending their meanings. I however believe that I have been able to surface the nuances of *Taittirīya-Bhāṣyam*. I hope this work will be of great value to students of Advaita Vedānta who wish to have a better understanding of the great tradition that is Advaita Vedānta.

I bow down with reverential gratitude to all the great masters of Advaita Vedānta of the past, from whom I have learnt indirectly through their texts, and of present being my Spiritual Guru, His Holiness Swami Dayananda Saraswati (1930–2015) from whom I have directly learnt. In this context, I am reminded of the following couplet:

yad-atra dūṣaṇaṁ kiñcit, tan-na teṣāṁ, mamaiva tat ।
yad-atra bhūsaṇaṁ kiñcit, tattu teṣāṁ, na vai mama ॥

Whatever deficiency found in this work, does not belong to those masters, rather it is mine, whereas whatever clarity found in this work belongs to them and not to me.

It is difficult to put in words what I owe to my Spiritual Guru Pujya Swami Dayananda Saraswati, under whose feet I studied the Upaniṣads, *Bhagavadgītā*, Catussūtrī of *Brahmasūtra* and many Prakaraṇa Granthas. My eternal gratitude to Pujya Swami Dayananda Saraswatiji who so kindly wrote the Foreword to this book.

My gratitude to Swami Swahananda's *Taittirīyopaniṣad*, whose explanations I have used as endnotes in three chapters of this text.

My deep appreciation for Dr Satish and Shri Sugavanam Krishnan for having gone through the manuscript minutely and suggesting changes, and Medha Michika who so kindly worked out the *rūpasiddhi* of "Upaniṣad".

My grateful thanks to Shri Akshay Kumar, for nursing me back to health through Jindal Naturecure Institute, and Smt. Payal Parija, for her consistent support during my years of studies and research.

I put forward my special gratitude to Shri Susheel Kumar Mittal, Director, D.K. Printworld, for his continuing support in publishing my work. But for his support and encouragement this work would not have reached the readers so soon.

Makara Saṅkrānti **Atmaprajnananda Saraswati**
15 January 2016

Contents

Acknowledgement

AT the outset, I express my profound gratitude to *Īśvara* in the form of Lord Śrī Medhā Dakṣiṇāmūrti for the successful completion of this book.

I deeply appreciate DDCE of Utkal University, Vani Vihar, which enabled me to complete my Masters in Sanskrit. After successful completion of my MA, all my teachers of PG Department of Sanskrit, Utkal University, individually mentioned below, inspired me to pursue my Ph.D.

I express my sincere gratitude to my teacher Dr Subash Chandra Dash, Senior Lecturer of P.G. Department of Sanskrit, Utkal University for his valuable guidance and constant help to complete this book on time.

I express my deep respect and gratitude to Prof. Gopal Krushna Dash, Head of the Department of Sanskrit, Utkal University and his team of teachers: Prof. Alekh Charan Sarangi, Ex. Vice-Chancellor, Sri Jagannatha Samskrta Visvavidyalaya, Puri and Ex. HOD, Prof. Prafulla Kumar Mishra, Prof. Raghu Nath Panda, Prof. Radha Madhab Dash, Prof. Prativa Manjari Rath and Dr Dina Bandhu Tripathy for their continued grace, goodwill, encouragement, advice and guidance for the completion of this book.

My appreciation to all the members of staff of P.G. Department of Sanskrit, Utkal University for their kind and timely cooperation.

I extend my sincere appreciation to the authorities of Parija Library of Utkal University, Seminar Library of P.G. Department of Sanskrit, Utkal University, Swami Dayananda Saraswati Library at Rishikesh and Coimbatore, State Library and Museum Library, Bhubaneswar, for permitting me to use the library resources for my research work.

My special deep appreciation to Mr Sanjaya Kumar Rout, without whose timely assistance this book would not have seen the light of the day.

I offer my *praṇāms* to Lord Śrī Medhā Dakṣiṇāmūrti, for providing me good health, a functioning mind and memory, and invisible inspiration to complete this book.

8 January 2010 **Atmaprajnananda Saraswati**

Note on Transliteration

In this study, Devanāgarī characters are transliterated according to the scheme adopted by the "International Congress of Orientalists" at Athens in 1912, and since then generally acknowledged to be the only rational and satisfactory one. In it, the inconsistency, irregularity and redundancy of English spelling are ruled out. The letters f, q, w, x and z are not called to use. One fixed value is given to each letter. Hence, a, e, i and g always represent अ, ए, इ and ग् respectively, and never ए, इ, ऐ and ज् or other values which they have in English. The letters t and d are always used for त् and द् only. One *tialde* (˜), one accent, four macrons (¯) and ten dots (2 above, 8 below) are used to represent adequately and correctly all Sanskrit letters. The letter c alone represents च्. Since the natural function of h will be to make the *aghoṣa* into *ghoṣa* (e.g. kh, ch, ṭh, th, ph, gh, jh, ḍh, dh, bh), it would be an anomaly for a scientific scheme to use it in combinations like ch and sh for giving च् and ष् values; hence ch here is छ् and sh स् ह्. The vowel ऋ is represented by ṛ because ri is legitimate for रि only, is out of place, and the singular ṛi is an altogether objectionable distortion. The *tialde* (˜) over n represents ञ् ñ. Accent mark over s gives श् ś; dots above m and n give *anusvāra* (ं), ṁ and ङ्, ṅ, respectively. Dots below h and r give *visarga* (:) ḥ, and ऋ ṛ, respectively. Dots below s, n, t and d give their corresponding cerebrals ष्, ण्, ट् and ड्, ṣ, ṇ, ṭ and ḍ; and macrons (¯) over a, i, u and r give आ, ई, ऊ, and ॠ ā, ī, ū, ṝ respectively. Macrons (¯) are not used to lengthen the quantity of e and o, because they always have the long quantity in Sanskrit. Sanskrit words are capitalized only where special distinctiveness is called for, as in the opening of a sentence, title of books, etc. The scheme of transliteration in full is as follows:

अ a,	आ ā,	इ i,	ई ī,
उ u,	ऊ ū,	ऋ ṛ,	ॠ ṝ,
ए e,	ऐ ai,	ओ o,	औ au,
	ं ṁ,	: ḥ	

क् k,	ख् kh,	ग् g,	घ् gh,	ङ् ṅ,
च c,	छ् ch,	ज् j,	झ jh,	ञ् ñ,
ट् ṭ,	ठ् ṭh,	ड् ḍ,	ढ् ḍh,	ण् ṇ,
त् t,	थ् th,	द् d,	ध् dh,	न् n,
प् p,	फ् ph,	ब् b,	भ् bh,	म् m,
य् y,	र् r,	ल् l,	व् v,	
श् ś,	ष् ṣ,	स् s,	ह् h	

Abbreviations

AdhBhā	*Brahmasūtra-Adhyāsa-Bhāṣya*
AiUp	*Aitareya Upaniṣad*
Aṣ	*Aṣṭādhyāyī*
AV	*Atharvaveda*
BṛUp	*Bṛhadāraṇyaka Upaniṣad*
BhGī	*Bhagavadgītā*
BhāPu	*Bhāgavata Purāṇa*
BrSū	*Brahmasūtra*
BGSB	*Bhagavadgītā-Śāṅkara-Bhāṣya*
BSSB	*Brahmasūtra-Śāṅkara-Bhāṣya*
BUB	*Bṛhadāraṇyaka-Upaniṣad-Bhāṣya*
BUBV	*Bṛhadāraṇyaka-Upaniṣad-Bhāṣya-Vārttika*
ChāUp	*Chāndogya Upaniṣad*
DevīMā	*Devī Māhātmya*
GarPu	*Garuḍa Purāṇa*
ĪśāUp	*Īśāvāsya Upaniṣad*
KaUp	*Kaṭha Upaniṣad*
KaiUp	*Kaivalya Upaniṣad*
KeUp	*Kena Upaniṣad*
KUSB	*Kaṭha-Upaniṣad-Śāṅkara-Bhāṣya*
MaBh	*Mahābhāṣya*
MaBhā	*Mahābhārata*
MaSm	*Manusmṛti*
MahUp	*Mahānārāyaṇa Upaniṣad*
MaiUp	*Maitrāyaṇī Upaniṣad*
MāUp	*Māṇḍūkya Upaniṣad*
MāṇKā	*Māṇḍūkya Kārikā*

MukUp	*Muktikā Upaniṣad*
MuṇUp	*Muṇḍaka Upaniṣad*
MuṇUpŚāBhā	*Muṇḍaka-Upaniṣad-Śāṅkara-Bhāṣya*
NaiSi	*Naiṣkarmyasiddhi*
NyāSū	*Nyāya-Sūtra*
PadPu	*Padma Purāṇa*
Pañ	*Pañcadaśī*
PañVi	*Pañcapādika Vivaraṇa*
PāṇŚi	*Pāṇinīya Śiksā*
PrUp	*Praśna Upaniṣad*
ṚVBhā	*Ṛgveda-Bhāṣya*
ṚVS	*Ṛgveda-Saṁhitā*
ŚaṅDig	*Śaṅkara-Digvijaya*
ŚvUp	*Śvetāśvatara Upaniṣad*
ŚYV	*Śukla-Yajurveda*
SiLeSaṁ	*Siddhāntaleśasaṁgraha*
SubUp	*Subāla Upaniṣad*
SV	*Sāmaveda*
TaSaṅ	*Tarka-Saṅgraha*
TaSaDī	*Tarka-Saṁgraha Dīpikā*
TaiĀr	*Taittirīya Āraṇyaka*
TaiBr	*Taittirīya Brāhmaṇa*
TaiSa	*Taittirīya-Saṁhitā*
TaiUp	*Taittirīya Upaniṣad*
TUB	*Taittirīya-Upaniṣad-Bhāṣya*
TUBV	*Taittirīya-Upaniṣad-Bhāṣya-Vārttika*
UpSā	*Upadeśa Sāhasrī*
Va	*Vanamālā*
VāSaṁMā	*Vajasaneya Saṁhitā Mādhyandina*
VePa	*Vedānta-Paribhāṣā*
VeSā	*Vedāntasāra*
ViCū	*Vivekacūḍāmaṇi*
ViSaNā	*Viṣṇusahasranāma*
YoSū	*Yogasūtra*

1

Introduction to Vedānta

Indian Philosophical Systems

INDIAN philosophy is generally discussed in terms of six major orthodox (*āstika*) schools, and three major heterodox (*nāstika*) schools. These words normally convey a division into theists and atheists. However, this is not the meaning implied when these terms are used to denote the schools of Indian philosophy. *Āstika* systems are those that accept the authority (*pramāṇattvam* of the Vedas as a valid means of knowledge) of the Vedas, whereas *nāstika* systems are those who reject it.[1] The *āstika* systems are the *ṣaḍ-darśana*s, the six systems of Indian philosophy – Nyāya, Vaiśeṣika, Sāṁkhya, Yoga, Mīmāṁsā and Vedānta. The *nāstika* systems are Cārvāka, Jainism and Buddhism.

The Vedas

The Vedic corpus that is accepted as *pramāṇa* by the *āstika* philosophies has four sections – Saṁhitā, Brāhmaṇa, Āraṇyaka, and Upaniṣad. Saṁhitā has Sūktas or hymns. Brāhmaṇa contains the technical know-how of the fire ritual. Āraṇyaka has *mantra* and *upāsanā*s that are practised in the forests (i.e. not for *gṛhastha*s). Upaniṣads normally appear in the last part of Āraṇyaka and deal with spiritual philosophy. Some Upaniṣads

---

1 The rejection was more due to (i) the inability of a person to grow during the same lifetime, and (ii) the *hiṁsā* involved in some of the rituals which shocked the sensitivity of both Mahāvīra and the Buddha.

are exceptions and appear in Saṁhitā[2] and Brāhmaṇa[3] too. Thus Upaniṣads, as they appear in the last part of the Vedas, are called Vedānta. There are 108 Upaniṣads, out of which ten are famous. Since Upaniṣads are mostly philosophical, they are found in prose. However, there are Upaniṣads like *Taittirīyopaniṣad*, *Gaṇapatyatharvaśirṣopaniṣad* and *Īśāvāsyopaniṣad* that have *svaras*.

These four sections are mapped to the four *āśramas*. A *brahmacārī* is supposed to study the Saṁhitā. A *gṛhastha* is supposed to follow the Brāhmaṇa. A *vānaprasthī* is supposed to follow the Āraṇyaka. A *sannyāsī* is supposed to study the Upaniṣads.

Apauruṣeyatvam of the Vedas

Orthodox Indian thoughts maintain that the Vedas are revealed literature, i.e. they are not authored by any human being. Thus, the Vedas are said to be impersonal (*apauruṣeya*), and hence unquestionable. They are referred to as *Śruti* (that which is heard), and is accepted to be what was envisioned by the Vedic seers (*ṛṣi*s).

It is the Mīmāṁsā that rejects the view that the Veda was ever composed by anybody. Nyāya-Vaiśeṣika ascribes its authorship to *Īśvara*. The position of Ācārya Śaṅkara about this view is midway between the two. Like the Mīmāṁsā, but unlike the Nyāya-Vaiśeṣika, he admits that the Veda is *apauruṣeya*. However, he redefines that word to make it signify not that the Veda has no author and is timeless, but that it is produced or, more properly, resuscitated at the beginning of each *kalpa*, by one that cannot interfere either with its content, or with the order of its words. In the case of works like *Raghuvaṁśa*, the author composes it as he likes. On the other hand, in case of the Vedas, the first creator of the Veda in every cycle who is *Īśvara*, repeats it

---

2 *Īśāvāsya Upaniṣad* is the 40th chapter of the *Śukla-Yajurveda Saṁhitā*.

3 *Praśna*, *Muṇḍaka* and *Māṇḍūkya Upaniṣad* are in the *Gopatha Brāhmaṇa* of *Atharvaveda* (Paippalāda Śākhā).

anew, but precisely as it was in the other cycles (*pravāha-nityam*). That is, the Veda is self-existent in this view also; only it is not the self-same Veda that always is, but a series of what may be described as re-issues of a timeless (*pravāha-nityam*) edition, which goes back to the beginningless time. This view is not different in substance from the Mīmāṁsā view, excepting that it finds a place for *Īśvara* in the doctrine. (Mīmāṁsā does not accept *Īśvara*).

As per Swami Dayananda Saraswati:

i. Agnihotra and other ritual *karma*s are not matters of inference. There is no other way of knowing these *karma*s than Veda.

ii. There is no other *pramāṇa* for knowing *Ātmā* to be *Brahman,* which is *jagatkāraṇam* and *Parameśvara*. Veda is *pramāṇa* for *ātmajñānam*.

iii. It is not *pauruṣeya,* because it is not born out of one's thinking box, not born of one's inference, or insight. If it occurs in somebody's head (a *ṛṣi*), he calls himself "I am a *draṣṭā*". These statements are revelation, hence they are called seers. Veda has to come from *Īśvara,* because nobody else knows what *Īśvara* is.

iv. This knowledge is *apauruṣeyam,* because the *jīveśvara aikyam* equation is not a matter of inference. It is not *pratyakṣa,* much less inference. *Īśvara* Himself has to reveal the knowledge.

v. *Apauruṣeyatvam* is an attitude, *apauruṣeyatvam* is no authorship. For any knowledge, any way there is no authorship. One discovers.

vi. If you have to learn Vedānta, you have to treat Vedas as *pramāṇa*. There is no other way. It is not a system of philosophy. *Vedānto nāma upaniṣat pramāṇam* (*Ve Sā*-3) "what is Vedānta is Upaniṣad as *pramāṇa*".

vii. Veda/Vedānta is *pramāṇa* because it is – *anadhigata, abādhitam* and *phalavat arthabodhakatvam*.[4]

viii. Although most philosophical systems are discussed in the *Brahmasūtra*, Vedānta is not a philosophical system.

Unlike in the Western philosophical systems, who wanted to keep religion and God out of their search for their basic question about the human being, this world and the creator; in India, religion and philosophy are together. Scholars have created a system out of the Vedas/Vedānta, nevertheless *Īśvara* and *devatās* are an integral part of the whole philosophy.

Introduction to Vedānta

Vedānta (Upaniṣads) is the last word in search of the truth about the individual *jīva*, this *jagat* and the creator. Vedānta represents the doctrine of the total identity of the subject and object, beyond which human reason, thought and experience cannot go. This vision is held even by a farmer in a village (that all that is here is *Bhagavān* or *Bhagavān* is everywhere).

Knowledge of Upaniṣads Goes Outside India

Among the works comprising Vedic literature, the Upaniṣads were the first to attract the attention of the Western scholars and their wide and well-deserved praise. Several of these works were translated into Persian in Moghul times. Dara Shikoh[5] (CE

---

4 *Vedānta Paribhāṣā* of Dharmaraja Adhvarindra.

5 Dara devoted much effort towards finding a common mystical language between Islam and Hinduism. Towards this goal, he completed the translation of fifty Upaniṣads from its original Sanskrit to Persian in 1657, so it could be read by Muslim scholars. His translation is often called *Sirr-e-Akbar* (*The Greatest Mystery*), where he states boldly, in the Introduction, his speculative hypothesis that the work referred to in the Quran as the *Kitab al-maknun* or the *Hidden Book* is none other than the Upaniṣads. His most famous work, *Majma-ul-Bahrain* (*The Confluence of the Two Seas*), was also devoted to a revelation of the mystical and pluralistic affinities between Sūfic and Vedāntic speculation (Wiki, accessed on 15 May 2014). →

1615-1668), the eldest son and the legitimate heir of Emperor Shah Jehan (CE 1592–1666) and Mumtaz Mahal was attracted by the Upaniṣads and had them translated into Persian language.

Subsequently from Persian language, they were translated into Latin about the beginning of the nineteenth century. It was through this Latin translation that they came to be known for the first time in Europe. Arthur Schopenhauer (CE 1788–1860), the German philosopher, who can be termed one of the greatest European thinkers during his time, admired them through these translations.

> The Upaniṣads were translated from Sanskrit into Persian by, or it may be, for Dara Shukoh (1640-59), the eldest son of Shah Jehan, an enlightened prince, who openly professed liberal religious tenets of the great Emperor Akbar, and even wrote a book intended to reconcile the religious doctrines of Hindus and Mohammedans. He seems to have heard of the Upaniṣads during his stay in Kashmir in 1640. Afterwards, he invited several paṇḍits from Banaras to Delhi, who were to assist him in the work of translation. The translation was

---

← Dara Shikoh, the elder brother of Aurangzeb, was a Sanskrit scholar. He translated the *Īśāvāsyopaniṣad* into Persian. He was a seeker of Truth, and in his search for the Truth, studied *Quran*, Old Testament, New Testament, and the Vedas with the help of some *paṇḍits*. As a result of his search, he made the following remarks, "After gradual research, I have come to the conclusion that long before all heavenly books like Quran, Old Testament and New Testament, etc. God had revealed to the Hindus, through the *ṛṣis* of yore, of whom Brahmā was the chief, his four Books of Knowledge (*Ṛgveda*, *Yajurveda*, *Sāmaveda* and *Atharvaveda*). A fortunate person, who relinquishing the selfishness of his polluted mind, for the sake of God, being free from bias, will study my translation of the *Īśopaniṣad*, the Word of God, will attain salvation and be free from death, fear and misery."

For such sayings, the Muslim *mullāh*s declared him a heretic and had him killed by his sectarian brother Aurangzeb, who seized the Mogul throne.

> finished by 1657. Three years after the accomplishment of the work, in 1659, the prince was put to death by his brother Aurangzeb, in reality, no doubt, because he was the eldest son and legitimate successor of Shah Jehan, but under the pretext that he was an infidel, and dangerous to the established religion of the empire.[6]

However, neither any translation under Akber's reign (CE 1556-1586), nor the translations of Dara Shikoh attracted the attention of the European scholars until the year CE 1775. In that year, Anquetil Duperron, the famous traveller and discoverer of the Zend Avesta, received one MS. of the Persian translation of the Upaniṣads, sent to him by M. Gentil, the French resident at the court of Shuja-ud-daula, and brought to France by M. Bernier. After receiving another MS, Anquetil Duperron collated the two and translated the Persian translation into French (not published) and into Latin. The Latin translation was published in CE 1801 and 1802.

Meaning of the Word Vedānta

Standing at the end of the Veda, the Upaniṣads came to be known as "Vedānta" (end of the Veda) being a locational name, much as the metaphysics of Aristotle owed its designation to its being placed after physics in his writings. Therefore, the concluding part of the Vedas, i.e. the Upaniṣads is Vedānta. However, the word (Vedānta) which at first only indicated the position of the Upaniṣads in the collection, later developed the significance of the aim or fulfilment of Vedic teaching, it being permissible to use *anta* in Sanskrit, like its equivalent "end" in English, in both these senses.

Subsequently, Vedānta as a technical term, did not only mean the last portions of the Veda, or chapters placed, as it were, at the end of a volume of Vedic literature, but the end, i.e. the object,

---

6 Cf. Sacred Books of the East, vol. I: *The Upaniṣads*, Introduction, p. lvii, tr. F. Max Müller, Motilal Banarsidass.

the highest purpose of the Veda.

1. There are of course, passages, like the one in *Taittirīya Āraṇyaka*, where Vedānta means simply the end of the Veda, *yo vedādau svaraḥ prokto vedānte ca pratiṣṭhitaḥ*,[7] meaning "The *oṁ* which is pronounced at the beginning of the Veda, and has its place also at the end of the Veda". Here *vedānta* stands simply in opposition to *vedādau*, and it is impossible to translate it as Sāyaṇa does, by Vedānta or Upaniṣad.
2. Vedānta, in the sense of philosophy, occurs in *Taittirīya Āraṇyaka*, in a verse of *Mahā Nārāyaṇa Upaniṣad*, repeated in *Muṇḍaka Upaniṣad* III.2.6, and elsewhere, *vedānta-vijñāna-suniścitārthāḥ* (those who have well understood the object of the knowledge arising from the Vedānta),[8] (and not "from the last book of the Veda"); and *Śvetāśvatara Upaniṣad* of *Kṛṣṇa-Yajurveda* – *vedānte paramaṁ-guhyam*[9] (the highest mystery in the Vedānta).
3. Afterwards, it is used in plural also, e.g. *Kṣurikopaniṣad*,[10] *puṇḍariketi vedānteṣu nigadyate* "it is called *puṇḍarīka* in the Vedāntas", i.e. in *Chāndogya* and other Upaniṣads, as the commentator says, but not in the last books of each Veda.[11]

From many angles, Upaniṣadic vision (*jīveśvara-aikyam*) is indeed the Vedāntic vision. The Vedic literature can be

---

[7] *MahUp* XII.17.

[8] Also in

vedānta-vijñāna-suniścitārthāḥ sannyāsa-yogād-yatayaḥ śuddhasattvāḥ ।
te brahmaloke tu parāntakāle parāmṛtā(t) parimucyanti sarve ॥
– *MuṇUp* III.2.6; *MahUp* XII.15; *KaiUp* I.4

[9] *ŚvUp* VI.22.

[10] Of *Kṛṣṇa-Yajurveda*.

[11] Sacred Books of the East, vol. I: *The Upaniṣads*, Introduction, p. lxxxvi.

grouped into four distinct sections – Saṁhitā, Brāhmaṇa, Āraṇyaka, and Upaniṣad.[12] The Saṁhitā portion contains the *mantras*. The *mantras* are hymns, prayers, and formulae for the fire rituals. These Saṁhitās are four – *Ṛk, Yajus, Sāma,* and *Atharva.* The Brāhmaṇa portions of the Vedas is explanatory treatise on the *mantras*, for the performance of fire rituals. The Āraṇyakas are forest-books attached to the Brāhmaṇa that give philosophical interpretations to the latter by allegorizing them as well as prescribing various types of meditations (*upāsanās*). Lastly, there are the Upaniṣads that deal with the knowledge of *Brahman.*

The concluding portions of the Vedas contain the Upaniṣads. They are called Vedānta (*veda + anta*: end of the Veda). The term is very apt, since like most Sanskrit terms, there is a *śleṣa* or rhetorical figure involved. Sanskrit roots are multi-significant or multivalent. Besides literally expressing the fact that Upaniṣads form the concluding part (*avasāna-bhāga*) of the Vedas, the term also expresses the idea that the Upaniṣads represent the "aim" or "goal" of the Vedas. Being known as the crown or summit of the Vedas (*śruti-śiras*), the Sanskrit word *anta,* like the English word "end", may be used to mean both "terminus" and "aim". The aim or goal of Vedānta, both as applied to the Upaniṣads as well as the philosophical systems of that name, concerns the nature of *Brahman.*

In its widest sense, the term Vedānta means, "The Upaniṣads, the *Brahmasūtra,* and other treatises that help to understand their meaning, such as *Bhagavadgītā* and commentaries on them".[13]

As stated above, the Vedāntic schools derive their name of Vedānta from the fact that they claim to interpret the Upaniṣads, as well as having founded their individual systems upon them. Their difference lies primarily in that, while the

---

[12] See charts 1-5.

[13] *VeSā* 3.

Chart 1: Ṛgveda*

Ṛgveda-Śākala-Saṁhitā	*Brāhmaṇa*	*Āraṇyaka*	*Upaniṣads*	*Mahāvākya*	*Śāntimantraḥ*	*Priest*
1,028 *sūktas*, 10,580 *ṛcās*, 153,826 words, 432,000 syllables (as per Śaunaka) 10 *maṇḍalas*/ or 8 *aṣṭakas*						
Available Śākhās						Ṛtvik
Śākala Saṁhitā (extant)	*Aitareya* (extant)	*Aitareya*	*Aitareya*	*prajñānaṁ brahma* (*AiUp* V.3)	*vaṅg me manasi pratiṣṭhitā*	
Bāṣkala Saṁhitā (in fragments)			*Bāṣkala*			
Āśvalāyana Saṁhitā (extant)						
Śāṅkhyāyana Saṁhitā (extinct)	*Kauṣītaki* (extant)/or *Śāṅkhyāyana*	*Kauṣītaki*	*Kauṣītaki*- (extant)			
Māṇḍūkāyana Saṁhitā (extinct)	*Paiṅgi*					

* *Ṛṣi:* Paila; original *śākhā*s are twenty-one as per *Caraṇavyūha*.

Chart 2: Śukla-Yajurveda*

Śukla-Yajurveda Saṁhitā	*Brāhmaṇa*	*Āraṇyaka*	*Upaniṣads*	*Mahāvākya*	*Śāntimantraḥ*	*Priest*
Available Śākhās						
Kāṇva (2,086 *mantras*)	*Śatapatha-Kāṇva* (100 chapters) As big as *Ṛgveda*	*Śatapatha*	*Īśāvāsya* (40th chapter)			Adhvaryu
Mādhyandina (1,975 *mantras*, 111 less than *Kāṇva*)	*Śatapatha-Mādhyandina* (100 chapters)	*Bṛhadāraṇyaka*	*Bṛhadāraṇyaka*	*ahaṁ brahmāsmi* (*BṛUp* I.4.10)	*pūrṇamadaḥ pūrṇamidam*	

* *Ṛṣi*: Yājñavalkya; original *śākhās* in *Śukla-Yajurveda* are fifteen as per *Caraṇavyūha*.

Chart 3: Kṛṣṇa-Yajurveda*

Kṛṣṇa-Yajurveda Saṁhitā	*Brāhmaṇa*	*Āraṇyaka*	*Upaniṣads*	*Mahāvākya*	*Śāntimantraḥ*
Available Śākhās					
Taittirīya	*Taittirīya*	*Taittirīya*	*Taittirīya, Mahānārāyaṇa*		*śaṁ no mitra śaṁ varuṇaḥ—*
Kaṭha	*Kaṭha*		*Kaṭha*		*sa ha navavatu—*
Maitrāyaṇī	*Maitrāyaṇī*	*Maitrāyaṇī*	*Maitrāyaṇī*		
Kapiṣṭhala	*Satyāyanī Bhallaka*		*Śvetāśvatara*		

* *Ṛṣi*: Vaiśampāyana; original *śākhās* are ninty-four as per *Caraṇavyūha*.

Chart 4: Sāmaveda*

Sāmaveda Saṁhitā	*Brāhmaṇa*	*Āraṇyaka*	*Upaniṣads*	*Mahāvākya*	*Śāntimantraḥ*	*Priest*
Available Śākhās						
Kauthumīya (1,875 songs)		No *Āraṇyaka*	*Chāndogya*	*tat tvam asi* (*ChUp* VI.8.7)	*āpyāyantu mamāṅgāni*	Udgātā
Jaiminīya or Talavakāra (1,687 songs)	*Jaiminīya* (or *Talavakāra*)	*Talavakāra* (*Jaiminīya Upaniṣad Brāhmaṇa*) Or *Gāyatri Upaniṣad*	*Kena* (or *Talavakāra*)			
Rāṇāyanīya	*Tāṇḍya* (*Pancaviṁśa*) *Ṣaḍviṁśa* *Sāma-vidhāna* *Ārṣeya* *Daivatādhyāya* *Mantra* *Saṁhitopaniṣad* *Vaṁśa*					

* *Ṛṣi*: Jaimini; original *śākhās* are 1,000 as per *Caraṇavyūha*.

Chart 5: Atharvaveda*

Atharvaveda Saṁhitā	*Brāhmaṇa*	*Āraṇyaka*	*Upaniṣads*	*Mahāvakya*	*Śāntimantraḥ*	*Priest*
Available-Śākhās						Brahmā
Śaunaka (extant) 20 *kāṇḍas* 598 hymns, 5,038/5,977 verses		No Āraṇyaka			*bhadraṁ karṇebhiḥ*	
Paippalāda (extant)	*Gopatha*		*Muṇḍaka, Māṇḍūkya, Praśna*	*ayamātmā brahma* (*MāṇUp* 2)		
Dānta (extinct) *Pradānta* (extinct) *Snāta* (extinct) *Sautna* (extinct) *Brahmadāvala* (extinct) *Devavarśata* (extinct) *Caraṇavaidyā* (extinct)						

* *Ṛṣi* : Sumantu; original *śākhā*s are fifty as per *Caraṇavyūha*.

non-dualistic tradition propounds an acosmic view, the theistic tradition of Vedānta (Vaiṣṇava Vedānta)[14] uphold a cosmic view of *Brahman*.

Prasthānatraya of Vedānta

The Upaniṣads, *Bhagavadgītā* and *Brahmasūtra* are known as the *prasthānatraya* (triple foundation/cannon of Vedānta). *Prasthāna* means "foundation" and thus, these three constitute the three foundations of revelation (Śruti), remembrance (Smṛti) and reason (Nyāya). They are respectively known as, the Upaniṣads or Śruti-prasthāna, *Bhagavadgītā* or Smṛti-prasthāna and *Brahmasūtra* or Nyāya-prasthāna.[15]

As stated above, the Vedas are referred to as Śruti, and since the Upaniṣads form part of the Vedas, their name as Śruti-prasthāna is justified. *Bhagavadgītā* stands next to the Upaniṣads with reference to authoritativeness, and is considered almost an equal. *Bhagavadgītā* (Song of the Lord) contains the message of Lord Kṛṣṇa to the humanity. It forms part of the epic, *Mahābhārata*,[16] which is a Smṛti (remembered text). Thus, *Bhagavadgītā* is known as the Smṛti-prasthāna. *Brahmasūtra* represents the standpoint of reason because it sets forth the Vedāntic teachings in a logical order. It is also called *Uttara-Mīmāṁsā-Sūtra* since it is an enquiry into the final sections of the Vedas; *Vedānta-Sūtra* since it is the aphoristic text of Vedānta; *Śārīraka-Sūtra* since it is concerned with the

---

14 The principal Vaiṣṇava schools are:
Viśiṣṭādvaita of Rāmānuja (CE 1017–1137);
Dvaitādvaita of Nimbārka (CE 1165);
Dvaita of Madhva (CE 1199–1276);
Śuddhādvaita of Vallabha (CE 1479–1531); and
Acintya-Bhedābheda of Caitanya (CE 1486–1534).

15 See Chart 6.

16 Bhīṣma-Parva, Chapters 25-42.

Chart 6: Prasthānatraya (Advaita Vedānta Literature)

Śruti-prasthāna	*Smṛti-prasthāna*	*Nyāya-prasthāna*
Upaniṣads (10)	*Bhagavadgītā*	*Brahmasūtra / Śārīraka-Sūtra / Vedānta-Sūtra*
1. *Īśā*	All the 17 chapters*	Has 4 adhyāyas
2. *Kaṭha*		
3. *Muṇḍaka*		Each *adhyāya* with 4 *pādas*
4. *Praśna*		Total 16 *pādas*
5. *Aitareya*		
6. *Kena*		Each *pāda* with few *adhikaraṇas*
7. *Taittirīya*		Total 191 *adhikaraṇas*
8. *Chāndogya*		
9. *Māṇḍūkya*		Each *adhikaraṇa* has few *sūtras*
10. *Bṛhadāraṇyaka*		Total 555 *sūtras*

The above are studied along with *Śāṅkara-Bhāṣyam*.

* Śaṅkara has written his commentary on *Bhagavadgītā* from Chapter II.11 only when Bhagavān Kṛṣṇa starts the teaching with the *śloka* — *aśocyan anvaśocastvaṁ prajñāvādāṁśca bhāṣase*.

nature and destiny of the embodied *jīva*; and *Bhikṣusūtra*[17] since those who are most competent to study this are the *sannyāsīs* (renunciates) who are *bhikṣus*.[18]

Thus, we see that the basic sourcebook of Vedānta, and therefore its basic doctrine, is based upon Śruti and supported by Smṛti and reasoning (Nyāya). In light of this, the central teaching of all three sourcebooks will be posited to be one and the same, i.e. *Brahman*.

Difference between Veda and Vedānta

Vedānta is a body of teaching found at the end of the Veda. The Vedas, four in number *Ṛk, Yajus, Sāma* and *Atharva*, are each loosely divided into two sections. The first section deals with (i) *dharma* – religious ethics that includes *karma* – religious actions, (ii) *artha* – other special actions to achieve security, and (iii) *kāma* – pleasures. This section, called the *karmakāṇḍa* is very bulky, understandably so, since it deals with human desires and actions required to fulfil those desires.

The last section of the Vedas is called *jñānakāṇḍa* (knowledge section). It is very much shorter because the subject matter is a single desire for (iv) *mokṣa* – freedom from the sense of limitation. The fulfilment of that desire is not through actions, which are many, but through knowledge, which is singular with regard to the particular thing to be known.

---

17 *Brahmasūtra* is referred to by Pāṇini as *Bhikṣusūtra* in his *Aṣṭādhyāyī* IV.3.110: *pārāśaryaśilālibhyāṁ bhikṣu-naṭa-sūtrayoḥ*.

18 The alternative title *Bhikṣusūtra* to *Brahmasūtra* was proposed by Pandit Gopinath Kaviraja. However, Pandit Udayavira Sastri strongly opposed this move, clarifying that the text authored by Bhikṣu-Pañcaśikha, the disciple of Kapila, of Parāśara *gotra* is originally titled *Bhikṣusūtra* (a text on Sāṁkhya). – Visnudev Rakesh, Gurukul Kangdi University, Haridwar

Subject Matter of Vedānta

Therefore, although it may appear strange, but the subject matter of the Vedānta is completely different from the subject matter of the Vedas. While the first three *puruṣārthas*, namely *dharma, artha* and *kāma,* are the subject matter of the Vedas, Vedānta, i.e. Upaniṣads, deals only with the ultimate *puruṣārtha,* i.e. *mokṣa.* This will be clear if we use *anubandha-catuṣṭaya* method.

Anubandha-Catuṣṭaya

The four essential factors of any treatise are grouped as *anubandha-catuṣṭaya.*[19] They are *viṣaya, prayojanam, adhikārī* and *sambandha.*

Viṣaya (Subject Matter)

In Vedānta, the subject matter is *mokṣa* – freedom, whereas in the Vedas, the subject matter is all the other three pursuits – *dharma, artha* and *kāma.*

Prayojanam (Purpose)

The *karmakāṇḍa* portion of the Vedas describes varieties of rituals and sacrifices, as the means to fulfil various desires entertained by an equally large number of people. In contrast, the *jñānakāṇḍa* that contains the Upaniṣads, has the knowledge of identity between the *jīva* and *Brahman* as the main[20] topic. The pursuit here is *mokṣa* – freedom from the sense of limitation.

---

[19] *VeSā* 5.

[20] There are other topics as well – *vidyāstuti, adhikāritvam, anadhikārīs,* importance of the *guru/guru-paramparā,* nature of the individual *jīva,* nature of *Īśvara, jīveśvara-aikyam, sṛṣṭikrama* (cosmology), *Īśvara* being the creator (rather manifest) of this overwhelming *jagat,* law of *karma,* a continuing *jīva,* reincarnation as per one's *karma,* concept of *jīvanmukti,* etc.

Adhikārī (Eligible Person)

A student of Vedānta is vastly different from a student of the Vedas. Sadānanda defines the *adhikārī* as one who has completed studying the Vedas and has performed immense charity – *asmin janmani janmāntare vā*[21] and is *sādhana-catuṣṭaya-sampannaḥ.*[22] In fact, now he/she wants to know the *vastu,* and the relationship between him/her and the Lord if he is there, and the overwhelming world around him/her – *jīva, jagat* and *Īśvara.*

Sambandha (Relationship)

i. Śāstra and Subject Matter = *Pratipādaka–Pratipādya.* The Upaniṣads or the Vedāntic texts play the part of the revealer (*pratipādaka*) while the subject matter is the revealed (*pratipādya*). Thus, the relation between the text and the purpose however is the same in case of the Vedas and Vedānta.

ii. Subject Matter and Knowledge = *Sādhana–Sādhya* or *Pramāṇa–Prameya.*

iii. *Jñānam* and *mokṣa* = *Sādhana–Sādhya* (but no time gap is involved. *Jñānam* is *mokṣa*).

The Philosophy of Vedānta

Vedānto nāma upaniṣat pramāṇam.[23] The study of Upaniṣads is not a mere intellectual exercise. Just as the eyes are the only means to know the form and colour, a *pramāṇa,*[24] similarly Upaniṣad is the only means, to know the truth of myself, to get out of this constant buffeting of sorrow and pain, and the incessant cycle of birth and death, which is the common lot of the mortal. *Tarati*

---

21 *VeSā* 6.

22 See Chart 7.

23 *VeSā* 3.

24 See Chapter 2 on Concept of Pramāṇa.

Chart 7: Sādhana-Catuṣṭaya

Viveka	*Vairāgya*	*Śamādi-Ṣaṭka-sampatti*	*Mumukṣuttvam*
Nityānitya-vastu-viveka	*Ihāmutra-phala-bhoga-virāga*		*Moktum-icchā-mumukṣā. Tasya bhāvaṁ mumukṣuttvam*

Śama	***Dama***	***Uparati***	***Titikṣā***	***Śraddhā***	***Samādhānam***
Withdrawing the mind from everything else except listening to the scriptures	Restraining physical manifestation of any negative emotions	Withdrawing the mind from drifting back to the objects of senses	Being unruffled by extreme situations over which one does not have immediate control	Faith in the Śruti statements as unfolded by the *guru*	Applying the restrained mind in listening to the scriptures

śokam ātmavit[25] is the promise of Śruti.

It is with this spirit of a quest that the study of the Upaniṣads is approached. The very purpose of human life is vitiated if it ends without this knowledge. *Iha ced avedīt atha satyam asti, na ced iha avedīt mahatī vinaṣṭi*, mourns *Kenopaniṣad*.[26] In *Bṛhadāraṇyaka*, Yājñavalkya tells Gārgī, *etad akṣaram aviditvā 'smāllokāt praiti, sa kṛpaṇaḥ.*[27] *Śravaṇa, manana, nididhyāsana*[28] of the Upaniṣad alone, done with *śraddhā* at the feet of the right *guru*, is enough to make the *adhikārī* student grasp the meaning of the *mahāvākya upadeśa – tat tvam asi*[29] after which there is no question of sorrow.

Meaning of the Word Upa-ni-ṣad

The word "Upaniṣad" has been variously explained by old Indian commentators, but their explanations cannot be regarded as historically or philologically accurate, since what the commentators have done is merely to read into the word, the meaning of which as a result of long use, it had come to possess by that time. While thus the commentators give us no help, we fortunately find the word used in the Upaniṣads themselves, and there it generally appears as synonymous with *rahasya* (secret). That should have been its original meaning.

Etymologically the word is equivalent to sitting *sad*, nearby (*upa*), devotedly (*ni*) – meaning that *vidyā* which is obtained by going near (*upa*) the knowledge, and learning with commitment (*ni* = *niścayena*). And in course of time, it came to signify the secret instruction imparted at such private sittings.[30] That the

---

25 *ChāUp* VII.1.3.

26 *KeUp* II.5.

27 *BṛUp* III.10.

28 *ātmāvāre draṣṭavyaḥ, śrotavyaḥ, mantavyaḥ, nididhyāsitavyaḥ – BṛUp* II.4.5 and IV.5.6, Yājñavalkya–Maitreyī Saṁvāda

29 *ChāUp* VI.8.7, VI.9.4, VI.10.3, VI.11.3, VI.12.3, VI.13.3, VI.14.3, VI.15.3 and VI.16.3.

30 *PrUp* I.1-2.

teaching of Upaniṣads was regarded as a mystery, and that much care and anxiety were bestowed upon keeping it from the ineligible, lest it should be misunderstood or misapplied, come out in several Upaniṣads[31, 32, 33] and *Bhagavadgītā*.[34]

---

31 *Muṇḍakopaniṣad* III.2.10 says: *tad etad-ṛcā-abhyuktam:*
kriyāvantaḥ śrotriya brahmaniṣṭhāḥ,
svayaṁ juhvata ekarṣi śraddhayantaḥ ।
teṣām-eva-etāṁ brahmavidyā vadeta,
śirovrataṁ vidhivad-yestu cirṇam ॥

Meaning: This very rule has been declared in the following Vedic *ṛcā/mantra*: "This knowledge of *Brahman* should be passed on to them alone, who are engaged in the practice of disciplines, well-versed in the Vedas, and devoted to *Īśvara/Brahman*, who personally offer oblations to the fire called Ekarṣi with faith, and by whom the vow of holding the fire on the head (also means a *sannyāsī*, with shaven head) has been duly accomplished."

32 *tad-etat satyam ṛṣiraṅgirāḥ provāca naitad-acīrṇavrato 'dhīte* । – *MuṇUp* III.2.11

Meaning: Seer Aṅgiras spoke this Truth in the days of yore. No one, who has not observed the vow (who does not have spiritual inclination), should study this.

33 The concluding two *mantras* of *Śvetāśvatara Upaniṣad* highlight the eligibility of the student:

vedānte paramaṁ guhyaṁ purākalpe pracoditam ।
nā 'praśāntāya dātavyaṁ, na 'putrāyāśiṣyāya vā punaḥ ॥ – VI.22

Meaning: This highest mystical knowledge in the Vedānta (Upaniṣads) was taught in the previous cycle/eon. It is not to be given to one, whose passions have not been subdued; nor to one, who is not a worthy son, nor to an unworthy disciple.

yasya deve parā bhaktiḥ yathā deve tathā gurau ।
tasyaite kathitā hyārthāḥ prakāśante mahātmanāḥ ॥ – VI.23

Meaning: These Truths, when taught, shine forth only in that great person, who has supreme devotion to *Īśvara*, and an equal degree of devotion to the spiritual teacher (*guru*).

34 *Bhagavadgītā* XVIII.67 says:

→

The meaning of the word *upa-ni-ṣad* is explained elaborately by Ācārya Śaṅkara, in his *sambandha-bhāṣya* in *Kaṭhopaniṣad* (and casually in *Bṛhadāraṇyaka*). He defines the word *upa-ni-ṣad* in his introduction to this commentary as "leading to acquisition of the knowledge of *Brahman*". The word *upa-ni-ṣad* is derived from the root √*ṣadḷ* of first conjugation (*Bhvādi-gaṇa*), as well as sixth conjugation (*Tudādi-gaṇa*) in the text *Dhātupāṭha*. The meaning of the root √*ṣadḷ* however is same in both the places, as *viśaraṇa-gati-avasādaneṣu*. There are two prefixes *upa* and *ni*, before the root. *Viśaraṇa* means destruction, here meaning destruction of ignorance (*avidyā*), the root cause of *saṁsāra*. *Avasāna* means putting an end to *avidyā-kāma-karma*. The above two meanings are in the negative sense. The positive meaning is denoted by the word *gati*, meaning the knowledge that takes one to *Brahman*. Hence, the meaning is, that knowledge which takes one to *Brahman*. The *kvip* affix, which is a zero-affix, is added after the root, bringing in the meaning of the agent. Please see Appendix B for the work-out.

Another meaning of Upaniṣad by Swami Dayananda Saraswati (b. 1930), founder of "Ārṣa Vidyā" tradition is:

> *upa* (*sāmipyena*), *ni* (*nitarām*), *sat* (*sthitam*) – always there, as oneself alone is that *mokṣa* in the form of *brahma-svarūpa*. You can take *upaniṣat* as *parama-rahasyaṁ brahmavidyā* that is given to you by *śāstra*, or you can say it is the *phala*, *mokṣa*, *parama śreyaḥ*, that is always there, non-separate from you. Thus *ni* + *sad* becomes *ni* + *ṣad* after certain grammatical rules. *Sat* is there in the sense of *sthiti* – a different *dhātu*[35] altogether. Both meanings are *satyam*.

← *idaṁ te nātapaskāya nābhaktāya kadācana* ।
na cāśuśrūṣave vācyaṁ na ca māṁ yo 'bhasūyati ॥

Meaning: This (all that I have taught you) should never to be spoken by you to one, who is devoid of austerities or devotion, nor to one, who does not render service, nor to one who cavils at Me (*Īśvara*).

[35] *'ṣṭhā' – gati-nivṛttau – Bhvādi-gaṇa*.

Number of Upaniṣads

There are several works that have been given the name Upaniṣads – over 200 being reckoned. A great majority of them in fact appear to be of comparatively recent times, and do not deserve to be given the lofty status of the Upaniṣads. Even among the classical Upaniṣads, chronological differences are traceable; but generally speaking, they all exhibit a familiarity both in their thoughts and in the language. According to *Muktikopaniṣad* (I.1.11-13). Upaniṣads are 1,180,[36] one of each *śākhā* of the Vedas. However only 200 are brought to light[37] until now, many of which clearly bear the stamp of modernity. Of these, 108 are listed attached to the four Vedas and are categorized.[38] A complete text of all the 108 Upaniṣads is available with commentary by Śrī Upaniṣad Brahmendra Yogin (whose original name is Śrī Rāmacandrendra Saraswatī,[39] belonging to Shri Kanchi Kamakoti Peetham,

---

36 *Viṣṇu Purāṇa* also mentions the number of *śākhās* to be 1,180, out of which, *Sāmaveda* had the largest number of *śākhās*, i.e. 1,000. In *Ṛgveda* there were 21, in *Yajus* 109 (*Śukla-Yajurveda* 15, and *Kṛṣṇa-Yajurveda* 94) and in *Atharvaveda* 50.

37 By the Theosophical Publishing House, Adyar, Chennai, India.

38 See Appendix for the list of 108 Upaniṣads with their respective Vedas, at the end of this book.

39 Upaniṣad Brahmayogī is the title of Rāmacandrendra Saraswatī, a great *sannyāsī* and Advaitin, who is credited with having written commentaries on all 108 Upaniṣads of *Muktikopaniṣad*. His works have been translated and published by the Adyar Library and Research Centre. He was born Śvarāma of Vādhūla *gotra* in Brahmapuram, a village on the River Palār. This would date to the middle of the eighteenth century, based on tales of his association, as an older contemporary, with Tyāgarāja (CE 1767–1847).

His *sannyāsa* name was Rāmacandrendra, but he came to be known for his scholarship by names such as Upaniṣad Brahmayogī, Upaniṣad Brahmendra and Upaniṣad Brahman. His commentaries on all 108 Upaniṣads of the Muktikā canon were the fulfilment of a wish of his father Śivakāmeśvara. Besides these, he was also →

Kanchi), disciple of Swāmi Vāsudevendra. The entire group besides the 10 major Upaniṣads is divided into six categories,[40] namely (i) Sāmānya Vedānta (25), (ii) Sannyāsa Vedānta (17), (iii) Yoga Vedānta (20), (iv) Śaiva Vedānta (14), (v) Śākta Vedānta (8), and (vi) Vaiṣṇava Vedānta (14). All these Upaniṣads in the six categories are available as separate books with original texts, the commentary of Upaniṣad Brahmendra Yogin, and the English translation of some of them published by Adyar Library and Research Centre, Adyar, Chennai.

The *Muktikopaniṣad* associates each one of them with one Veda or the other, although only five are seen as part of the Veda in its existing form. However, there is evidence to believe that some more might have been part of some Saṁhitā or Brāhmaṇa in the past, from which they have been separated and became detached subsequently. The ten major Upaniṣads belonging to the four Vedas on which Śaṅkara Bhagavatpāda wrote commentaries are:

Ṛgveda	–	*Aitareya*
Kṛṣṇa-Yajurveda	–	*Taittirīya, Kaṭha*
Śukla-Yajurveda	–	*Īśa, Bṛhadāraṇyaka*

← the author of independent works such as *Paramādvaita-Siddhānta-Paribhāṣā* and *Upeya-Nāma-Viveka*. A prolific author, he annotated the colophons of each of his works with the number of *grantha*s contained in it, presumably to prevent interpolation. On this basis, his works amount to over 45,000 *grantha*s.

http://hinduebooks.blogspot.in/2010/09/108-upanishads-with-sanskrit-commentary.html

[40] I would however not assign much importance to this division, since presence of a *mahāvākya* or *akhaṇḍārthabodha-vākya* is the only distinguishing feature of any Upaniṣad. Categorizing Upaniṣads into Yoga, Śaiva, Śākta and Vaiṣṇava appears to me as an effort to bring these denominations up to the level of Upaniṣads. Vedāntins are non-sectarians. Although they relate to *Īśvara,* the form is not important.

Sāmaveda – *Kena, Chāndogya*

Atharvaveda – *Muṇḍaka, Māṇḍūkya, Praśna*

Each of the four Vedas contains Upaniṣads that are taught in the Advaita tradition to show the *ekavākyatā* of all the four Vedas. Śaṅkara Bhagavatpāda selected the above ten out of the numerous Upaniṣads (available to him then) to comment upon them, being careful enough to select from all the four Vedas. The reason was to show the *ekavākyatā* of the Vedas, i.e. the non-difference between the *Brahman-Ātmā*. Second, it is considered adequate to study these ten Upaniṣads. After completing these ten Upaniṣads, one can study the others independently with the help of whatever commentary is available and arrive at the purport of the Upaniṣads.

īśa-kena-kaṭha-praśna-muṇḍaka-māṇḍūkya-tittiriḥ ।
aitareyaṁ ca chāndogyaṁ bṛhadāraṇyakaṁ tathā ॥[41]

Table 1.1 shows that of the ten Upaniṣads, four are parts of some well-known Saṁhitā or Brāhmaṇa.

> The number of Upaniṣads translated by Dara Shikoh amounts to 50; their number as given in *Mahāvākya-Muktāvalī*, and in the *Muktikopaniṣad* is 108. Prof. Weber thinks that their number, so far as we at present, may be reckoned at 235.[42] However, in order to arrive at so high a number, every title of an Upaniṣad would have to be counted separately, while in several cases it is clearly the same Upaniṣad, which is quoted under different names. In an alphabetical list, which Weber published in 1865, the number of real Upaniṣads reached 149. To that number Dr Burnell[43] in his catalogue added 5, Prof. Haug 16, making the sum total to 170.[44]

We are discussing mainly about the earliest set of Upaniṣads.

---

41 *MukUp* I.1.30.

42 Weber, *History of Sanskrit Literature*, p. 155 n.

43 *Indian Antiquary*, II: 267.

44 Sacred Books of the East, vol. I: *Upaniṣads*, p. lxviii.

Table 1.1: Upaniṣads as part of Saṁhitas or Brāhmaṇas

Upaniṣads	*Vedas*	*Portion*	*Details*
Īśāvāsya	*Śukla-Yajurveda Saṁhitā*	Saṁhitā	In the Saṁhitā section, 40th chapter of *Śukla-Yajurveda Saṁhitā* – both Kāṇva and Mādhyandina Śākhā, with minor variation
Kena	*Sāmaveda*		
Kaṭha	*Kṛṣṇa-Yajurveda*		
Praśna	*Atharvaveda* Paippalāda Śākhā	Brāhmaṇa	In *Gopatha Brāhmaṇa*, is in prose form
Muṇḍaka	*Atharvaveda* Paippalāda Śākhā	Brāhmaṇa	In *Gopatha Brāhmaṇa*
Māṇḍūkya	*Atharvaveda* Paippalāda Śākhā	Brāhmaṇa	In *Gopatha Brāhmaṇa*, is in prose form
Taittirīya	*Kṛṣṇa-Yajurveda* Taittirīya Śākhā	Āraṇyaka	The seventh, eighth and ninth chapters of the *Taittirīya Āraṇyaka*
Aitareya	*Ṛgveda* Śākala Śākhā		
Chāndogya	*Sāmaveda*		
Bṛhadāraṇyaka	*Śukla-Yajurveda*	Āraṇyaka	Is part of *Śukla-Yajurveda-Vājasaneya-Brāhmaṇa* of Kāṇva Śākhā. It is an Āraṇyaka as well.

Thereafter in the later times, most scholars turned sectarian. Over the centuries, varieties of texts gave themselves (or were tagged) the suffix – "Upaniṣad" to their title. That was perhaps meant to provide those texts a halo of authority and an elevated position in the hierarchy of traditional texts. The thoughts in most of such texts were neither fresh nor universal. Most of those texts were theistic and sectarian in their approach and were, therefore, classified according to their affiliations such as Vaiṣṇava, Śaiva, Śākta, etc. With that, the spirit of enquiry, also vanished. Each one was busy championing his cause, putting down the other. There was neither the spirit, nor the wisdom of enquiry.

Now, there are as many Upaniṣads as one can list; there is no definite number. According to some, there are more than 360 Upaniṣads, which include the major and the minor ones; the ancient and the not-so-ancient; some well known and some hardly known.

Therefore, "Upaniṣads" usually stands for the first ten (*Īśāvāsya, Kena, Kaṭha, Praśna, Taittirīya, Aitareya, Chāndogya, Bṛhadāraṇyaka, Muṇḍaka* and *Māṇḍūkya*); followed by the other three (*Kauṣītaki, Śvetāśvatara* and *Jābāla*).

Taittirīya Upaniṣad

Yajurveda has been handed down to us, in two recensions – *Kṛṣṇa-Yajurveda* and *Śukla-Yajurveda*. There is a story regarding the origin of *Kṛṣṇa-Yajurveda*. Vyāsa's disciple Vaiśampāyana had twenty-seven disciples. One of them was Yājñavalkya, son of Brahmarāta. One day the *ṛṣi*s decided that, one who does not reach the Meru Mountain within a week, will get the curse of *brahmahatyā*. Vaiśampāyana could not reach for some reason. His nephew died because of an injury in his foot. Vaiśampāyana called all his disciples and ordered them to perform atonement ritual for him. Yājñavalkya did not want to be part of the group that he considered inferior to him. Vaiśampāyana did not appreciate his arrogance in calling his brāhmaṇa disciples as inferior. He disowned Yājñavalkya and ordered him to return all the knowledge taught by him. Yājñavalkya threw up all the scriptures learnt by him from Vaiśampāyana. His other disciples picked it up in form of Tittiri birds on Vaiśampāyana's order. Thus, this *śākhā* is known as Taittirīya-Śākhā. Subsequently, Yājñavalkya became the visionary of many *śākhā*s by meditating on the sun, which came to be known as *Śukla-Yajurveda*. This story is not available in any Upaniṣad or Brāhmaṇa. However, Pāṇini has written *tittiri-varatantu-khaṇḍikokhacchaṇ*.[45] This is

---

[45] *Aṣ* IV.3.102.

presented in a different way in *Kṛṣṇa-Yajurveda-Anukramaṇikā* – that Veda Vyāsa's disciple Vaiśampāyana handed over this recension to Yāska, and Yāska to Tittiri. Tittiri's disciples are Taittirīya.[46]

Taittirīya Upaniṣad belongs to *Kṛṣṇa-Yajurveda*, while *Īśāvāsya* and *Bṛhadāraṇayaka* belong to *Śukla-Yajurveda*. Of the two recensions (*śākhās*), Taittirīya (of *Kṛṣṇa-Yajurveda*) and Vājasaneyī (of *Śukla-Yajurveda*), the Taittirīya recension is older and more important of the two. It contains a Saṁhitā, a Brāhmaṇa and an Āraṇyaka. In Taittirīya recension, the Saṁhitā and the Brāhmaṇas are mixed together, unlike in the Vājasaneyī, where they are distinctly separate. This is the reason why the *śākhā* is called *Kṛṣṇa* (mixed, not black, as popularly translated) *Yajurveda*. The seventh, eighth and ninth chapters of *Taittirīya Āraṇyaka* constitute *Taittirīya Upaniṣad*; and they are respectively known as Śīkṣāvallī, Brahmānandavallī and Bhṛguvallī, named after the beginning of each chapter. Śīkṣāvallī is also known as *Saṁhiti Upaniṣad*, since the study of *saṁhitā* forms part of it. The remaining two *vallīs* are together called *Vāruṇi Upaniṣad*, because they deal with the knowledge of the *Brahman* (*brahma-vidyā*) as taught by Varuṇa. Each of these chapters is divided into various *anuvāka*s (sections). There are twelve *anuvāka*s in Śīkṣāvallī, nine in Brahmānandavallī and ten in Bhṛguvallī.

Taittirīya Upaniṣad is very popular among those who learn Vedic chanting in the strictly traditional manner, followed by *Mahānārāyaṇa Upaniṣad*, which is the tenth and concluding chapter of *Taittirīya Āraṇyaka*.

---

46 See Swāmi Vidyānanda Giri's Preface to *Taittirīya Upaniṣad*, Kailash Ashram.

Significance[47] of Taittirīya Upaniṣad in the Study of Vedānta

Taittirīya Upaniṣad is one of the ten principal Upaniṣads. Śaṅkara's *bhāṣyam* (commentary) on this Upaniṣad and Sureśvarācārya's *vārttika*[48] (verse-commentary that seeks to explain both the Upaniṣad and Śaṅkara's *bhāṣyam* thereon), enhance its importance. This Upaniṣad is a classic for four of its outstanding teachings:

i. For *svarūpa lakṣaṇa* (the definition of the essential nature of *Brahman*). The second chapter, the Brahmānandavallī's *mantra – satyaṁ jñānam anantaṁ brahma*[49] is the *svarūpa lakṣaṇa* of *Brahman*.

ii. *Taṭastha lakṣaṇa* (incidental nature of *Brahman* as the cause of the universe) which is presented in Bhṛguvallī, the third

---

[47] This concluding part is the presentation by my spiritual *guru* Swami Dayananda Saraswati. Nobody has explained *Taittirīya Upaniṣad* with *Śāṅkarabhāṣyam* as well as he has done in all his five long-term courses. The reason why I selected *Taittirīya Upaniṣad* as my topic was to study it again, make it my own and have a grip over it. *Taittirīya Upaniṣad* still baffles me, it is like Śaṅkara's *Bhāṣyam*, *prasanna-gambhīra*. Second, since it lends itself to chanting, it may appear fairly simple compared to *Chāndogya*, *Bṛhadāraṇyaka* and of course *Māṇḍūkya*. But it can pull the carpet under one's feet, the moment one thinks one has got it right.

[48] Independent exposition of a *bhāṣyam* in verse-form, e.g. Sureśvarācārya's *Taittirīya* and *Bṛhadāraṇyaka-Bhāṣya-Vārttikam*, based on Śaṅkara's *Taittirīya* and *Bṛhadāraṇyaka Bhāṣyam* respectively.

ukta-anukta-duruktānāṁ cintā yatra pravartate ।
taṁ granthaṁ vārttikaṁ prāhur-vārttikājña manīṣiṇaḥ ॥

Thus, the *vārttikas*, in other words, were *sūtras* intended to correlate, modify and supplement the original *sūtras*..It is said, Śaṅkara gave the freedom to Sureśvara to write *vārttikam* on his *Taittirīya* and *Bṛhadāraṇyaka Bhāṣyam*.

[49] *TaiUp* II.1.

chapter: *yato vā imāni bhūtāni jāyante* । *yena jātāni jīvanti* । *yatprayantyabhisaṁviśanti* ।[50]

iii. For the method of discrimination between the self and the non-self through an enquiry into fivefold sheath (*pañca-kośa-viveka*).[51]

iv. For *ānanda-mīmāṁsā*[52] (the calculus of happiness) that points to *Brahman* as happiness par excellence.

Brahman as the abhinna-nimitta-upādāna-kāraṇa of the Jagat

Apart from the above, *Brahman* being the *nimitta-kāraṇa* as well as the *upādāna-kāraṇa* is explicitly brought out in *Taittirīya*. The creation had baffled the *ṛṣi*s and it continues to baffle the scientists, the astrophysicists until the present. Brahmānandavallī gives a model of this creation stating:

> *tasmāt vā etasmāt ātmanaḥ ākāśaḥ sambhūtaḥ* । *ākāsād vāyuḥ* । *vāyor-agniḥ* । *agner-āpaḥ* । *adbhyaḥ pṛthivī* । *pṛthivyā oṣadhayaḥ* । *oṣadhībhyo 'nnam* । *annāt puruṣaḥ* ।[53]

Therefore, this *jagat* is nothing but the *vastu*. This is the Śruti-*pramāṇa* for *Brahman* being the *upādāna-kāraṇa* of this *jagat*.

The same *vallī* goes ahead to establish *Brahman* as the *nimitta-kāraṇa* of this *jagat:*

> *so 'kāmayata* । *bahu syāṁ prajāyeyeti* । *sa tapo' tapyata* । *sa tapastaptvā* । *idaṁ sarvam asṛjata* । *yadidaṁ kiṁca* । *tat sṛṣṭvā* । *tad evānuprāviśat* ।[54]
>
> *raso vai saḥ*।[55]

---

[50] *TaiUp* III.1.

[51] Ibid. II.1-5 and III.2-5.

[52] Ibid. II.8.

[53] Ibid. II.1.

[54] Ibid. II.6.

[55] Ibid. II.7.

bhiṣā 'smād vātaḥ pavate । *bhiṣodeti sūryaḥ* । *bhiṣā 'smād-agniścendraśca* । *mṛtyur-dhāvati pañcama iti* ।[56]

In all these sentences, the *nimitta-kāraṇa* is brought out very well.

Chāndogya Upaniṣad deals mainly with the *upādāna-kāraṇa*. In *Taittirīya* alone, the *nimitta-kāraṇa* is brought out clearly. The *bhāṣyam* is also beautiful and elaborate. Bhāṣyakāra Śaṅkara has given his best in *Taittirīya*.

Besides, as one studies this Upaniṣad, one is struck by the remarkable sequence, both chronological and logical, in the presentation of the subject matter. Śikṣāvallī explains the scriptural rites and meditations, which are *bahiraṅga-sādhanā*s (external aids to the attainment of *brahmajñānam*). While the performance of rites in a spirit of dedication to the Lord leads to purification of the mind (*cittaśuddhi*), the practice of meditation in the manner in which they are prescribed by the scripture without desiring results thereof, helps one to have concentration of the mind (*citta-naiścalyam*). Only a person whose mind is purified, and who is capable of concentration, is eligible for the study of Vedānta. *Śravaṇam* (listening to the scriptures), *mananam* (rational reflection) and *nididhyāsanam* (repeated contemplation) are the *mukhya-antaraṅga-sādhanā*s (principal internal aids to the attainment of knowledge). Eligibility is a prerequisite for *śravaṇam*, lack of which may not be fruitful. For a qualified seeker, the nature of *Brahman-Ātmā* has been set forth though the study of the various Śruti statements in the Brahmānandavallī. Bhṛguvallī purports to teach *mananam* (the method of reflection on the teachings of Śruti statements). The discipline of *mananam* should follow *śravaṇam*. Varuṇa did not tell Bhṛgu directly or immediately, what *Brahman* is. On the contrary, he formulated a definition of *Brahman*, and made Bhṛgu inquire in a systematic way into that definition, with a view to find out *Brahman* by himself. The *anvaya-vyatireka* method that

---

56 *TaiUp* II.8.

Bhṛgu followed enabled him to discriminate *Brahman-Ātmā* from *anna, prāṇa, manas, vāk,* etc. and finally obtain the knowledge of *Brahman-Ātmā*.

Taittirīya Upaniṣad quoted in the Brahmasūtra

Brahmasūtra is an analytical text. It analyses various apparently contradictory statements of the Śruti and arrives at the *tātparyam,* (the purport, the essential meaning). Ṛṣi Bādarāyaṇa has quoted extensively from *Taittirīyopaniṣad* in *Brahmasūtra* and it is impossible to comprehend *Brahmasūtra* without assimilating the subject matter of *Taittirīyopaniṣad*.

In the whole of 555[57] *sūtras* of *Brahmasūtra,*[58] there is only one *sūtra* that deals with the *lakṣaṇa* of *Brahman* – *janmādyasya yataḥ* ।[59] and this *sūtra* is based on *yato vā imāni bhūtāni jāyante* । *yena jātāni jīvanti* । *yatprayantyabhisaṁviśanti* । Such is the importance of *Taittirīyopaniṣad*.

57 545 *sūtras* as per Rāmānuja, and 564 as per Madhva.

58 This difference might be due to splitting of certain *sūtras*, or combining certain others.

59 *BrSū* I.1.2.

2

Concept of Pramāṇa in Indian Philosophy

Pramāṇas in Indian Philosophy

As stated in the previous chapter, there are six major *āstika* systems and three major *nāstika* systems in Indian philosophy. The number of *pramāṇa*s accepted by them become very important in their basic tenets and doctrines. According to each system, the number of *pramāṇa*s accepted as valid, depends upon the types of knowledge that are recognized (Table 2.1).

The Cārvākas – Materialists School accept only one *pramāṇa*: *pratyakṣa* (perception) as the only *pramāṇa*.

The Buddhists and the Vaiśeṣikas accept two *pramāṇa*s: *pratyakṣa* and *anumāna*. Vaiśeṣikas reduce *upamāna* and *śabda* to *anumāna*.

The Sāṁkhya, Yoga, Viśiṣṭādvaita, Dvaita accept three *pramāṇa*s: *pratyakṣa, anumāna* and *śabda*.

The Nyāya School accepts four *pramāṇa*s: *pratyakṣa, anumāna, śabda* and *arthāpatti*. *Śabda* in Nyāya includes both *apauruṣeya* (the Vedas) and *pauruṣeya* (*āptavākya*).

The Prābhākara Mīmāṁsā School accepts five *pramāṇa*s: *pratyakṣa, anumāna, śabda, arthāpatti* and *upamāna*. Incidentally, *śabda* as a *pramāṇa* as per Prābhākara Mīmāṁsā School continues to this day to represent only the Vedas.

The Bhāṭṭa Mīmāṁsā School accepts six *pramāṇa*s: *pratyakṣa, anumāna, śabda, arthāpatti, upamāna* and *anupalabdhi*.

Table 2.1: Pramāṇas Accepted in Indian Philosophical Systems

Pramāṇa	*Cārvāka* (1)	*Buddhism/ Jainism/ Vaiśeṣika*[1] (2)	*Sāṁkhya/ Yoga*[2] (3)	*Nyāya* (4)	*Prābhākara Mīmāṁsā* (5)	*Bhātta Mīmāṁsā* (6)	*Advaita Vedānta* (6)
Pratyakṣa (perception)	*	*	*	*	*	*	*
Anumāna (inference)		*	*	*	*	*	*
Arthāpatti (presumption)				*	*	*	*
Upamāna (comparison)					*	*	*
Anupalabdhi (non-apprehension)						*	*
Śabda (words)	Labelled *nāstika*, since it does not accept *śabda-*	Buddhism, Jainism labelled *nāstika*, since these do not accept *śabda-pramāṇa*	*	* *Apauruṣeya & pauruṣeya*	* Only Vedas *Apauruṣeya*	* *	* Only *Apauruṣeya*

[1] Vaiśeṣikas (*āstika*) reduce *upamāna* and *śabda* to *anumāna*.

[2] *Pratyakṣānumānāgamah, pramṇāni-Yogasūtra* I.7.

The Advaita recognizes all the six *pramāṇas* – *pratyakṣa, anumāna, śabda, arthāpatti, upamāna* and *anupalabdhi* accepted by the Bhāṭṭa Mīmāṁsā School and generally agrees with it with certain modifications. For example, Vedas are supposed to be merely reissues of an eternal edition of knowledge, perception is meant only for empirical purposes.

Background of Pramāṇa-Śāstra

The word *pramāṇa* signifies the essential means of arriving at valid knowledge. The whole system of Nyāya is based on *pramāṇa*. In fact, Nyāya-Śāstra is alternatively known as Pramāṇa-Śāstra. *Pramā* means "knowing an object as it is": *tadvati tat prakārānubhavaḥ pramā*. Another definition of *pramāṇa* is: *pramāyāḥ karaṇam, pramāṇam*. Alternatively, *yathārthānubhavaḥ pramā* (actual experience is *pramā*). To know a rope as rope is *pramā*. If we see a snake instead of the rope, it is *apramā: ayathārtha-anubhavaḥ apramā*.

Pramāṇas as per Advaita Vedānta

True knowledge (*yathārtha-jñāna*) is determined by *pramāṇa* and all *ācāryas* admit that a *pramāṇa* is a valid means of knowledge. Advaita Vedānta recognizes six *pramāṇas* and they are: *pratyakṣa* (perception), *anumāna* (inference), *arthāpatti* (presumption), *upamāna* (comparison), *anupalabdhi* (non-apprehension) and *śabda* (scriptural testimony only). Śaṅkara has adopted in his Advaita Vedānta system, these six *pramāṇas* as the valid means of knowledge.

1. *Pratyakṣa*

Pratyakṣa means perception (from the root √*akṣ* – to reach + *prati* = against, back). It is a valid means of knowledge (*pramāṇa*) for every school of Indian philosophy including the Cārvākas.

According to Nyāya, *pratyakṣa* is knowledge generated by sense–object contact. *Pratyakṣa* is defined as *indriyārtha-*

sannikarṣajanyaṁ jñānaṁ pratyakṣam,[3] meaning "direct perception takes place when there is a contact between the senses and the object". Perception is a direct means of knowledge and does not depend upon any other means of knowledge. It is to be noted here that *anumāna, arthāpatti, upamāna, anupalabdhi* and *śabda* (*pauruṣeya / āptavākyam,* not *śruti*), depend upon *pratyakṣa* as the *mūla-pramāṇa*. *Anumāna* cannot be arrived at without seeing part of the statement. *Upamāna* also cannot be made without seeing the example. *Śabda* (*pauruṣeya / āptavākyam*) also has to be perceptible. Gautama defines *pratyakṣa* as: *akṣam akṣaṁ pratityutpadyate iti pratyakṣam* (knowledge born of sensory perception, such as eyes is *pratyakṣa*).

Later Naiyāyikas recognized two kinds of perception: (i) *laukika* (ordinary), and (ii) *alaukika* (extraordinary) to include God's perception and the supernormal perception of the *yogīs*. The Nyāya School also recognizes both (i) *bāhya* (external), and (ii) *mānasa* (internal) perceptions.

The Nyāya system lays down a logical condition for valid knowledge that it should not contradict the real nature of the object. *Pratyakṣa* should be *avyabhicārī*.

2. *Anumāna*

Anumāna is another means of valid knowledge. It literally means knowledge afterwards. The word *anumāna* is derived from the root √*mā* = *māne,*[4] to measure, prepare, display. *Anu* = *paścāt* (along, after) + *māna; jñāna,* meaning "the knowledge that takes place afterwards". Thus, *anumāna* literally means, "after knowledge", i.e. knowledge that "follows other knowledge". Inferential knowledge is knowledge that results through the instrumentation of some other knowledge (*jñāna-kāraṇaka-*

---

3 *TaSaṅ* 32, p. 79.

4 √*mā* = *māne* in *Adādigaṇa*, 2nd conjugation; √*māṅ* = *māne śabde ca* in *Juhotyādigaṇa*, 3rd conjugation; √*māṅ*= *māne* in *Divādigaṇa*, 4th conjugation.

jñānam). In *anumāna,* first, the *liṅga* (minor term) is seen, then by *liṅga* or *hetu,* the *sādhya-sambandha-jñāna* or *vyāpti-jñāna* (invariable concomitance) takes place. This *sādhya* (major term) is known as *anumiti.* Since this knowledge takes place after *liṅga-darśana,* this is known as *anumāna*. The classic example is, *parvato vahnimān, dhūmatvāt, yathā mahānasaḥ.*

Anumāna is produced through the instrumentality of the knowledge of invariable concomitance (*vyāpti*). Hence, inference is indirect knowledge. (*Pratyakṣa* is the only direct knowledge.)

The Nyāya School claims that there are five factors of a syllogism – *anumāna*. This is known as *pañca-avayavi-nyāya*. The properties of the five factors are thus:

i. ***Pratijñā***: objective/proposition to be proved or established is *pratijñā: sādhya nirdeśaḥ pratijñā.*[5] It is a logical statement that has to be proved. *Parvato vahnimān* (this mountain has fire) is the *pratijñā,* which has to be established.

ii. ***Hetu***: reason, logic. It states the reason/logic for the establishment of the proposition. The definition of *hetu* is: *udāharaṇa-sādharmyāt sādhya-sādhanaṁ hetuḥ.*[6] In the above classic example, the *hetu* is *dhūmatvāt* (because it has smoke). The objective is to establish the presence of fire, through the presence of smoke.

iii. ***Udāharaṇa***: Definition is *sādhya-sādharmyāt tad-dharmmabhāvī dṛṣṭānta udāharaṇam.*[7] Or *vyāpti pratipādakam udāharaṇam.*[8] To present an example in support of the *pakṣa* (major term) is *udāharaṇa*. In the above example, the *udāharaṇa* is *yatra yatra dhūmaḥ, tatra tatra vahniḥ, yathā mahānasaḥ* (whatever has smoke, has fire, just as a kitchen).

---

5 *NyāSū* I.1.33.

6 Ibid. I.1.34.

7 Ibid. I.1.36.

8 *TaSaDī*.

iv. *Upanaya*: application of the universal concomitance to the present case. In *upanaya*, the *vyāpti* is used in the current situation. *Tathā parvataḥ* (similarly this mountain).

v. *Nigamana*: conclusion drawn from the preceding propositions. Definition: *hetvapadeśāt pratijñāyāḥ punar-vacanaṁ nigamanam*. In the above example *ata eva parvato vahnimān* (hence, the mountain has fire) is the *nigamana*.

It is interesting to note that Mīmāṁsā as well as Advaita Vedānta claim only three members to be needed in a syllogism, and they may be comprised either the first three (i) *pratijñā, hetu* and *udāharaṇa*, or the last three (ii) *udāharaṇa, upanaya* and *nigamana*.[9] Buddhism goes still further and claims that only two members of a syllogism are necessary: *udāharaṇa* and *upanaya*.

3. *Arthāpatti*

Arthāpatti is defined as: *anyathā anupapatti* (otherwise it is not possible). *Arthāpatti* means presumption. It is an act of postulating something to account for what apparently clashes with experience, and is therefore, in the nature of hypothesis. Sometimes two rival theories are equally plausible, but appear mutually incompatible. In such cases, a presumption is to be made. It is "assumption of some unperceived fact, in order to reconcile some inconsistency in perceived facts". For instance, in the statement – *pīno devadatto divā na bhuṅkte* (the fat Devadatta does not eat during the day), there is apparent contradiction because of two facts: (i) fat Devadatta does not eat during day, (ii) but, he does not lose weight. These two contradictory statements are reconciled with *arthāpatti pramāṇa* that he must be eating during night. *Arthāpatti* is more than one-step inference. However, at the best, it remains an inference.

Arthāpatti is of two kinds: (i) *śruta-arthāpatti* (postulation from what is heard), and (ii) *dṛṣṭa-arthāpatti* (postulation from what is seen). *Arthāpatti* is a valid means of knowledge (*pramāṇa*)

---

[9] *avayavāśca traya eva – VePa*, Chapter II, p. 75.

for the Nyāya, both the Mīmāṁsā schools and Advaita Vedānta.

Prābhākara school says that, where it involves an element of doubt as to the truth of the two irreconcilable facts of perception, there *arthāpatti* helps to remove the doubt.

According to Bhāṭṭa school, doubt is not the basis of presumption. The basis is the conflict of the two well-known facts. This is the difference between presumption and inference, and hence presumption should not be treated simply as inference.

Advaita Vedānta says that, there is neither a doubt nor a conflict, but merely an inexplicable fact that needs explaining. It posits that presumption is the framing of an explanatory hypothesis, based on the knowledge of the fact to be explained.

4. *Upamāna*

Definition is: *sādṛśya-pramākaraṇam upamānam. Upamāna* (comparison/example or similarity) is another valid means of knowledge – *upamāna* is that *pramāṇa*, through which, an unknown object is known, with a known object, based on same or comparable characteristics. *Prasiddha-sādharmyāt sādhya-sādhanam-upamānam.*[10] The classic example is: a person going to the forest is told that a bison is like a cow.

In *upamāna*, we acquire the knowledge of a new thing, through its resemblance with another thing previously well known. *Upamāna* reveals two facts – the knowledge of a new object not perceived before, and a well-known object perceived before, and the knowledge of resemblance between the both. *Upamāna* however should not be confused with analogy of the Western Logic.

Upamāna is a valid means of knowledge accepted by Nyāya, Mīmāṁsā and Advaita Vedānta. Both Kumārila (around CE 660 – older contemporary of Śaṅkara (CE 780–820)) and Prabhākara (CE 650–720) hold that *upamāna* is the knowledge of similarity

10 *NyāSū* I.1.6.

of the remembered cow, with the perceived bison. Advaita Vedānta agrees with Mīmāṁsā, as far as it goes. However, the former also includes in its definition, the knowledge of similarity between the perceived object to the remembered one (*smṛti*). Mīmāṁsā stops with the knowledge of the similarity between the remembered object with the perceived one.

Nyāya differs here, as it holds that, *upamāna* is the knowledge of *sādṛśya* (similarity) of an unknown object (e.g. a wild cow/ bison) with a familiar object (e.g. a cow).

Vaiśeṣika, Sāṁkhya, Yoga, Buddhism and Jainism do not accept *upamāna* as a *pramāṇa*. The Vaiśeṣikas treat *upamāna* within *anumāna*. Sāṁkhya consider it as *pratyakṣa*. The famous Buddhist philosopher Diṅnāga (CE 480–540) treats it as *pratyakṣa*. These contentions are neutralized in *Nyāya-Siddhānta-Muktāvalī*.

5. *Anupalabdhi or Abhāva (Non-apprehension)*

Anupalabdhi means non-cognition, non-apprehension, non-perception. By dint of this *pramāṇa*, non-existence (*abhāva*) is cognized. It should be remembered that Advaita Vedānta recognizes *abhāva* as a *bhāva-padārtha*, as *abhāva* does not mean void (*śūnya*). The absence of an object is known due to its non-perception. For example, we perceive the locus (*adhikaraṇa*) of a pot. When the pot is removed, from its locus, we perceive the locus (*adhikaraṇa*) of the non-existence (*abhāva*) of the pot (*bhūtale ghaṭo na*) and not non-existence per se.

Dharmarāja Adhvarīndra (around CE 1550–1650) discusses four kinds of non-existence (*abhāva*),[11] and they are: (i) previous non-existence (*prāgabhāva*), (ii) non-existence on destruction (*pradhvaṁsābhāva*), (iii) absolute non-existence (*atyantābhāva*), and (iv) mutual non-existence (*anyānyobhāva*).

Śabara Svāmī (beginning of CE) regards *anupalabdhi* as an independent valid means of knowledge. It is a specific *pramāṇa*,

---

[11] *VePa*, Chapter VI, p. 137.

by which negation is known, e.g. the absence of a pot on my hand (*karatale ghaṭo nāsti)*. The Bhāṭṭa Mīmāṁsakas and the Advaita Vedāntins hold that *abhāva* (non-existence) is known through non-cognition.

The above two schools are the only schools to accept non-cognition as a separate *pramāṇa* (valid means of knowledge). Just as positive apprehension of some existent through a valid means of knowledge is a way of cognizing; so is non-apprehension of something, another way of cognizing according to these two schools.

The critics say that this is merely a variant of perception and not really a separate source of cognition. However, since it is the specific cause of immediate knowledge of non-existence that is not produced by any other means of knowledge, it deserves a place in the list of valid *pramāṇa*.

Prabhākara, like some Vaiśeṣikas, does not recognize *anupalabdhi* as an independent means of knowledge. He rejects non-existence as an ontological reality and *anupalabdhi* as a distinct means of knowledge.

6. *Śabda*

Śabda (from the root √*śabd* = *śabdakriyāyām* – to make sound, *Curādigaṇa*, 10th conjugation) means sound, word. Technically, it means verbal testimony, verbal knowledge, scriptural authority. *Śabda* is an independent means of valid knowledge. *Śabda*, however, for all intents and purposes remains an external authority (that is why it requires *śraddhā* for acceptance). The definition *āptopadeśaḥ śabdaḥ*[12] (the sayings of an *āpta-puruṣa* are *śabda-pramāṇa*). And he who speaks the truth is an *āptaḥ*. *Āptavākyaṁ śabda* । *āptastu yathārtha-vaktā*.[13]

Indian philosophers lay down certain conditions before a

---

[12] *NyāSū* I.1.7.

[13] *TaSaṅ* VII.1, p. 119.

reference is made to a revealed text. They are: (i) the revealed truth should be extra-empirical (*anadhigata*), (ii) it should not be contradicted (*abādhitam*) by other *pramāṇa*,[14] and (iii) the reason should foreshadow what revelation states. In view of the majority of Indian philosophical systems, reason by itself is incapable of discerning the whole truth. It may often lead to two or more plausible conclusions, and without the aid of revelation, it is impossible to avoid sceptism.

According to Nyāya, *śabda-pramāṇa* is the testimony of a trustworthy person – one who knows the truth and communicates it correctly. Nyāya recognizes two kinds of *śabda*: *dṛṣṭārtha* and *adṛṣṭārtha*.

i. *Dṛṣṭārtha* operates within this empirical world. It is testimony relating to perceptible objects. All that has been said in the scriptures about perceptible objects such as medicines, rainfall, rites, ceremonies, etc. fall under this category.

ii. *Adṛṣṭārtha* deals with areas not perceptible, i.e. what the scriptures say about life after death: *puṇya, pāpa, svarga, karma-phala*, continuity of the *jīva, Īśvara*.

According to Mīmāṁsā, however, the purport of *śabda-pramāṇa* lies in the injunctive texts of the ritual sections of the Vedas, i.e. Brāhmaṇas.

According to Advaita Vedānta, the truth revealed by *śabda* is non-difference of the *jīva* with *Īśvara*.

In case of scriptural testimony, the revealed truth should be *anadhigata* – new or extra-empirical. Secondly, what is revealed should be *abādhitam* – not contradicted by other means of knowledge. It also must have *phalavat arthabodhakatvam*. It must give something which is *phalavat* – it must have meaning

---

[14] *tatra smṛtivyāvṛttaṁ pramātvam-anadhigata-avādhita-arthaviṣayaka-jñāntvam* । *smṛti-sādhāraṇantu avādhitārtha-viṣayaka-jñānatavam* ।
– *Ve-Pa*, Chapter I

> and value (whether it is *putrakāmeṣṭi* or *brahmajñānam*), and at the same time it should not be available by any other means of knowledge. *Śruti-pramāṇa* reveals that which is *anadhigata*. It reveals a *vastu* that is not known by other *pramāṇas*. Śruti is the only *pramāṇa* for *brahmavastu*.
>
> – Swami Dayananda Saraswati

Requisite Factors of Śabda-pramāṇa

In *śabda-pramāṇa*, the knowledge takes place from a sentence. It becomes imperative now to know what constitutes a sentence, and how to get its meaning. To know the meaning of any sentence, four conditions are necessary – *ākaṅkṣā*, *yogyatā*, *āsatti* / *sannidhi* and *tātparya*.

i. *Ākāṅkṣā* means expectancy, mutual affinity between words, syntax. Different words in a sentence must be related to each other. When one says, "bring", a natural desire is created in the mind of the listener as to "what". When one says, *gām ānaya* (bring the cow), that desire is fulfilled and the sentence conveys a meaning.

Words must be compatible in order to fulfil this condition. A mere group of words such as like – "Hari milk calf" does not convey any meaning, hence is not a valid sentence.

ii. *Yogyatā* means congruity or special fitness. It consists in there being no contradiction among the meanings of the words of a sentence; "fire is cold", goes against our experience. Or "sprinkle with fire", makes the sentence meaningless, since it is impossible to do such.

iii. *Āsatti* or *sannidhi* means proximity, nearness. It is a formal condition that the words must possess to constitute a sentence. The words that make up a sentence, must be proximate or contiguous in time when they are spoken, or in space, when they are written. If there is a long gap between two words, then the sentence will not be meaningful. After saying "bring" if one takes a long time to say "the cow", then it is not a meaningful sentence. Similarly, if the words are one after another without required gap, the sentence is not meaningful. Thus, *āsatti* consists in the articulation of words, without undue delay.

iv. *Tātparya* means purport/intent. The meaning of a sentence depends upon the purport of the speaker. According to Nyāya – *vaktur-icchā tu tātparyam* (purport/intent is the intention of the speaker). A word may have more than one meaning. Depending on the context, one has to decipher the meaning. *Saindhava* means the horse of the state of Sindhu or a kind of salt. If one asks "bring *saindhava*" while eating, one has to understand the meaning as salt. However, while going out if one says, "bring *saindhava*" one has to understand it as the horse. In common parlance, the meaning of a sentence is understood depending on the context.

The other division of *śabda*, based on *vṛtti*, is discussed in Chapter 9.

3

The Five Śānti-mantras in Taittirīya

Importance of Vedic Prayer

PRAYING to *Īśvara* is an integral part in the pursuit of self-knowledge. One cannot bypass *Īśvara*. In this pursuit, the *śānti-mantra*s play a significant role. Interestingly, out of the ten *śānti-mantra*s (*Daśaśānti*) that is traditionally chanted before any Upaniṣadic *upadeśa,* five are from *Taittirīya Upaniṣad.* In the *Pañcaśānti* also, three are from *Taittirīya Upaniṣad.* If one goes through the free translations of the five *śānti-mantra*s, one would observe that the prayers are always for knowledge and not material wealth. Even the prayer for good health and proper functioning of the faculties is ultimately for self-knowledge.

Vedānta and Worship

Although, in the study of Vedānta, there is no specific worship, nevertheless it is very important for one to relate to *Īśvara.* Otherwise, the pursuit becomes a mere intellectual exercise. And, since the *sannyāsī*s are eligible to pursue this, relating to *Īśvara* is never abandoned, although they have been freed from rituals, by the scriptures. This is clearly evident in the Upaniṣads, the *śānti-mantra*s.

Difference between Upāsanā and Self-Knowledge

Various *upāsanā*s are there in the Upaniṣads. *Upāsanā*s are stepping stones to self-knowledge. While rituals help in obtaining *cittaśuddhi, upāsanā*s help in gaining *citta-naiścalyam.* This has been elaborately dealt with in Chapter 5 (Sīkṣāvallī). It is to be understood that, while in *upāsanās*, duality is still there; in knowledge, duality is not there. Hence, self-knowledge is the highest that can be gained in this life.

First Śāntimantraḥ

This invocatory verse originally appears in *Ṛgveda*.[1]

ॐ ॥ शं नो मित्रः शं वरुणः। शं नो भवत्वर्यमा । शं न इन्द्रो बृहस्पतिः । शं नो विष्णुरुरुक्रमः। नमो ब्रह्मणे । नमस्ते वायो । त्वमेव प्रत्यक्षं ब्रह्मासि । त्वमेव प्रत्यक्षं ब्रह्म वदिष्यामि । ऋतं वदिष्यामि । सत्य वदिष्यामि । तन्मामवतु । तद्वक्तारमवतु । अवतु माम् । अवतु वक्तारम् ॥ ॐ शान्तिः शान्तिः शान्तिः ॥

oṁ śaṁ no mitraḥ śaṁ varuṇaḥ । *śaṁ no bhavatvaryamā* । *śaṁ na indro bṛhaspatiḥ* । *śaṁ no viṣṇur-urukramaḥ* । *namo brahmaṇe* । *namaste vāyo* । *tvameva pratyakṣaṁ brahmāsi* । *tvameva pratyakṣaṁ brahma vadiṣyāmi* । *ṛtam vadiṣyāmi* । *satyaṁ vadiṣyāmi* । *tan-mām avatu* । *tad vaktāram avatu* । *avatu mām* । *avatu vaktāram* । *oṁ śāntiḥ śāntiḥ śāntiḥ* ।

– *TaiUp* I.1

May Mitra, the Sun deity be auspicious to us. May Varuṇa, the Ocean deity be auspicious to us. May Aryamā, the Lord of the manes be auspicious to us. May Indra, the king of the *devatās*, and Bṛhaspati, the preceptor of the *devatās* be auspicious to us. May Viṣṇu, the all-pervasive, sustainer of the creation be auspicious to us. May Urukrama, Lord Vāmana be auspicious to us. Salutations to *Brahman* (Hiraṇyagarbha/ *Saguṇa-Brahman*). Salutations to Vāyu, the Wind deity. You (Vāyu)! are indeed the perceptible *Brahman*. I understand (declare) you to be the perceptible *Brahman*. I declare you as the right understanding. I understand you to be the truthfulness in speech. May that Truth protect me. May that Truth protect my Teacher. May it protect me. May it protect the Teacher. May there be peace, peace, peace.

---

1 *śaṁ no mitraḥ śaṁ varunaḥ śaṁ no bhavatvaryamā* ।
śaṁ na indro bṛhaspatiḥ śaṁ no viṣṇur-urukramaḥ ॥ – *ṚVS* I.90.9

Second Śāntimantraḥ

शं नो॑ मि॒त्रः शं वरु॑णः । शं नो॑ भवत्वर्य॒मा । शं न॒ इन्द्रो॑ बृह॒स्पतिः॑ । शं नो॑
विष्णु॑रुरु॒क्रमः॑ । नमो॒ ब्रह्म॑णे । नम॑स्ते वायो । त्वमे॒व प्र॒त्यक्षं॒ ब्रह्मा॑सि । त्वामे॒व
प्र॒त्यक्षं॒ ब्रह्म॑वादिषम् । ऋ॒तमं॑वादिषम् । स॒त्यमं॑वादिषम् । तन्मामां॑वीत् ।
तद्व॒क्तार॑मावीत् । आवी॑न्माम् । आवी॑द्व॒क्तारम्॑ । ॐ शान्तिः॑ शान्तिः॑
शान्तिः॑ ॥

*śaṁ no mitraḥ śaṁ varuṇaḥ ǀ śaṁ no bhavatvaryamā ǀ śaṁ
na indro bṛhaspatiḥ ǀ śaṁ no viṣṇur-urukramaḥ ǀ namo
brahmaṇe ǀ namaste vāyo ǀ tvameva pratyakṣaṁ brahmāsi ǀ
tvāmeva pratyakṣaṁ brahmāvādiṣaṁ ǀ ṛtamavādiṣam ǀ
satyamavādiṣam ǀ tanmām-āvīt ǀ tad-vaktāram-āvīt ǀ āvīn-
mām ǀ āvīd-vaktāram ǀ oṁ śāntiḥ śāntiḥ śāntiḥ ǀ   – TaiUp I.12*

May Mitra, the Sun deity be auspicious to us. May Varuṇa,
the Ocean deity be auspicious to us. May Aryamā, the lord
of the manes, be auspicious to us. May Indra, the king of
the *devatā*s and Bṛhaspati, the preceptor of the *devatā*s be the
source of auspiciousness to us. May Viṣṇu, the all-pervasive,
sustainer of the creation, be auspicious to us. May Urukrama,
Lord Vāmana be auspicious to us. Salutations to *Brahman*
(Hiraṇyagarbha/*Saguṇa-Brahman*). O Lord Vāyu! Salutations
to you. You are indeed the perceptible *Brahman*. I have
understood (declared) you to be the perceptible *Brahman*. I
have understood (declared) you to be the right understanding.
I have declared you to be the Truth/truthfulness. That Truth
protected me. That Truth protected the teacher. That Truth
protected me. That Truth protected the teacher. May there be
peace, peace, peace.

The deities mentioned in this *anuvāka* were invoked at the
outset to ward off all the obstacles on the path of the seeker
of *brahmajñānam*. The various acts of meditation were then
prescribed to purify the mind of the student of *brahma-vidyā*. It
is assumed that they have brought about the necessary result. It
now remains for the student to offer gratitude to the *devatā*s who
have helped in preparing the way; otherwise, the wrong-doing

of ingratitude may still prevent the aspirant from reaching the goal. This is the purpose of this *uttaraśānti*.

Third Śāntimantraḥ

यः॒छन्द॑सामृष॒भो विश्व॑रू॒पः । छन्दो॒भ्योऽध्य॒मृता॒त्सम्ब॒भूव॑ । स मेन्द्रो॑ मे॒धया॑ स्पृणोतु । अ॒मृत॑स्य देव॒ धार॑णो भू॒यासम् । शरीरं॑ मे॒ विच॑र्षणम् । जि॒ह्वा मे॒ मधु॑मत्तमा । कर्णा॑भ्यां भूरि॒ विश्रु॑वम् । ब्र॒ह्मणः॒ कोशो॑ऽसि मे॒धया॒ पिहि॑तः । श्रु॒तं मे॑ गोपाय ।

yaśchandasāṁ ṛṣabho viśvarūpaḥ | chandobhyo 'dhyamṛtāt sambabhūva | sa mendro medhayā spṛnotu | amṛtasya deva dhārano bhūyāsam | śarīraṁ me vicarṣaṇam | jihvā me madhumattamā | karṇābhyāṁ bhūri viśruvam | brahmaṇaḥ kośo 'si medhayā pihitaḥ | śrutaṁ me gopāya | – TaiUp I.4

(That *Oṁkāra*) which manifested from the hymns of the Vedas, is the greatest among the Vedic *mantras*, and is endowed with manifold forms. May that Lord (*Oṁkāra*) strengthen me with intelligence. O Lord! May I become the possessor of the immortal wisdom. May my body be healthy. May my speech be extremely sweet and agreeable.[2] May I listen (to the scriptures) repeatedly through (my) ears. You are the sheath (abode) of *Brahman*, (which is) veiled by worldly knowledge. May you protect what is studied to by me.

This *anuvāka* is a prayer addressed to *Īśvara*, the giver of all wishes, seeking mental power and physical fitness, without which the knowledge of *Brahman* is not possible. This is chanted for *medhā*.

Fourth Śāntimantraḥ

अ॒हं वृ॒क्षस्य॒ रेरि॑वा । की॒र्तिः पृ॒ष्ठं गिरे॑रि॑व । ऊ॒र्ध्व॑पवित्रो वा॒जिनी॑व स्व॒मृत॑मस्मि । द्रवि॑णं स॒वर्च॑सम् । सु॒मेधा॑ अ॒मृतो॑क्षितः । इति त्रि॒शङ्कोर्वे॑दानु॒वचनम् ॥

ahaṁ vṛkṣasya rerivā | kīrtiḥ pṛṣṭhaṁ gireriva | ūrdhvapavitro

---

[2] *madhurā ca vāk* (speech should be sweet) says Vyāsa in *MaBhā*, Ādi-Parva, 88.12.

vājinīva svamṛtam-asmi । *draviṇaṁ savarcasam* । *sumedhā amṛtokṣitaḥ* । *iti triśaṅkor-vedānuvacanam* । – *TaiUp* I.10

"I am the propeller of the Tree (of the Universe). My glory is as high as a mountain-peak. I am the cause and am pure. I am auspicious and immortal as (the effulgence of) the Sun. I am the effulgent (because of self-knowledge) wealth with divine intuition (or the wealth of self-knowledge has been obtained by me). I am imperishable and immutable." This is Sage Triśaṅku's declaration of self-knowledge.

From the topical context it appears that this is a *mantra* for *svādhyāya/japa*. By *svādhyāya/japa*, the mind gets ready for the knowledge to take place. This is the declaration of Sage Triśaṅku after recognizing his true nature. The repetition of this *mantra* prepares the mind for discovery of its meaning. This is chanted for *jñānam*.

Recitation of the Veda should not be missed by anyone seeking welfare and *mokṣa*. However, it will not be feasible for all to repeat and study the whole or even considerable portion of the Veda daily. Therefore, this "post-self-knowledge declaration" is provided by Sage Triśaṅku as a suitable substitute for the Veda, to be of use to those who aspire for self-knowledge.

Fifth Śāntimantraḥ

स॒ह नांववतु । स॒ह नौं भुनक्तु । स॒ह वी॒र्यं॑ करवावहै । ते॒ज॒स्वि ना॒वधींतमस्तु॒ ।
मा विद्वि॒षावहै॑ ॥ ॐ शान्ति॒ः शान्ति॒ः शान्तिंः ॥

oṁ sa ha nāvavatu । *sa ha nau bhunaktu* । *saha vīryaṁ karavāvahai* । *tejasvināvadhītamastu* । *mā vidviṣāvahai* । *oṁ śāntiḥ śāntiḥ śāntiḥ* । – *TaiUp* II

May He (the Lord) indeed protect both of us (the teacher and me). May He indeed nourish both of us. May we together acquire the capacity (to study and understand the scriptures). May what is studied, be brilliant. May there not be disagreement between both of us (the teacher and the disciple). May there be peace, peace, peace.

4

Taittirīya-Upaniṣad-Bhāṣyam

Definition of Bhāṣyam

WE have many sourcebooks on Indian philosophical systems. They are not easy to comprehend even to scholars who have a command over the allied disciplines, i.e. Vyākaraṇa, Nyāya, Mīmāṁsā, Śikṣā, etc. Hence, commentaries (*bhāṣyam*) were written by great masters on the original texts, to facilitate comprehension by the readers. The first extant commentary is *Mahābhāṣya* by Patañjali, which is on the sourcebook *Aṣṭādhyāyī* of Maharṣi Pāṇini. The definition of a *bhāṣyam* is as under:

> *sūtrārtho varṇyate yatra vākyaiḥ sūtrānusāribhiḥ* ।
> *svapadāni ca varṇyante bhāṣyaṁ bhāṣyavido viduḥ* ॥[1]

As per this definition, a *bhāṣyam* must explain all the *sūtra*s of the original text as per the intended meaning and defend them. In case, the *bhāṣyakāra* brings in his own statements to defend the ideas of the original text, he must explain that also. This is how a *bhāṣyam* differs from a *vṛtti*, which is a simple translation of the original text. A *vṛttikāra* need not defend the ideas of the author.

The earliest commentary in *Mahābhāṣya*-style was seen after 300 years in Śabara Swāmi's (first century CE) *bhāṣyam* on *Pūrva-Mīmāṁsā-Sūtra* of Maharṣi Jaimini. It was again seen after 700 years in Ācārya Śaṅkara's *Brahmasūtra-Bhāṣyam*. That is why, whereas Patañjali is known as *mahābhāṣyakāra*, Śaṅkara is known as *bhāṣyakāra* (like Sureśvara is fondly known as *vārttikakāra*,

---

[1] Cf. Introduction to commentary on *Mahābhāṣya*.

and Ānandagiri as *ṭīkākāra*). Śaṅkara is crisp and convincing. Śaṅkara's *bhāṣyam* is regarded as *prasanna* (pleasant), clear and easily intelligible, as well as *gambhīra* (profound) (as described by Vācaspati Miśra,[2] the *bhāmatikāra*).

Śaṅkara's *Taittirīya-Upaniṣad-Bhāṣyam* is profound unlike his *Kaṭhopaniṣad-Bhāṣyam* where there is not much *pūrvapakṣa* and *siddhānta*. In *Taittirīya-Upaniṣad-Bhāṣyam*, Śaṅkara has refuted many contentions of other philosophical systems, as well as has explained elaborately some debatable areas of the text.

In his *Taittirīya-Upaniṣad-Bhāṣyam*, Śaṅkara at times, introduced, either at the beginning, or at the end, or in the middle of a section, as the occasion demands, lengthy discussions on issues raised by the text, for the sake of clarification of the issues. There are five such lengthy discussions in his commentary on the *Taittirīya Upaniṣad*, and in three of them, he begins the discussion in his characteristic style with a stress on enquiry (*cintana*).[3]

Śīkṣāvallī: First Anuvāka (Futility of Karma)

In the first of these that occurs as an introduction to the first section of the Śīkṣāvallī, Śaṅkara says that freedom (*mokṣa*) cannot be attained by means of ritual action (*karma*). His argument is, whatever is produced is subject to time, and since freedom is the nature of the Self, which is timelessness, ritual action is not a means thereto.[4] Freedom is positive, and so it is no argument to say that, though produced by *karma* it can be timeless like *pradhvaṁsābhāva*, that is said to have a beginning,

---

2 *natvā viśuddhavijñānaṁ śaṅkaraṁ karuṇākaram* ।
bhāṣya-prasanna-gambhīraṁ tat-praṇīta vibhajyate ॥

3 *atraitaccintyate vidyākarmaṇor-vivekārtham* । – *TUB* I.11
tatraitaccintyam । *katham anuprāvisad-iti* । – Ibid. II.6
tatraitaccityam । *ko 'yam-evaṁvit, kathaṁ vā saṁkrāmati-iti* । – Ibid. II.8

4 *na hi nityaṁ kiñcid-ārabhyate loke, yad-ārabdhaṁ tad-anityam-iti* । *ato na karmārabdho mokṣaḥ* । – Ibid. I.1

but no end.[5] Śaṅkara says: "Freedom consists in remaining in one's own self on the cessation of the material cause, viz. ignorance (*avidyā*) and desire (*kāma*) on account of which one resorts to action *karma*. The Self, as such, is *Brahman*, and the knowledge of *Brahman* leads to the removal of ignorance."[6]

Śīkṣāvallī: Eleventh Anuvāka (Futility of Karma)

Discussion on the futility of *karma* is repeated again in the end of the eleventh *anuvāka* of Śīkṣāvallī. The main aim of the discussion is to ascertain whether freedom can be attained by:

i. *karma* alone,

ii. or by *karma* aided by knowledge,

iii. or by *karma* and knowledge combined,

iv. or by knowledge aided by *karma*,

v. or by knowledge alone.

By showing the untenability of the first four alternatives, Śaṅkara maintains that freedom can be attained by knowledge alone (v). His reply is:

i. What is produced by *karma* is perishable, and since freedom, as stated earlier, is not subject to time, *karma* cannot be a means to freedom.

ii. The futility of *karma* cannot be overcome by bringing knowledge as an aid to it. Śaṅkara declares that what is eternal, cannot be produced even if there are 100 scriptural texts to the contrary.[7]

iii. Nor can it be said that freedom can be attained by the combination of knowledge and *karma*. Śaṅkara rules out

---

5 *pradhvaṁsābhāvavan-nityo 'pi mokṣa ārabhya eveti cet, na, mokṣasya bhāvarūpatvāt* । – *TUB* I.1

6 Ibid. I.1.

7 *na hi vacanaśatenāpi nityam-ārabhyate, ārabdhaṁ vā avināsi bhavet* । – Ibid. I.11

this possibility:

(a) First on the ground that the result of *karma* is different from that of knowledge. *Karma* is required for: (i) *utpatti* – origination of a thing, or (ii) *āpti* – the attainment of a place/state (e.g. by going to a village), or (iii) *saṁskāra* – purification (e.g. cleaning a copper vessel), or (iv) *vikāra* – modification of a thing (e.g. milk becoming curd).[8] However, freedom is not any of these to be accomplished by *karma*.

(b) Further, the combination of knowledge and *karma* is not possible because of their mutual opposition. "Knowledge which relates to the reality wherein agency (*kartṛtvam*) and other factors are absent is opposed to *karma* which can only be brought about by accessories which are opposed to knowledge."[9]

iv. The fourth alternative also has to be ruled out in view of the mutual opposition between *karma* and knowledge.

Śaṅkara, therefore, concludes that

v. freedom can be attained by knowledge alone.

Brahmānandavallī: First Anuvāka (Sṛṣṭikrama)

In the first section of Brahmānandavallī, *Brahman-Ātmā* is presented as the cause of the world. The Upaniṣad says, "From that (*Brahman*) indeed, from this Self, the space is born, from the space the air . . . ." Commenting on this Śaṅkara says: "From that *Brahman*, that is identical with the Self, space (*ākāśa*) was created. Space means that which possesses the attribute of sound, and provides space for all things that have forms. From that space, air (*vāyuḥ*) which has two attributes, its own attribute of touch and

---

8 In the vision of the Upaniṣad, freedom can never be accomplished by *karma* – *nāsti akṛtaḥ kṛtena* । – *MuṇUp* I.1.12

9 *pravilīna-kartrādi-kāraka-viśeṣatattva-viṣayā hi vidyā, tad-viparīta-kāraka-sādhyena karmaṇā virudhyate* । – *TUB* I.11

the attribute of sound of its cause (*ākāśa*). The verb, "was created" in each of these statements is understood by implication." He then proceeds to explain the creation of fire, water and earth, and of plants, food and human being following the same sequence as given in the Upaniṣad.

There are two questions that can be raised here, in order to vindicate the non-dual nature of the ultimate nature of the *Brahman-Ātmā*.

Q.1: Is the creation of the world real? The question may be rephrased as follows, "Is *Brahman* real, or the incidental cause of the world?" *Brahman* is said to be one and non-dual, immutable and impartite, neither a cause nor an effect. Nevertheless, the Upaniṣad speaks of *Brahman* as the cause of the world. If so, what is the sense in which *Brahman* is said to be the cause of the world according to Advaita Vedānta? Śaṅkara does not discuss this question in this context. However, *vārttikakāra* Sureśvara argues on various grounds that the creation of the world is not real, and *Brahman* is only the incidental cause of the world through *avidyā*.[10]

Q.2: The other question is whether *Brahman* itself is the cause of everything from space onwards, or whether *Brahman* is the cause of space alone. This question arises because Śruti says that from the Self, space came into being, and from space, air was created, and from air, fire was produced, etc. Śaṅkara has not resolved this issue in *Taittirīya*, though he has answered this question in his commentary on *Brahmasūtra*.[11]

However, this ambiguity has been explained by Sureśvara. He says that *Brahman* itself is the cause of everything. *Brahman* through *avidyā* is the cause of space, and the same *Brahman*, which has assumed the form of space, or which remains conditioned as space through *avidyā*, is the cause of air.

---

10 *TUBV* II.140-65.

11 *BSSB* II.3.10 and II.3.13.

Similarly, *Brahman* alone, which has assumed the form of air through *avidyā*, is the cause of fire. The same explanation holds well in other cases also.[12] According to Advaita, no element by itself independent of *Brahman* can be the cause of another element.

Brahmānandavallī: Third, Fourth and Fifth Anuvākas

Taittirīya Upaniṣad enumerates five sheaths – *annamaya, prāṇamaya, manomaya, vijñānamaya* and *ānandamaya* – presented from gross to subtle. Generally viewed, it appears as though *Taittirīya Upaniṣad* speaks of each sheath as the self of the earlier sheath, i.e. *prāṇamaya* as the self of *annamaya, manomaya* as the self of *prāṇamaya* and so on, and finally it speaks of *ānandamaya* as the self of *vijñānamaya*. The statement – *tasyaiṣa eva śārīra ātmā* । *yaḥ pūrvasya* – occurs in the third,[13] fourth and fifth *anuvāka*s of Brahmānandavallī. Śaṅkara explains this text, as it occurs in each of these *anuvāka*s from the standpoint of the *vṛttikāra*, who holds the self, comprising happiness (*ānandamaya*), the fifth in the series, as the real Self or *Brahman*,[14] and finally rejects in his commentary on the fifth *anuvāka*. Śaṅkara maintains on various grounds that the self, comprising happiness cannot be *Brahman*, rather it is the conditioned-self. However, he does not give any indication in the third and fourth *anuvāka*s as to whether his explanation of the text *tasyaiṣa eva śārīra ātmā* । *yaḥ pūrvasya* is from

---

12 *TUBV* II.153.

13 Śaṅkara explains this text in the third section as follows: *tasya pūrvasya annamayasya eṣa śarīre annamaye bhavaḥ śārīra ātmā* । *kaḥ? ya eṣa prāṇamayaḥ* ।

14 Acyutakṛṣṇānanda Tīrtha explains Śaṅkara's position as follows: *"tasyaiṣa eva" iti vākyam-ānandamayo brahmeti vadatāṁ vṛttikārāṇaṁ matena vyācaṣṭe* । *ata evānandamaya-adhikaraṇe vṛttikāramate sthitvā ānandamaya-paryāyastham-idaṁ vākyaṁ tasya pūrvasyeti padayor-ittham-eva vyavahitānvaya-pradarśanena vyākhyātam ācāryaiḥ* । See *Vanamālā*, Chinmaya Foundation of Education and Culture, Madras, 1981, pp. 136-37.

the standpoint of the *vṛttikāra*, or his own explanation. One has to wait until one comes to his commentary on the fifth *anuvāka*. The method adopted by Śaṅkara when he discusses this issue in both *Brahmasūtra-Bhāṣyam* and *Taittirīya-Upaniṣad-Bhāṣyam* is the same, first to state all the view of *vṛttikāra* as the prima facie view, and then present the conclusion (*siddhānta*) according to Advaita. The issue whether the self consisting of happiness is the real Self or the conditioned-self is discussed in the Ānandamaya-adhikaraṇa of *Brahmasūtra*. In the beginning, Śaṅkara explains the *sūtra*s 12-19 that constitute the Ānandamaya-adhikaraṇa from the standpoint of the *vṛttikāra*, then criticizes it, and states his final view in the course of his commentary on the nineteenth *sūtra*, and before concluding his commentary on this *adhikaraṇa*, he shows how these *sūtra*s have to be interpreted.[15] It may be mentioned here that Sureśvara smelling the danger of such interpretation, and to forestall the difficulty in understanding the text *tasyaiṣa eva śārīra ātmā* । *yaḥ pūrvasya* interprets it from the standpoint of Advaita in the beginning. After presenting *vṛttikāra*'s view as the prima facie view in the first two verses, he criticizes it elaborately in seventeen verses in his *vārttika*.[16]

Brahmānandavallī: Fifth Anuvāka and Bhṛguvallī: Sixth Anuvāka – Parity (Ānandamaya same as Brahman?)

There is an argument given in the justification of the view that *ānandamaya* in the fifth *anuvāka* of Brahmānandavallī refers to *vastu – Brahman*, and not the conditioned-self. Śaṅkara does not refer to this argument, which focuses its attention on the parity of reasoning between Bhṛguvallī and Brahmānandavallī. Sureśvara however has explained this in detail, clarifying that the *ānandamaya* in the fifth section of Brahmānandavallī is the conditioned-self, and not *Brahman*.[17]

---

15 *idaṁ tu iha vaktavyam – BSSB* I.1.19

16 *TUBV* II.325-41.

17 Ibid. II.332-40.

I am inclined to produce here *in toto*, the clarification by Swami Dayananda Saraswati:

> In the Ānandamaya-adhikaraṇa of *Brahmasūtra*, uses the kind of analysis that shows the importance of *sampradāya*, and consistent logic. One *vṛttikāra* argues that, the meaning of *ānandamaya* is *ātmā*. Śaṅkara demolishes the entire argument. He shows that *ānandamaya* cannot be the *vastu*. *Ānandamayaḥ* there is a *lakṣaṇa* to point out *Parātmā*. He shows that *ānandamayaḥ* is not *abhyasta* (repetition), *ānandam* (*Brahman*) alone is *abhyasta*. It is *ānanda*, and not *ānandamayaḥ*, which is *abhyāsa* as the *svarūpa* of *Para-Brahman*. Śaṅkara shows that *mayaṭ* there indicates *vikāra*, and not *prācūrya*. If it was *prācūrya*, there would have been *pratiyogī-leśa*. *Tad brahma* alone is what is pointed out by the *ānandamaya vākya*, because *Brahman* is *pratiṣṭhā*.
>
> The *vṛttikāra* comes back with a different meaning, but Śaṅkara has made his point. Śaṅkara's reasoning is particularly lucid, and the clarity of his arguments reflects a thorough understanding of the tradition of logical analysis. The *vṛttikāra* and other *ācārya*s who came after Śaṅkara could go forward on the road he made, but some used it only to support their own theologies (Rāmānuja, Madhva).

Brahmānandavallī: Sixth Anuvāka (Anupraśnāḥ) – The Three Questions

The sixth section of Brahmānandavallī contains certain questions raised by the disciple for clarifying his doubts, after listening to the instruction given by the teacher.

Q. 1: The first question is: whether *Brahman* exists or not.

Q. 2: The second question is: whether an ignorant person, after departing from this world, attains *Brahman* or not.

Q. 3: And the third question is: whether a wise person does, or does not attain *Brahman*.

A.1: According to Śaṅkara, the first question is answered by Upaniṣad beginning from the text, *so 'kāmayata* । *bahu syāṁ prajāyeyeti* (II.6) until *sa yaścāyaṁ puruṣe, yaścāsāvāditye, sa ekaḥ* (II.8) by giving various reasons such as: (i) the phenomena of creation, (ii) acquisition of joy, and (iii) functioning of life which prove the existence of *Brahman*.

A.3: The third question, whether a man of knowledge attains *Brahman* or not, is answered, according to Śaṅkara, by the Upaniṣad in the passage beginning from *sa ya evaṁ vit* (II.8).

A.2: Śaṅkara is of the view that the Upaniṣad does not answer separately the second question, whether an ignorant man attains *Brahman* or not, as the answer to the third question also contains the answer to the second one.[18]

Vārttikakāra Sureśvara however does not agree with Śaṅkara's explanation (Table 4.1). According to Sureśvara, the first question that relates to the existence of *Brahman* is answered by the Upaniṣad beginning from *so 'kāmayata, bahu syāṁ prajāyeyeti* (II.6) up to *eṣa hyevānandayāti* (II.7). The third question whether a person of knowledge attains *Brahman* or not, says Sureśvara, is answered by *Taittirīya Upaniṣad* in the text, *yadā hyevaiṣa etasminnadṛśye 'nātmye 'nirukte 'nilayane 'bhayaṁ 'pratiṣṭhāṁ vindate* । *atha so 'bhayaṁ-gato bhavati* । (II.7). The second question relating to the fate of the ignorant person is also answered according to Sureśvara in the text, *yadā hyevaiṣa etasminn-ud-aram-antaraṁ kurute* । *atha tasya bhayaṁ bhavati* (II.7). Sureśvara holds that *Taittirīya Upaniṣad* in the sixth and seventh sections of Brahmānandavallī answers all the three questions raised by the disciple.[19] According to Sureśvara, even the question about the ignorant person is directly answered by the Upaniṣad text (*śabdāt*), and not by implication (*arthāt*).

---

[18] *tatra vidvān-samaśnute na samaśnuta iti, anupraśno'ntyaḥ; tad-apākaraṇāya-ucyate* । *madhyamo 'nupraśno 'antyāpākaraṇād-apākṛta iti, tad-apākaraṇāya na yatyate* । – *TUB* II.8

[19] *TUBV* II.539-42.

Table 4.1: Views of Śaṅkara and Sureśvara on the Three Questions in the Sixth Anuvāka of Brahmānandavallī

Question		*Śaṅkara*	*Sureśvara*
1.	Whether *Brahman* exists or not?	Answered by Śruti from *so 'kāmayata* । *bahu syāṁ prajāyeyeti* । (II.6) up to *sa yaścāyaṁ puruṣe, yaścā-sāvāditye, sa ekaḥ* । (II.8) by giving various reasons such as: (i) the phenomena of creation, (ii) acquisition of joy, (iii) functioning of life, etc. which prove the existence of *Brahman*.	Beginning from, *so 'kāmayata* । *bahu syāṁ prajāyeyeti* । (II.6) until *eṣa hyevā-nandayāti* (II.7).
2.	Whether an ignorant person, after departing from this world, attains *Brahman* or not?	The Upaniṣad does not answer separately the second question, whether an ignorant man attains *Brahman* or not, as the answer to thethird question also contains the answer to the second one.	Answered in the passage'*yadā hyeva-aiṣa etasminn-ud-aram-antaraṁ kurute*। *atha tasya bhayaṁ bhavati* । (II.7)
3.	Whether a wise person does or does not attain *Brahman*?	Answered by the Upaniṣad in the passage beginning from *sa ya evaṁ vit* (II.8).	Answered in the passage: *yadā hye-vaiṣa etasminnadṛ-śye'nātmye'nirukte-'nilayane 'bhayaṁ-pratiṣṭhāṁ vindate. atha so 'bhyaṁ gato bhavati* । (II.7)

Brahmānandavallī: Sixth Anuvāka (Praveśa-śruti)

The discussion that occurs in the sixth section of Brahmānandavallī is concerned about the meaning of the entry text (*praveśa-śruti*), "having created that, into that very world It (*Brahman*) entered". After considering various possibilities by which one may try to understand the meaning of this text, the opponent concludes that this text has to be ignored, as it does not convey any meaning. Śaṅkara argues that this text purports to convey the knowledge of *Brahman*, which is the central theme of the chapter (*vallī*), through an account of the creation of space, air, fire, etc. The entry of the Self into the cavity of the intellect has been stated with a view to show that, the association of the Self with the mind causes knowledge of *Brahman* to take place, because the mind that is proximate to the Self has the power of illumination.[20]

Brahmānandavallī: Eighth Anuvāka

Advaita which maintains that *Brahman*, the Ultimate Reality, is non-dual and that, one attains freedom by *brahmavidyā* has to clarify certain issues such as "Who is the knower of *Brahman*? How does he attain *Brahman*? Is the attainer different from or the same as *Brahman*?" There are critics who urge that, since the attainer is different from the attained, the theory of non-dualism is untenable. They also urge that, in order to make the term "attainment" meaningful in the literal sense, the Advaitin must accept duality between the attainer and the attained. The discussion that occurs in the eighth section of Brahmānandavallī, focuses its attention on these issues. The substance of Śaṅkara's argument may be stated as follows: It is the *jīva* that is the knower of *Brahman*. On the authority of *Taittirīya*'s statement, "The knower of *Brahman* attains the highest", it has to be said that one attains the highest that is *Brahman* through knowledge. Since the *jīva* in its essential nature is identical with *Brahman*, the attainer and the attained are not different, and so there is no danger to the theory of non-dualism. It is well known that knowledge removes ignorance. Since knowledge alone is prescribed as the means of attaining *Brahman*,[21] it follows that the non-attainment

---

20 *evam-antaḥkaraṇa-guhātmā-sambandho brahmaṇa upalabdhihetuḥ* । *sannikarṣāt, avabhāsātmakatvāc-ca antaḥakaraṇasya* । – *TUB* II.6

21 *vidyāmātropadeśat* । *vidyāyāśca dṛṣṭaṁ kāryam-avidyānivṛttiḥ, tacceha vidyāmātram ātmaprāptau sādhanam-upadiśyate* । – *TUB* II.8

of *Brahman* is because of ignorance, and that its attainment is through knowledge. In short, the *jīva* due to ignorance identifies itself with the physical body, the *prāṇa*, the mind, etc. which are non-Self; and through knowledge, it distinguishes the Self from the non-Self and remains as *Brahman*.[22] If the *jīva* were different from *Brahman*, it cannot become or remain as *Brahman* through knowledge. Hence, the attainment of *Brahman* by the *jīva* should not be understood in the literal sense of acquisition of something new, otherwise not attained. According to Śaṅkara, the word "attainment" here means, knowledge alone.[23]

Brahmānandavallī: Fourth and Ninth Anuvākas (yato vāco nivartante)

The *Taittirīya Upaniṣad* statement *yato vāco nivartante* occurs twice in Brahmānandavallī, in the fourth as well as the ninth sections. However, the context in the two sections is different. Śaṅkara does not explain the meaning of this text in the fourth section, where it occurs first in the context of *manomaya-kośa*. He however brings out the difference in the meaning of the text, while commenting on it in the ninth section, where the context is non-dual *Brahman*. Sureśvara however specifically clarifies that since the context in the fourth section is *manomaya-kośa*, the text does not refer to *Brahman*.[24]

Bhṛguvallī: Tenth Anuvāka

The last of the discussions occurs in the tenth and concluding section of Bhṛguvallī. Śaṅkara emphasizes here that, though the Self is free from the worldly existence involving the relation of experience and experiencer, it is nevertheless ascribed to the Self

---

22 *yā hi brahmavidyayā svātmaprāptirupadiśyate sā-avidyākṛtasya annādiviśeṣātmana ātmatvenādhyāropitasya anātmano 'pohārthā* ।
– *TUB* II.8

23 *tasmāt na prāptiḥ saṅkramaṇam . . . jñānamātraṁ ca saṅkramaṇam-upapadyate* । – Ibid.

24 *TUBV* verse 306.

through ignorance[25] and that, since the *jīva* in its essential nature is identical with *Brahman*, sorrow, fear and other characteristics of transmigratory existence do not really belong to it.[26]

Like his other commentaries, Śaṅkara's *Taittirīya-Upaniṣad-Bhāṣyam* is both lucid and profound (*prasanna–gambhīra*). Śaṅkara sets forth the central teaching of Advaita within the framework of scripture, supporting scripture by reasoning. While reasoning is guided by Śruti, Śruti in its turn is ably supported by reasoning. Śaṅkara makes full use of flawless reasoning in support of his interpretation of Śruti, and thereby shows that the teaching of Śruti meets the demands of reason. He is neither dogmatic in his exposition of Śruti, nor does he indulge in dry reasoning. He shows that the model of creation, the principle of cause–effect relation (*kāraṇa–kārya*), the enquiry into the five sheaths, the study of the calculus of happiness and the analysis of the subject–object epistemology, reinforce the truth of non-duality that constitutes the central teaching of Śruti (Upaniṣads). Citing passages from Smṛti and Itihāsa,[27] that are considered to be secondary scripture, Śaṅkara shows that his teaching is not only based on Śruti, but is also in harmony with other scriptural authorities such as Smṛti and Itihāsa. To Śaṅkara, the truth is known from Śruti and is corroborated by reasoning.

Śaṅkara sets forth the teaching of Advaita with devotion to Śruti, respect for reasoning. He is unsurpassed in facility of style and magnificence of diction, profundity of thought and richness

---

25 *kāryaviṣaya eva bhojya-bhoktṛtvakṛtaḥ saṁsāro, na tvātmani-iti* । – *TUB* III.10

26 *na* । *trāsāder-duḥkhasya ca upalabhyamānatvāt nopalabdhṛ-dharmatvam* । – Ibid.

27 Śaṅkara quotes from *Manusmṛti* in three places in his *Taittirīya-Upaniṣad-Bhāṣyam* – once in his commentary on I.1, and twice in his commentary on I.11. He quotes from *Mahābhārata* twice – once in his commentary on I.4 and again on III.1. He also quotes from *Āpastamba-Dharmaśāstra* in his commentary on I.11.

of imagery, and his writings that are quite numerous, exhibit a remarkable consistency throughout. There is nothing in Śaṅkara of ephemeral and parochial, the mid-rib of his philosophy is timeless and universal.

Śaṅkara constructs his system of philosophy on the triple foundation of Śruti, *yukti* and *anubhava*, and bases his critique of other systems precisely on these very grounds. He was interested in the true knowledge of the *vastu*. He gave importance to Śruti because it was the authoritative words of the *ṛṣis*. He emphasized *yukti* since it is an aid to the understanding of Śruti. However, in the examination of other systems of philosophy, he displayed his subtle logical acumen and put forth such arguments that were in fact devastating to some schools as can be seen in Chapter 10.

5

Śīkṣāvallī

Introduction to Śīkṣāvallī

THE first chapter is named Śīkṣāvallī after the first word of the chapter. It deals with *karma*s and *upāsanā*s that are preparatory steps for the knowledge of *Brahman*.

Taittirīya starts with elaborate instructions to the student entering the portals of *brahma-vidyā*, to prepare him to receive the teaching. A razor sharp, alert, acute intellect is a prerequisite for this study. Apart from this, the intellect must be tranquil, free from *rāga-dveṣa* – any abiding likes and dislikes, and all the negative traits such as anger, jealousy, etc. that go with *rāga-dveṣa*.

Śīkṣāvallī is mainly concerned with *saguṇa-vidyā*, the knowledge of *Saguṇa-Brahman*. It gives an account of the various *upāsanā*s (meditations) to be practised by the spiritual aspirant for attaining *citta-naiścalyam* – ability to stay with a topic for a length of time, which facilitates the knowledge of *Brahman*. While the performance of *karma* without specific desire (*niṣkāma-karma*) purifies the mind (*cittaśuddhi*) and creates a desire for knowledge (*vividiśā*), the practice of meditation is conducive to the concentration of mind (*citta-naiścalyam*) and development of the intellect. It is with this view to help the spiritual aspirant to qualify for the *nirguṇa-vidyā*, the knowledge of the unconditioned *Brahman* that Śīkṣāvallī proceeds to explain the different meditations.

Summary of the Twelve Anuvākas

Śāntimantraḥ

Of the twelve *anuvākas* (sections) in Śīkṣāvallī, the first section contains a prayer to the gods for the removal of obstacles in the way of *saguṇa-vidyā*.

Śikṣā-śāstrārtha-saṅgrahaḥ

The second section deals with *śikṣā* (the science of phonetics) and stresses that there should not be any indifference or complacency in the recital of the text.

Saṁhitopāsanam

Meditation on the *saṁhitā* is taught in the third section that will secure fruits of this world as well as the future world. If a person meditates on the *saṁhitā* without any desire for results such as cattle (wealth) and heaven, he will attain *cittaśuddhi* (purification of the mind) that is necessary for the attainment of *brahmajñānam*.

Medhādi-siddhyarthā Āvahanti-homa-mantrāḥ

The fourth section gives an account of the *mantras* that are to be recited along with offering of the oblations, for attaining good memory, sound health, intelligence and wealth.

Vyāhṛtyupāsanam

The fifth section teaches meditation on the *vyāhṛtis*; that is conducive to the attainment of independent sovereignty.

Manomayatvādi-guṇaka-brahmopāsanayā Svārājya-siddhiḥ

The sixth section gives instruction on the meditation of *Saguṇa-Brahman* as located in *hṛdayākāśa* (the cavity of the heart, i.e. mind), and as possessed of such attributes as "formed of mind" for mediocre students.

Pṛthvivyādyupādhika-pañca-brahmopāsanam

Meditation on *Saguṇa-Brahman* as endowed with perceptible qualities is taught in the seventh section, meant to help relatively average students/aspirants.

Praṇavopāsanam

The eighth section teaches meditation on *oṁ*; that is a means for attaining *Saguṇa-Brahman* (Hiraṇyagarbha), in accordance with the manner, in which it is meditated upon. This meditation is for the benefit of advanced students.

Svādhyāya-praśaṁsā

The ninth section stresses the importance of the duties enjoined by Śruti and Smṛti such as the study of scripture, performance of rites, having ethical values and attitudes, fulfilment of family and social obligations, along with the practice of *upāsanā*.

Brahmajñāna-prakāśaka-mantraḥ

The entire *mantra* of the tenth section is to be recited by the student, as such a recital is conducive to the attainment of purification of mind and thereby *brahmajñānam*. In this *mantra*, Sage Triśaṅku gives expression to his experience after *brahmajñānam*.

Śiṣyānuśāsanam

The eleventh section contains the post-instruction of the teacher to the students returning home after the completion of their studies. It is intended to show that the performance *vaidika* as well as *laukika karma*s are conducive to the rise of knowledge.

Uttara-Śāntimantraḥ

In the last section of the *vallī*, the disciple expresses his gratitude to the gods for protecting him and his teacher.

First Anuvāka: Śāntimantraḥ

ॐ ॥ शं नो॑ मि॒त्रः शं वरु॑णः । शं नो॑ भवत्वर्य॒मा । शं न॒ इन्द्रो॒ बृह॒स्पति॑ः । शं नो॒ विष्णु॑रुरुक्र॒मः । नमो॒ ब्रह्म॑णे । नम॑स्ते वायो । त्वमे॒व प्र॒त्यक्षं॒ ब्रह्मा॑सि । त्वमे॒व प्र॒त्यक्षं॒ ब्रह्म॒ वदिष्यामि । ऋ॒तं व॑दिष्यामि । स॒त्यं व॑दिष्यामि । तन्माम॑वतु । तद्व॒क्तार॑मवतु । अव॑तु॒ माम् । अव॑तु व॒क्तार॑म् ॥ ॐ शान्ति॒ः शान्ति॒ः शान्ति॑ः ॥

oṁ śaṁ no mitraḥ śaṁ varuṇaḥ । *śaṁ no bhavatvaryamā* । *śaṁ na indro bṛhaspatiḥ* । *śaṁ no viṣṇur-urukramaḥ* । *namo brahmaṇe* । *namaste vāyo* । *tvameva pratyakṣaṁ brahmāsi* । *tvameva pratyakṣaṁ brahma vadiṣyāmi* । *ṛtam vadiṣyāmi* । *satyaṁ vadiṣyāmi* । *tan-mām avatu* । *tad vaktāram avatu* । *avatu mām* । *avatu vaktāram* । *oṁ śāntiḥ śāntiḥ śāntiḥ* । – I.1

May Mitra be the source of auspiciousness to us. May Varuṇa be the source of auspiciousness to us. May Aryamā be the source of auspiciousness to us. May Indra and Bṛhaspati be the source of auspiciousness to us. May Viṣṇu, the all-pervasive, sustainer of the creation be auspicious to us. May Urukrama, Lord Vāmana be auspicious to us.[i] Prostrations to *Brahman* (Hiraṇyagarbha). O Lord Vāyu! Prostrations to you. You are the perceptible *Brahman*.[ii] I declare you to be the perceptible *Brahman*. I declare you as the right understanding. I declare you as the Truth. May that Truth protect me. May that Truth protect my teacher. May that Truth protect me. May it protect the Teacher. *Oṁ*. May there be peace, peace, peace.[iii]

This invocatory verse originally appears in *Ṛgveda*.[1] The deities invoked here may be regarded as the delegates, among whom *Īśvara* distributes some of His powers. They may also be conceived as His manifestations. *Ṛgveda* declares that Indra, Mitra, Varuṇa and the rest are but manifestations of that single truth, named variously by the sages.[2] Mitra, Varuṇa and Aryamān are three

---

1 *śaṁ no mitraḥ śaṁ varunaḥ śaṁ no bhavatvaryamā* ।
śaṁ na indro bṛhaspatiḥ śaṁ no viṣṇururukramaḥ ॥ – *ṚVS* I.90.9

2 *indraṁ mitraṁ varunam-agnim-āhur-atho divyaḥ sa suparṇo garutmān* । →

of the Ādityas[3] (deities of the heavenly sphere) mentioned in *Ṛgveda*.

Mitra is the guardian spirit of the *prāṇavṛtti* (the in-breathing activity) and the day. He calls people to activity, sustains the earth and the sky, and beholds all with unwinking eyes.

Varuṇa is the deity of the waters in the firmament and the sea. Sāyaṇa has presented him as the deity of the night.[4] He is commonly associated with Mitra, and is celebrated as the king of gods, and the lord of the universe. In the hymns, several great attributes and functions are ascribed to him, such as presiding over the waters in the firmament and the sea, upholding heaven and earth, possessing extraordinary power and wisdom, hating falsehood, seizing transgressors with his *pāśa* (noose), pardoning wrong-doings and bestowing immortality. In *Ṛgveda*, twelve *sūkta*s are dedicated to Varuṇa.

Aryamān is the regent of the sun and the eyes. He is the chief of the *pitṛ*s (the manes) and the Milky Way is called his path.

Indra is the governor of the atmosphere and the upper regions. He presides over the gods. A vanquisher of the demons of darkness and a benefactor of humans, his power and energy are devoutly praised in the Vedas, and he is most frequently invoked. In *Ṛgveda*, 200 hymns are dedicated to Indra. Besides, in fifty more *sūkta*s he is praised along with other deities.

Bṛhaspati is the deity in whom piety and righteousness are personified. He is also the god of wisdom and eloquence. He is therefore deemed appropriately the genius of speech and intellect, while Indra is considered that of strength of the hand.

← *ekaṁ sad-viprā bahudhā vadantyagniṁ yamaṁ mātariśvānam āhuḥ* ||

– Ibid. I.164.46

3 The twelve Ādityas are Viṣṇu, Indra, Vivasvat, Mitra, Varuṇa, Pūṣan, Tvaṣṭā, Bhaga, Aryamān, Dhātā, Sautṛ and Aṁśa. They signify the twelve months of a year.

4 *ṚVBhā* VII.87.1.

Viṣṇu is often invoked with Indra. He is the personification of light and the sun, especially in his striding over heaven in three steps, "explained as denoting the threefold manifestation of light in the form of fire, lightning, and the sun, or as designating the three daily stations of the sun in his rising, culminating and setting". He is also considered the chief of the Ādityas and the guardian spirit of the feet; and finally he is identified with the all-pervading Reality. In *Ṛgveda*, five *sūkta*s are dedicated to Viṣṇu.

Just as a person is looked upon an embodiment of the universe, the deities who rule over the cosmic functions are also conceived to have their corresponding rulership in the personality of the human being. Hence, it is appropriate that these gods are propitiated, without which the attainment of the highest wisdom is not possible.

Second Anuvāka: Śīkṣā-śāstrārtha-saṅgrahaḥ

After peace-invocation, the teacher begins with a brief introduction to *śikṣā* (discipline of pronunciation). Since revelation of Truth is through words, one should have correct understanding of every letter, and its pronunciation. Hence, the teacher says that one should know all the factors necessary for right pronunciation. Correct pronunciation and knowledge of the *sandhi*s are emphasized, so that the meaning does not become distorted even slightly by incorrect pronunciation. Knowledge can take place only when the meaning is accurate and clear.

शीक्षां व्याख्यास्यामः । वर्णः स्वरः । मात्रा बलम् । साम सन्तानः । इत्युक्तः शीक्षाध्यायः ॥

śīkṣāṁ vyākhyāsyāmaḥ । *varṇaḥ svaraḥ* । *mātrā balam* ।
sāma santānaḥ । *ityuktaḥ śīkṣādhyāyaḥ* ॥ – I.2

We shall expound the science of phonetics. (It deals with) the alphabet, accent, pitch, effort, modulation/uniformity (of pace), and conjunction (of the letters). Thus has been taught the chapter on the discipline of phonetics.

In this *anuvāka,* we get the earliest systematic treatment of the science of phonetics. *Varṇa*s (alphabets/speech sounds) are the primary element in the structure of the language. They form themselves into syllables and words. A vowel sound is present in every syllable determining its accent and quantity. There are three important *svara*s (accents or tones) falling on vowels, known as *udātta* (acute), *anudātta* (grave) and *svarita* (circumflex). These determine the rhythm of the text. The vowels are *hrasva* (short), *dīrgha* (long) and *pluta* (prolated) with reference to the length of time required to pronounce them. One *mātrā* is one prosodical instant. The correct time taken to pronounce a *hrasva* vowel is one *mātrā* (prosodical instant), to pronounce a *dīrgha* vowel is two *mātrā*s and a *pluta* is three *mātrā*s. When articulate sounds are uttered, a certain force is to be exerted over the vocal organs in order to make the speech intelligible and effective; this is what is implied by *balam*. The term *sāma,* literally meaning likeness or similarity, denotes the rhythm to which the voice should be adjusted. Conjunctions (*santāna*) means successive flow of the juxtaposed vocal sounds. In the study of the Veda, attention should be given on all these factors. Failure to observe these principles renders pronunciations defective and detracts from the effect of the text studied. For, it is believed that the relation between word and its essence is timeless. The story of Tvaṣṭṛ, occurring in *Taittirīya Saṁhitā* II.4.12 and *Śatapatha Brāhmaṇa* I.5.2, is often cited as example to illustrate how the utterance of the word *indraśatru* with *udātta* accent on the first syllable instead of on the last produced fatal result, quite against Tvaṣṭṛ's intention. Pāṇini's *Śikṣā,*[5] and the first *āhnikam* of Patañjali's *Mahābhāṣya* also deal with this aspect.

---

[5] *mantro hinaḥ svarato varṇato vā, mithyāprayukto na tam-artham-āha* |
sa vāgvajro yajamānaṁ hinasti, yathendraśatruḥ svarato 'parādhāt ||
– *PāṇŚi* 52

In the Paśpaśāhnikam of *Mahābhāṣya*, Maharṣi Patañjali has given an illustrious example[6] stating: "words polluted by the defective utterance of vowels or other letters do not represent the desired meaning, since they are used in an incorrect manner, just as Tvaṣṭṛ, the demon, courted death from Indra, for reasons of incorrect pronunciation of the *svara* in the word *indraśatru*."

Various Upāsanās in Taittirīya

There are five *upāsanā*s in Śikṣāvallī elaborated in various *anuvāka*s. The third *anuvāka* deals with Saṁhitā-upāsanā, fifth with Vyāhṛti-upāsanā, sixth with Hiraṇyagarbha-upāsanā, seventh with Paṅkta-brahma-upāsanā and eighth with Praṇava-upāsanā.

*Upāsanā*s make the intellect unwavering (*citta-naiścalyam*) and razor sharp, while *karma* purifies the mind of all the negative tendencies (*citta-śuddhi*). For this purpose, *karma* as well as *upāsanā*s are elaborately dwelt upon in Śīkṣāvallī.

The young student is first led to see that he is not an isolated part of the universe (*mahaḥ*), which is *Brahman* that is *Ātmā*, is the basis for the *loka*s, *deva*s, the Vedas and *prāṇa*s. This *upāsanā* itself is enough to prepare the intellect to come out of its limited compass, and to gain a vision of the cosmic whole. There are many more such *upāsanā*s.

Third Anuvāka: Saṁhitā-Upāsanā

The third *anuvāka* (section) deals with Saṁhitā-Upāsanā – (meditation on the conjunction of the Vedic letters). There are five types of *sandhi*s in the Sanskrit language. However, here the five *sandhi*s take an allegorical or metaphysical meaning. The student is used to Vedic chanting and his mind is soaked in Vedic sounds. Hence, they can form ideal symbols of *upāsanā*.

---

6 *duṣṭaḥ śabdaḥ svarato varṇato vā, mithyāprayukto na tam-arthamāha* ।
sa vāgvajro yajamānaṁ hinasti, yathendraśatruḥ svarato 'parādhāt ॥
– *MaBh* I.2

Here the teacher gives an *upāsanā* on various *devatās*, keeping the conjunction of letters as the symbols, i.e. locus. This is an *upāsanā* with five subsidiary *upāsanās* connected with various aspects of the creation. Each subsidiary *upāsanā* involves meditation on four *devatās*. The whole scheme is considered as one *upāsanā* in which twenty *devatās* are meditated upon. Hence, this is as good as an *upāsanā* on the Hiraṇyagarbha, the total.

सह नौ यशः । सह नौ ब्रह्मवर्चसम् ।

saha nau yaśaḥ । *saha nau brahmavarcasam* । – I.3

May we both together become famous.[iv] May we both (attain) spiritual effulgence[v] together.

अथातः सꣳहिताया उपनिषदं व्याख्यास्यामः । पञ्चस्वधिकरणेषु । अधिलोकमधिज्यौतिषमधिविद्यमधिप्रजमध्यात्मम् । ता महासꣳहिता इत्याचक्षते ।

athātaḥ-saṁhitāyā upaniṣadaṁ vyākhyāsyāmaḥ । *pañcasvadhi-karaṇeṣu* । *adhilokam-adhijyautiṣam-adhividyam-adhiprajam-adhyātmam* । *tā mahāsaṁhitā ityācakṣate* । – I.3

Now, (since the student is familiar with Vedic chanting) we will expound the secret meaning of the conjunction[vi] of letters on five perceptible objects – the worlds, the luminaries, the knowledge, the progeny, (and) the self. (The wise) call them "the great conjunctions".

अथाधिलोकम् । पृथिवी पूर्वरूपम् । द्यौरुत्तररूपम् । आकाशः सन्धिः । वायुः सन्धानम् । इत्यधिलोकम् ।

athādhilokam । *pṛthivī pūrvarūpam* । *dyaur-uttararūpam* । *akāśaḥ sandhiḥ* । *vāyuḥ sandhānam* । *ityadhilokam* । – I.3

Now the teaching concerning the world is this: The earth is the prior form, the heaven is the latter form; the sky is the conjunction; air is the link. Thus concludes the meditation related to the worlds.

The annotator states that the earth and the rest stand for

the *devatās* (presiding deities) of those elements. The whole meditation helps to contemplate the cosmic immensities as interrelated, completely including all existence in a grand whole. By doing so, the mind goes beyond trifle occupations and attunes itself to the infinite.

> अथाधिज्यौतिषम् । अग्निः पूर्वरूपम् । आदित्य उत्तररूपम् । आपः सन्धिः ।
> वैद्युतः सन्धानम् । इत्यधिज्यौतिषम् ।
>
> *athādhijyautiṣam* । *agniḥ pūrvarūpam* । *āditya uttararūpam* ।
> *āpaḥ sandhiḥ* । *vaidyutaḥ sandhānam* । *ityadhijyautiṣam* ।
>
> – I.3
>
> Now the teaching on the luminaries is as follows: Fire is the former form, the sun is the latter form; the rain waters are the conjunctions; lightning is the link. Thus concludes the meditation related to the luminaries.

The Vedic seers looked upon light as a single entity that manifests on earth as fire, in the intermediate region as lightning and in heaven as the sun. This contemplation helps to steady the mind by dwelling on a unifying principle of cosmic magnitude, namely light, which has much resemblance with the ultimate principle to which the Upaniṣad ultimately points.

> अथाधिविद्यम् । आचार्यः पूर्वरूपम् । अन्तेवास्युत्तररूपम् । विद्या सन्धिः ।
> प्रवचनꣳसन्धानम् । इत्यधिविद्यम् ।
>
> *athādhividyam* । *ācāryaḥ pūrvarūpam* । *antevāsyuttararūpam* ।
> *vidyā sandhiḥ* । *pravacanam̐ sandhānam* । *ityadhividyam* ।
>
> – I.3
>
> Now follows the meditation dealing with the knowledge. The teacher is the prior form, the disciple is the latter form; knowledge is the conjunction; teaching/exposition is the link. Thus concludes the meditation related to knowledge.

The Upaniṣadic seer must have chosen the whole process of learning as a theme for meditation, because of the close relation existing between the *guru* and the disciple, who according to

Vedic conception, should live like a shadow (of the *guru*) for deriving the full benefit of learning. There is nothing greater or holier than knowledge,[7] hence its propagation and the factors involved therein deserve reverent meditation.

अथाधि॒प्रजम् । माता पू᳚र्वरू॒पम् । पितोत्त॑ररू॒पम् । प्र॑जा स॒न्धिः । प्रजनन॑ँ स॒न्धानम् । इत्यधि॒प्रजम् ।

athādhiprajam । mātā pūrvarūpam । pitottararūpam । prajā sandhiḥ । prajananaṁ sandhānam । ityadhiprajam ।

– I.3

Next is the meditation related to progeny. Mother is the prior form, father is the latter form; progeny is the conjunction, procreation is the link. Thus concludes the meditation related to progeny.

The union of the mother and father for the sake of progeny is treated as a sacred action, and the sages have deemed it worthy of holy reflection. The same idea is seen in *Bhagavadgītā* when Lord Kṛṣṇa says that He is the Kandarpa, the cause of procreation.[8]

अथाध्या॒त्मम् । अधराहनुः पू᳚र्वरू॒पम् । उत्तराहनुरुत्त॑ररू॒पम् । वाक् स॒न्धिः । जिह्व॑ा स॒न्धानम् । इत्यध्या॒त्मम् ।

athādhyātmam । adharāhanuḥ pūrvarūpam । uttarāhanurutta-rarūpam । vāk sandhiḥ । jihvā sandhānam । ityadhyātmam ।

– I.3

Now begins the meditation dealing with the individual. The lower jaw is the former form, the upper jaw is the later form; speech is the conjunction; the tongue is the link. Thus concludes the meditation related to the individual.

By *adhyātmam* (the self), the complete physical and psychological aspects of the human personality are denoted.

---

7 *na hi jñānena sadṛśaṁ pavitram iha vindyate* । – *BhGī* IV.38

8 *prajānāścāsmi kandarpaḥ* । – *BhGī* X.28

इतीमा महासꣳहिताः । य एवमेता महासꣳहिता व्याख्याता वेद । सन्धीयते प्रजया पशुभिः । ब्रह्मवर्चसेनान्नाद्येन सुवर्ग्येण लोकेन ॥

itīmā mahāsaṁhitāḥ । *ya evam etā mahāsaṁhitā vyākhyatā veda* । *sandhīyate prajayā paśubhiḥ* । *brahmavarcasenānnādyena suvargyeṇa lokena* । –I.3

Thus, these (five) are the great conjunctions. One, who meditates[vii] upon these great conjunctions as expounded above, is blessed with progeny, wealth of cattle, spiritual effulgence, agreeable food, and heavenly world.

The word *veda* here means meditation, since the section deals with meditation, and not knowledge.

Fourth Anuvāka:
Medhādi-siddhyarthā Āvahanti-homa-mantrāḥ

Next, we get a prayer for intelligence. The prayer is addressed to the Lord in the form of *Oṁkāra*. Moreover, the student prays for healthy body and sense-organs, so that he can discover his immortal nature.

यःछन्दसामृषभो विश्वरूपः । छन्दोभ्योऽध्यमृताथ्सम्बभूव । समेन्द्रो मेधया स्पृणोतु । अमृतस्य देव धारणो भूयासम् । शरीरं मे विचर्षणम् । जिह्वा मे मधुमत्तमा । कर्णाभ्यां भूरि विश्रुवम् । ब्रह्मणः कोशोऽसि मेधया पिहितः । श्रुतं मे गोपाय ।

yaśchandasām-ṛṣabho viśvarūpaḥ । *chandobhyo 'dhyamṛtāth-sambabhūva* । *samendro medhayā spṛṇotu* । *amṛtasya deva dhārano bhūyāsam* । *śarīraṁ me vicarṣaṇam* । *jihvā me madhumattamā* । *karṇābhyāṁ bhūri viśruvam* । *brahmaṇaḥ kośo 'si medhayā pihitaḥ* । *śrutaṁ me gopāya* । –I.4

That (*Oṁkāra*), which manifested from the hymns of the Vedas, is the greatest among the Vedic *mantra*s and is endowed with manifold forms. May that Lord (*Oṁkāra*) strengthen me with intelligence.[viii] O! Lord!, May I become the possessor of the immortal[ix] wisdom. May my body be healthy.[x] May my

> speech be extremely sweet and agreeable.[9] May I listen (to the scriptures) repeatedly through (my) ears. You are the sheath[xi] (abode) of *Brahman*, (which is) veiled by worldly knowledge. May you protect what is studied to by me.

This *anuvāka* is a prayer addressed to *Īśvara*, the giver of all wishes, seeking mental power and physical fitness, without which the knowledge of *Brahman* is not possible.

The epithet *ṛṣabha* according to traditional Advaitic interpretation refers to *oṁ*, the sound symbol of *Brahman*. The mystic syllable *oṁ* is set forth in the Upaniṣads as the object of profound meditation, and highest spiritual efficacy is attributed to it.

***Om in Various Upaniṣads*:** The origin of *om* is stated in *Chāndogyopaniṣad*.[10] It states:

> This sacred syllable was discovered by Prajāpati through meditation, for the benefit of the world. It is the quintessence of the Vedas, and that the entire speech is pervaded by it, just as a leaf is pervaded by the fibres. Indeed all this is *Oṁkāra*.

As words and objects are inseparable, similarly by including all the words through *Oṁkāra*, all the objects are also included. Hence, *Oṁkāra* is said to possess a manifold or universal form.

The unique exaltation of *oṁ* is found in *Māṇḍūkyopaniṣad*, where it is identified with all.[11] Everything is *Brahman* and this Self within is *Brahman*. This Self has four quarters.[12] It

---

9 *madhurā ca vāk* (speech should be sweet) says Vyāsa in *MaBhā* Ādi-Parva 88.12.

10 *tānyabhyatapattebhyo 'bhitaptebhya oṁkāraḥ saṁprāsravat-tadyathā śaṅkunā sarvāṇi parṇāni* । – *ChāUp* II.23.3

11 *oṁ ityetat akṣaram idaṁ sarvaṁ tasyopavyākhyānaṁ, bhutaṁ bhavad-bhaviṣyad-iti sarvam oṁkāra eva* । *yaccānyat trikālātītaṁ tadapi-oṁkāra eva* । – *MāUp* I.1

12 *sarvaṁ hi-etad brahma, ayamātmā brahma, so 'yamātmā catuṣpāt* ।
– Ibid. I.2

contains not only the three *mātrās*, but also the *amātrā* that is the transcendent Reality *turīya*.[13]

Kaṭhopaniṣad extols *oṁ* as the highest goal of all religious striving by affirming it to be the imperishable support and the best means for resting the mind.[14]

Muṇḍakopaniṣad asks the aspirant to meditate upon *Ātmā* as *oṁ*,[15] while the same text allegorically considers it as a bow[16] from which the arrow, i.e. the *Ātmā*, is sent to its mark, namely *Brahman*.

Praśnopaniṣad identifies *Oṁkāra* with *Para-Brahman* (*Nirguṇa-Brahman*) and *Apara-Brahman* (*Saguṇa-Brahman*), and considers it as the only *āyatana*, resting place or support to attain either of the above two aspects of *Brahman*.[17] Further, it states that, he who meditates with the help of it until departure is relieved of his wrong-deeds, just as a snake is relieved of its slough, and is lifted to the highest.[18]

---

13 *nāntaḥ-prajñaṁ na bahiṣ-prajñaṁ na ubhayataḥ-prajñaṁ na prajñāna-ghanaṁ na prajñaṁ-nāprajñam* । *adṛṣtam-avyavahāryam-agrāhyam-alakṣaṇam-acintyam-avyapadeśyam-ekātma-pratyaya-sāraṁ prapañcopaśamaṁ śāntaṁ śivam-advaitaṁ caturthaṁ manyante, sa ātmā sa vijñeyaḥ* । – Ibid. II.5

14 *sarve vedā yat-padam āmananti, tapāṁsi sarvāṇi ca yad-vadanti* ।
yad-ichanto brahmacaryaṁ caranti, tat te padaṁ saṅgraheṇa bravīmi ।
om-ityetat । – *KaUp* I.2.15

15 *arā iva rathanābhau saṁhatā yatra nāḍyaḥ* ।
sa eṣo 'ntaścarate bahudhā jāyamānaḥ ।। – *MuṇUp* II.2.6

16 *praṇavo dhanuḥ śaro hi-ātmā, brahma tat-lakṣyam-ucyate* ।
apramattena veddhavyaṁ, śaravat-tanmayo bhavet ।। – Ibid. II.2.4

17 *tasmai sa hovāco* । *etad vai satyakāma paraṁ-ca-aparaṁ ca brahma yad oṁkāraḥ* । *tasmād-vidvān-etena-eva-āyatanena-ekataram anveti* ।
– *PrUp* V.2

18 *yah punaretaṁ trimātreṇa-om-iti-anena-eva-akṣareṇa paraṁ puruṣam-abhidhyāyīta, sa tejasi sūrye sampannaḥ* । *yathā pādodaras-tvacā vinir-mucyata, evam ha vai sa pāpmanā vinirmuktaḥ; sa sāmabhir-unnīyate brahmalokaṁ* । *sa etasmat-jīvaghanāt-parāt-paraṁ puriśayaṁ puruṣam-īkṣate* । *tad-etau ślokau bhavataḥ* । – *PrUp* V.5

Bṛhadāraṇyakopaniṣad marks *oṁ* as identical with *ākāśa-Brahman* to serve as a means of meditation.[19]

In *Bhagavadgītā*, Bhagavān Kṛṣṇa declares that He is *Oṁkāra* in all the Vedas,[20] and that this monosyllabic *oṁ* should be uttered by a dying man for attaining the highest destiny,[21] and that it is the designation of *Brahman*.[22] He, who knows the meaning of *oṁ*, knows the Veda, says Manu.[23] There is no other holy symbol, so full of sacred potency or so short and easy to be uttered by a dying man, except this great *mantra*.

The Oṁkāra-Upāsanā is followed by a prayer for wealth. This is to be done in the form of a *homa*. Through this, one seeks wealth in the form of cattle, sheep, clothes, etc. Wealth is prayed for by the current student who is a future teacher, to facilitate the students' living in the *gurukulam* that he will have in the future. It may be sought for *gṛhasthāśrama* that follows the completion of *brahmacarya āśrama* (student life).

आवहन्ती वितन्वाना । कुर्वाणा चीरमात्मनः । वासाꣳसि मम गावश्च । अन्नपाने च सर्वदा । ततो मे श्रियमावह । लोमशां पशुभिः सह स्वाहा ।

āvahantī vitanvānā । kurvāṇā cīramātmanaḥ । vāsāṁsi mama gāvaśca । annapāne ca sarvadā । tato me śriyam āvaha । lomaśāṁ paśubhiḥ saha svāhā । –I.4

(O Lord!) Thereafter (having endowed me with intelligence and fitness), bless me with wealth that will immediately

---

19 *oṁ khaṁ brahma । khaṁ purāṇaṁ, vāyuraṁ kham-iti ha smāha kauravyāyaṇī-putraḥ; vedo 'yaṁ brāhmaṇā viduḥ; vedainena yad-veditavyam ।* – *BṛUp* V.1.1

20 *praṇavaḥ sarva-vedeṣu śabdaḥ khe pauruṣaṁ nṛṣu ।* – *BhGī* VII.8

21 *om-ityekākṣaraṁ brahma vyāharan-mām-anusmaran ।*
yaḥ prayāti tyajan dehaṁ sa yāti paramāṁ gatim ॥ – Ibid. VIII.13

22 *oṁ tat sad iti nirdeśo brahmaṇas-trividhaḥ smṛtaḥ ।*
brāhmaṇās tena vedāś ca yajñāś ca vihitāḥ purā ॥ – Ibid. XVII.23

23 *ādyaṁ yat-tryakṣaraṁ brahma trayo yasmin pratiṣṭhitāḥ ।*
sa guhyo 'nyastrivṛd-vedo yastaṁ veda sa vedavit ॥ – *MaSm* XI.265

bring, increase and preserve plenty of clothes for me, plenty of cattle for me, and plenty of food and drinks (for me) all the time, and plenty of fleecy/woolly animals along with other animals/cattle.

(The word *svāhā* indicates that this *mantra* is to be used in a *homa*.)

Then with an intention to become a great teacher to maintain the tradition, the student seeks the Lord's blessings so that many students with discipline and sincerity may come to him from various directions. The final prayer to the Lord is: "Let me purify myself in you and let us merge. O Lord! May you reveal yourself unto me and merge in me."

आमायन्तु ब्रह्मचारिणः स्वाहा । वि मा यन्तु ब्रह्मचारिणः स्वाहा । प्र मा यन्तु ब्रह्मचारिणः स्वाहा । दमायन्तु ब्रह्मचारिणः स्वाहा । शमायन्तु ब्रह्मचारिणः स्वाहा ।

āmāyantu brahmacāriṇaḥ svāhā । *vi mā yantu brahmacāriṇaḥ svāhā* । *pra mā yantu brahmacāriṇaḥ svāhā* । *damāyantu brahmacāriṇaḥ svāhā* । *śamāyantu brahmacāriṇaḥ svāhā* ।

–I.4

यशो जनेऽसानि स्वाहा । श्रेयान् वस्यसोऽसानि स्वाहा । तं त्वा भग प्रविशानि स्वाहा । स मा भग प्रविश स्वाहा । तस्मिन् सहस्रशाखे । नि भगाहं त्वयि मृजे स्वाहा । यथापः प्रवता यन्ति । यथा मासा अहर्जरम् । एवं मां ब्रह्मचारिणः । धातरायन्तु सर्वतः स्वाहा । प्रतिवेशोऽसि प्र मा भाहि प्र मा पद्यस्व ॥

yaśo jane 'sāni svāhā । *śreyān vasyaso 'sāni svāhā* । *taṁ tvā bhaga praviśāni svāhā* । *sa mā bhaga praviśa svāhā* । *tasmin sahasraśākhe* । *ni bhagāhaṁ tvayi mṛje svāhā* । *yathāpaḥ pravatā yanti* । *yathā māsā aharjaram* । *evaṁ māṁ brahmacāriṇaḥ* । *dhātarāyantu sarvataḥ svāhā* । *prativeśo 'si pra mā bhāhi pra mā padyasva* । –I.4

May many *brahmacārī*s (students) come to me. May many students with varied interests come to me. May many students with intelligence come to me. May many students with self-mastery come to me. May many students with controlled-mind come to me. May I become renowned (as a teacher) among the people. May I become superior[xii] and wealthier than common people. O Lord! May I merge into you. O Lord! May you merge[xiii] into me. O Lord! May I purify myself in you who have thousand forms.[xiv] O Lord! May many students come to me from far-off and different directions. May students come to me just as waters rush downwards, and just as the months rush towards the (next) year. (O Lord!) You are (like) a refuge. Reveal[xv] yourself unto me (and) enter into me.

These are invocations with which, oblations should be offered into the sacred fire for getting fortune and students. Wealth in the hands of an intelligent man is the means of doing religious and spiritual work, by which purity of mind is attained and then wisdom follows. From the teacher's standpoint the prayer is altruistic, for he is anxious to get a very large number of students, calm and free from external activities, as he is desirous to get wealth, food and clothing.

The indeclinable word *svāhā* marks the end of a *mantra* after repeating which, one oblation is offered into the sacrificial fire.

Fifth Anuvāka: Vyāhṛti Upāsanā

The four *vyāhrtis* – *bhūḥ, bhuvaḥ, suvaḥ* and *mahaḥ* – serve as symbols for meditating on various *devatās*. This is a group of four subsidiary *upāsanās*, and each subsidiary *upāsanā* consists of meditation on four *devatās* connected with various aspects of the creation.

भूर्भुवः सुवरिति वा एतास्तिस्रो व्याहृतयः । तासामु ह स्मै तां चतुर्थीम् ।
माहाचमस्यः प्रवेदयते । मह इति । तद् ब्रह्म । स आत्मा । अङ्गान्यन्या देवताः ।

bhūr-bhuvaḥ-suvar-iti vā etāstisro vyāhṛtayaḥ । tāsām u ha smaitāṁ caturthīm । māhācamasyaḥ pravedayate । maha iti । tad brahma । sa ātmā । aṅgānyanyā devatāḥ । – I.5

Bhūḥ, bhuvaḥ and *suvaḥ* – these are indeed the three *vyāhṛtis* (mystical utterances). Along with them, sage Māhācamasya[xvi] reveals the fourth (*vyāhṛti*) which is *mahaḥ*. That (*mahaḥ*) is (to be meditated as) Hiraṇyagarbha. He (Hiraṇyagarbha) is *Ātmā*. All other gods are (his) limbs.

भूरिति वा अयं लोकः । भुव इत्यन्तरिक्षम् । सुवरित्यसौ लोकः । मह इत्यादित्यः । आदित्येन वाव सर्वे लोका महीयन्ते ।

bhūriti vā ayaṁ lokaḥ । *bhuva ityantārikṣam* । *suvarityasau lokaḥ* । *maha ityādityaḥ* । *ādityena vāva sarve lokā mahīyante* ।

– I.5

Bhūḥ is (to be meditated as) this world. *Bhuvaḥ* is (to be meditated as) the intermediary space. *Suvaḥ* is (to be meditated as) the heaven. *Mahaḥ* is (to be meditated as) the sun. By the sun alone, all these worlds increase and prosper.

भूरिति वा अग्निः । भुव इति वायुः । सुवारित्यादित्यः । मह इति चन्द्रमाः । चन्द्रमसा वाव सर्वाणि ज्योतींषि महीयन्ते ।

bhūriti vā agniḥ । *bhuva iti vāyuḥ* । *suvārityādityaḥ* । *maha iti candramāḥ* । *candramasā vāva sarvāṇi jyotīṁṣi mahīyante* ।

– I.5

Bhūḥ is (to be meditated as) fire. *Bhuvaḥ* is (to be meditated as) air. *Suvaḥ* is (to be meditated as) the sun. *Mahaḥ* is (to be meditated as) the moon. By the moon alone, all these luminaries increase and prosper.

भूरिति वा ऋचः । भुव इति सामानि । सुवरिति यजूंषि । मह इति ब्रह्म । ब्रह्मणा वाव सर्वे वेदा महीयन्ते ।

bhūriti vā ṛcaḥ । *bhuva iti sāmāni* । *suvariti yajūṁṣi* । *maha iti brahma* । *brahmaṇā vāva sarve vedā mahīyante* । – I.5

Bhuḥ is (to be meditated as) *Ṛgveda*. *Bhuvaḥ* is (to be meditated as) *Sāmaveda*. *Suvaḥ* is (to be meditated as) *Yajurveda*. *Mahaḥ* is (to be meditated as) (*Saguṇa*) *Brahman* (*Oṁkāra*). By *Brahman* (*Oṁkāra*) alone, all the Vedas are glorified.

भूरिति वै प्राणः । भुव इत्यपानः । सुवरिति व्यानः । मह इत्यन्नम् । अन्नेन वाव सर्वे प्राणा महीयन्ते ।

bhūriti vai prāṇah । *bhuva ityapānaḥ* । *suvariti vyānaḥ* । *maha ityannam* । *annena vāva sarve prāṇā mahīyante* । – I.5

Bhūḥ is (to be meditated as) *prāṇaḥ*. *Bhuvaḥ* is (to be meditated as) *apānaḥ*. *Suvaḥ* is (to be meditated as) *vyānaḥ*. *Mahaḥ* is (to be meditated as) food. By food alone, all the *prāṇa*s are maintained.

ता वा एताश्चतस्रश्चतुर्धा । चतस्रश्चतस्रो व्याहृतयः । ता यो वेद । स वेद ब्रह्म । सर्वेऽस्मै देवाः बलिमावहन्ति ॥

tā vā etāścatasraścaturdhā । *catasraścatasro vyāhṛtayaḥ* । *tā yo veda* । *sa veda brahma* । *sarve 'smai devaḥ balim-āvahanti* ।
–I.5

Thus, these four (*vyāhṛtis*) comprised in a group of four and becoming fourfold (are to be meditated upon). One who knows (and meditates on) these four *vyāhṛti*s, knows Hiranyagarbha,[xvii] (and) all the gods[xviii] carry offerings to him.

The *vyāhṛti*s (mystical utterances) are used in connection with various Vedic rituals. They form a theme for internal meditations here. At present, there are seven *vyāhṛti*s – *bhūḥ, bhuvaḥ, suvaḥ, mahaḥ, janaḥ, tapaḥ* and *satya*. The fourth *vyāhṛti, mahaḥ* was revealed to Ṛṣi Māhācamasya through divine intuition. It is derived from a root √ syllable *maha* meaning to become great, or to grow without limit. The term *Brahman* also is derived from the root√ *bṛh – vṛdhhau* having the same meaning. Here, therefore, *mahaḥ* is equated with *Brahman* as *Ātmā* for the purpose of the meditation prescribed in this lesson.

In common usage, the word *ātmā* denotes the whole personality as distinguished from the limbs such as head, hands and feet. Here the fourth *vyāhṛti* takes the place of *Ātmā*; and the other three *vyāhṛti*s that precede take the position of the limbs of the body. By an originative injunction, it is laid down that one, who desires the rewards held out at the end of the *anuvāka*, should meditate that his *Ātmā* is *mahaḥ*, or Virāṭ, of which the *vyāhṛtis* representing the deities in the form of fire, sun, moon, *Oṁkāra*, food, etc. The sixteen divisions of the *vyāhṛtis* correspond to the *ṣoḍaśa-kalā puruṣa* mentioned in other Upaniṣads.[24] It is also suggested that the various worlds are but the limbs of Virāṭ.

Sixth Anuvāka: Hiraṇyagarbha-upāsanā

Manomayatvādi-guṇaka-brahmopāsanayā svārājya-siddhiḥ

In the sixth section, we get Hiraṇyagarbha-upāsanā. Here the mind is to be taken as the locus of *upāsanā*. This is to be done along with the *upāsanā* narrated in the fifth *anuvāka*, i.e. Vyahṛti-Upāsanā. Through this *upāsanā*, one attains oneness with Hiraṇyagarbha. After dropping the body, the *upāsaka* (the meditator) travels through the *susumnā-nāḍī*. Emerging through the top of the head, he attains oneness with Agni, Vāyu, Āditya and ultimately with Hiraṇyagarbha. Enjoying lordship over all, he attains boundless peace and joy. Even the gods bring offerings to him. This is the highest glory that one can attain through *upāsanā*.

स य एषोऽन्तर्हृदय आकाशः । तस्मिन्नयं पुरुषो मनोमयः । अमृतो हिरण्मयः । अन्तरेण तालुके । य एष स्तन इवावलम्बते । सेन्द्रयोनिः । यत्रासौ केशान्तो विवर्तते । व्यपोह्य शीर्षकपाले ।

sa ya eṣo 'ntarhṛdaya ākāśaḥ । *tasminnayaṁ puruṣo manomayaḥ* । *amṛto hiraṇmayaḥ* । *antareṇa tāluke* । *ya eṣa stana ivāvalambate* । *sendrayoniḥ* । *yatrāsau keśānto vivartate* । *vyapohya śīrṣakapāle* । –I.6

That eternal and effulgent Hiraṇyagarbha who is revealed through the mind (is to be meditated) in that locus which is the space within the heart.[xix] (*Susumnā nāḍī*[xx] passes through that part), which hangs down like a nipple between the two

---

[24] *PrUp* VI.1-5.

palates, is the path of Indra (Hiraṇyagarbha). (It comes out) [xxi] breaking open the crown of the head, where the roots of the hair are divided apart. That is the passage to (the world of) Hiraṇyagarbha.

भूरित्यग्नौ प्रतितिष्ठति । भुव इति वायौ । सुवरित्यादित्ये । मह इति ब्रह्मणि । आप्नोति स्वाराज्यम् । आप्नोति मनसस्पतिम् । वाक्पतिश्चक्षुष्पतिः । श्रोत्रपतिर्विज्ञानपतिः । एतत्ततो भवति । आकाशशरीरं ब्रह्म । सत्यात्म प्राणारामं मन आनन्दम् । शान्तिसमृद्धममृतम् । इति प्राचीनयोग्योपास्व ॥

bhūrityagnau pratitiṣṭhati । *bhuva iti vāyau* । *suvarityāditye* । *maha iti brahmaṇi* । *āpnoti svārājyam* । *āpnoti manasas-patim* । *vākpatiścakṣuspatiḥ* । *śrotrapatir-vijñānapatiḥ* । *etattato bhavati* । *ākāśaśarīraṁ brahma* । *satyātma prāṇārāmaṁ mana ānandam* । *śāntisamṛddham-amṛtam* । *iti prācīnayogyopāsva* । –I.6

(At the time of death, the *upāsaka*) merges into the fire,[xxii] which is in the form of *bhūḥ*; (he merges) into the air which is in the form of *bhuvaḥ*; (he merges) into the sun which is in the form of *suvaḥ*; (he merges) into Hiraṇyagrbha which is in the form of *mahaḥ*. (Having become Virāṭ[xxiii]) He attains sovereignty. He attains lordship over all the minds. He becomes the lord of speech, the lord of eyes, the lord of ears, and the lord of intellect. In addition to this, the following (attributes) are also there. Hiraṇyagarbha has an all-pervasive body like the space; and which consists of the entire universe with and without form. He has all the *prāṇa*s as the sporting ground. He has a mind[xxiv] that is the embodiment of *ānanda*. He is all peace, prosperity, and immortality. O! Prācīnayogya! May you meditate thus.

This *anuvāka* is indeed cryptic. For interpreting it, Śaṅkarācārya's commentary has been closely followed and words are supplied from it to construe the passage directly in an unbroken manner. According to Śaṅkara, this *anuvāka* lays down the accessories of the meditation taught in the preceding (fifth) *anuvāka*. It describes the place where (*Saguṇa*) *Brahman* (Hiraṇyagarbha) is to be worshipped as *mahaḥ*, the attributes that are to be remembered in the meditation, the passages by which *Ātmā* unites with the object of worship, and the location from where *Ātmā* enjoys the homage paid by the gods.

Seventh Anuvāka: Pāṅktabrahma-upāsanā

Now follows the Pāṅktabrahma-upāsanā. The entire universe is divided into six groups of five factors each. Each group is known as a *pāṅkta* (a group of five). Of these, three are at the objective level (*ādhibhautika*) and three are at the personal level (*ādhyātmika*). One complements the other. One should meditate upon the first three as identical with the second. This is also another type of Hiraṇyagarbha-upāsanā. The result is the same, viz. oneness with the Hiraṇyagarbha.

पृथिव्यन्तरिक्षं द्यौर्दिशोऽवान्तरदिशाः । अग्निर्वायुरादित्यश्चन्द्रमा नक्षत्राणि ।
आप ओषधयो वनस्पतय आकाश आत्मा । इत्यधिभूतम् । अथाध्यात्मम् ।
प्राणो व्यानोऽपान उदानः समानः । चक्षुः श्रोत्रं मनो वाक्त्वक् । चर्म माꣳसꣳ
स्नावास्थि मज्जा । एतदधिविधायऋषिरवोचत् । पाङ्क्तं वा इदꣳ सर्वम् ।
पाङ्क्तेनैव पाङ्क्तꣳ स्पृणोतीति ॥

pṛthivyantarikṣaṁ dyaurdiśo 'vāntaradiśāḥ । *agnir-vāyur-ādityaś-candramā nakṣatrāṇi* । *āpa oṣadhayo vanaspataya ākāśa ātmā* । *ityadhibhūtam* । *athādhyātmam* । *prāṇo vyāno 'pāna udānaḥ samānaḥ* । *cakṣuḥ śrotraṁ mano vāk tvak* । *carma-māṁsaṁ-snāvasthi majjā* । *etadadhividhāya ṛṣir-avocat* । *pāṅktaṁ vā idaṁ sarvam* । *pāṅktenaiva pāṅktaṁ spṛṇotīti* । –I.7

(i) The earth, the sky, the heaven, the (four) main quarters and the (four) intermediary quarters, (ii) the fire, the air, the sun, the moon and the stars, (iii) water, herbs (of healing), trees (of the forest), space and *virāṭ* – (these three groups of five factors) constitute *adhibhūta-pāṅktam*.

Now follow (the three groups of five factors) which constitute *adhyātma-pāṅktam*: (i) *prāṇa*,[xxv] *vyāna*, *apāna*, *udāna* and *samāna*,

> (ii) the eyes, the ears, the mind, speech and the skin, (iii) skin/ hide, flesh, muscles, bone and marrow. The sage who revealed them said, "the whole universe is based on a fivefold principle (*pāṅkta*s)". One set of (subjective three) *pāṅkta*s preserves the other set of (objective three) *pāṅkta*s.

The group under the elements, *adhibhūta*s includes the five great elements that constitute the universe, and their conspicuous products, ten in number. Overall, they form three sets of five. Under the heading *adhyātma-pāṅkta* come the subtle and gross bodies. The components of the first are included under two sets of five. The whole Virāṭ body is thus described. The worshipper of this aspect of *Brahman* attains Hiraṇyagarbha. The number five has its special significance, because of its familiarity in two Vedic connections. Yājñic worship which was the universal practice of Vedic culture has five factors; namely, the *yajamāna*, his wife, his son, and wealth which includes ingredients, human efforts, and gods. There is also a common Vedic metre called *paṅkti* having five lines of eight syllables each. The *ṛṣi* opens up a cosmic vision through this principle of five based on facts known to all.

Eighth Anuvāka: Oṁkāra-upāsanā

The eighth section deals with Oṁkāra-upāsanā. *Oṁkāra* is to be meditated on as *Brahman*. Through this meditation one attains *Brahman*, whether *Parā* or *Aparā*. The Upaniṣad talks about the glory of *Oṁkāra* in the following words. In all rituals, *Oṁkāra* is uttered during Vedic chanting, offering of oblations, etc. The very beginning of the Vedic studies is with *Oṁkāra*. Its utterance makes all pursuits holy and fruitful.

> ओमिति ब्रह्म । ओमितीद॑ सर्वम् । ओमित्येतदनुकृति ह स्म वा अप्योश्रावयेत्याश्रावयन्ति । ओमिति सामानि गायन्ति । ओ॑ शोमिति शस्त्राणि श॑सन्ति । ओमित्यध्वर्युः प्रतिगरं प्रतिगृणाति । ओमिति ब्रह्मा प्रसौति । ओमित्यग्निहोत्रमनुजानाति । ओमिति ब्राह्मणः प्रवक्ष्यन्नाह ब्रह्मोपाप्नवानीति । ब्रह्मैवोपाप्नोति ॥

om iti brahma । *om itīdaṁ sarvam* । *om ityetad-anukṛtir ha sma vā apyośrāvayetyāśrāvayanti* । *om iti sāmāni gāyanti* । *oṁ śom iti śastrāṇi śaṁsanti* । *om ityadhvaryuḥ pratigaraṁ pratigṛṇāti* । *om iti brahmā prasauti* । *om ityagnihotram anujānāti* । *om iti brāhmaṇaḥ pravakṣyannāha brahmopāpnavānīti* । *brahmaivopāpnoti* । –I.8

One should meditate upon *Oṁkāra* as *Brahman* because this entire (universe) is indeed *Oṁkāra*. (i) This *Oṁkāra* is also an expression of acceptance/compliance.[xxvi] (ii) Moreover, (the priests) direct (the assistant) to recite (to the gods) thus – "*oṁ*, may you recite" (to the gods). (iii) (The *Sāmaveda*-priest) chants the *Sāma-mantras* after uttering *Oṁkāra*. (iv) (The *Ṛgveda*-priest[xxvii]) chants the *Ṛg-mantras* after uttering *oṁ śom*. (v) The *Yajurveda*-priest[xxviii] expresses his permissions by uttering *Oṁkāra*. (vi) The *Atharvaveda*-priest[xxix] gives permission by uttering *Oṁkāra*. (vii) The priest[xxx] permits (the host) to perform *agnihotra*-ritual by uttering *Oṁkāra*. (viii) Desiring to learn the Vedas, the brāhmaṇa[xxxi] utters *Oṁkāra* with the intention "Let me attain Vedic knowledge". Indeed, he attains Vedic knowledge.

First, it is laid down that one should meditate purely upon *oṁ* without thinking of any intervening factor. For, *oṁ* is the manifesting word of *Īśvara*.[25] In practice, one should repeat the syllable *oṁ* with the mind fixed on its meaning, i.e. *Brahman*. Thus this universe, comprising name and form, is comprehended by *oṁ*, through the words in all the languages denoting the objects of the universe. In this manner, *oṁ* pervades all words and objects.

Personal Human Values (Antaraṅga-Sādhanā) in Taittirīya

It has been stated in the earlier (sixth) *anuvāka* that through *upāsanā*s one can get the sovereignty. This may lead to one's understanding that *karma*s (rituals) are futile and one may be

---

25 *tasya vācakaḥ praṇavaḥ – YoSū* I.27

inclined to question the use of everything else taught by the scriptures. To negate such understanding this *anuvāka* stresses the importance of *karma-yoga,* doing one's duties as per the scriptural injunctions. For this purpose, scriptural duties (*karma*) have also been dwelt upon in the Śīkṣāvallī. The text here emphasizes that they (*iti-kartavyatā*) too have their purpose preparing the student for *brahma-vidyā,* which is the subject matter of the next *vallī.*

Ninth Anuvāka: Svādhyāya-Praśaṁsā (Antaraṅga-sādhanā)

Having elaborately dealt with various *upāsanā*s, the Upaniṣad now emphasizes the importance of *karma* in the ninth section. The study of one's own Veda, truthfulness, righteousness, austerity, sense-control, mind-control, worship, hospitality to the guests and humanity, continuance of the family lineage, etc. should be followed. Of them, regular study of and teaching of one's own Veda is considered important.

It is to be noted here that, when these *upāsanā*s and *karma*s are done without desire for material ends, they prepare the mind for *brahma-vidyā* that is discussed in the next chapter.

ऋतं च स्वाध्यायप्रवचने च । सत्यं च स्वाध्यायप्रवचने च । तपश्च स्वाध्यायप्रवचने च । दमश्च स्वाध्यायप्रवचने च । शमश्च स्वाध्यायप्रवचने च । अग्नयश्च स्वाध्यायप्रवचने च । अग्निहोत्रं च स्वाध्यायप्रवचने च । अतिथयश्च स्वाध्यायप्रवचने च । मानुषं च स्वाध्यायप्रवचने च । प्रजा च स्वाध्यायप्रवचने च । प्रजनश्च स्वाध्यायप्रवचने च । प्रजातिश्च स्वाध्यायप्रवचने च । सत्यमिति सत्यवचा राथीतरः । तप इति तपोनित्यः पौरुशिष्टिः । स्वाध्यायप्रवचने एवेति नाको मौद्गल्यः । तद्धि तपस्तद्धि तपः ॥

ṛtaṁ ca svādhyāyapravacane ca । *satyaṁ ca svādhyāyapravacane ca* । *tapaśca svādhyāyapravacane ca* । *damaśca svādhyāyapravacane ca* । *śamaśca svādhyāyapravacane ca* । *agnayaśca svādhyāyapravacane ca* । *agnihotraṁ ca svādhyāyapravacane ca* । *atithayaśca svādhyāyapravacane ca* । *mānuṣaṁ ca svādhyāyapravacane ca* । *prajā ca svādhyāyapravacane ca* । *prajanaśca svādhyāyapravacane ca* । *prajātiśca svādhyāyapravacane ca* । *satyam-iti satyavacā rāthītaraḥ* । *tapa iti taponityaḥ pauruśiṣṭiḥ* । *svādhyāya-pravacane eveti nāko maudgalyaḥ* । *taddhi tapastaddhi tapaḥ* । –I.9

One should observe the following, righteousness/right understanding as per scriptures, along with study and teaching or reciting of the Vedas,[xxxii] truthfulness in speech and action along with study and teaching of the Vedas, austerities along with study and teaching of the Vedas, self-mastery along with study and teaching of the Vedas, composure along with study and teaching of the Vedas, tending the consecrated fires along with study and teaching of the Vedas, performance of the Agnihotra-ritual along with study and teaching of the Vedas, social obligations along with study and teaching of the Vedas, bringing up a family along with study and teaching of the Vedas, procreation at the ordained period of time along with study and teaching of the Vedas, (and) begetting grandchildren along with study and teaching of the Vedas. Sage Satyavacā also known as Rāthītara who never swerved from truth, held that truthfulness is the greatest practice. Austerity is the highest practice according to Sage Pauruśiṣṭi, who was in constant penance. The study and teaching of the Vedas is the highest duty according to Sage Nāka, the son of Sage Mudgala. That alone is true austerity, that indeed[xxxii] is true austerity.

Tenth Anuvāka: Brahmajñāna-prakāśaka-mantraḥ

From the topical context it appears that, the tenth section is a *mantra* for *svādhyāya/japa*. By *svādhyāya/japa*, the mind gets ready for the knowledge to take place. This is the declaration of Sage Triśaṅku after recognizing his true nature. The repetition of this *mantra* prepares the mind for discovery of its meaning.

अहं वृक्षस्य रेरिवा । कीर्तिः पृष्ठं गिरेरिव । ऊर्ध्वपवित्रो वाजिनीव स्वमृतमस्मि ।
द्रविणꣳ सवर्चसम् । सुमेधा अमृतोक्षितः । इति त्रिशङ्कोर्वेदानुवचनम् ॥

ahaṁ vṛkṣasya rerivā । kīrtiḥ pṛṣṭhaṁ gireriva । ūrdhvapavitro vājinīva svamṛtam-asmi । draviṇaṁ savarcasam । sumedhā amṛtokṣitaḥ । iti triśaṅkor-vedānuvacanam । – I.10

"I am the sustainer of the Tree (of the Universe). My glory[xxxiii] is as high as a mountain-peak. I am pure. I am auspicious and immortal[xxxiv] as (the effulgence of) the sun. I am the effulgent (because of Self-knowledge) wealth[xxxv] with divine intuition (or the wealth of Self-knowledge has been obtained by me). I am free from death and decay." This is Sage Triśaṅku's declaration of Self-knowledge.

It has been emphatically declared in the preceding section (ninth *anuvāka*) that the solemn recitation of the Veda should not be missed by anyone seeking welfare and *mokṣa*. However, it will not be feasible for all to repeat and study the whole or even considerable portion of the Veda daily. Therefore, this "post-Self-knowledge declaration" is provided by Sage Triśaṅku as a suitable substitute for the Veda, to be of use to those who aspire for Self-knowledge.

The analogy of tree is interesting here. A gigantic tree developing from the potentialities hidden in a small seed, rising high up in the vast sky, has always impressed the minds of sages, evoking sublime reflections. The sages have taken it as a profound symbol of *Īśvara* as manifest in the cosmos or extending beyond it. Other traditions than Vedic have reference to this universal symbol, both in the straight and in the inverted positions. Brahmavṛkṣa, Bodhidruma, Tree of Life, and the like are familiar terms in other cultures to which these belong.

In the Vedic tradition, the tree stands for both the Absolute Reality, as well as its manifestation (*jagat*). As the Absolute Reality, the erect Brahmavṛkṣa consists of a continuous stem with two parts, the one extending as the axis of the cosmos that maintains its existence, and the other branching above the universe. *Śvetāśvatara Upaniṣad*[26] states that the Great Being stands without a second, in its own glory, like an immovable tree. The same *mantra* is found in *Mahānārayaṇa Upaniṣad* XII.13. *Maitrāyāṇi Upaniṣad* VI.4 speaks of the one Aśvattha identified with *om*.

Ṛgveda X.31.7[27] and X.81.4[28] ask "What is that Tree, out of which heaven and earth were fashioned?" And *Taittirīya-Brāhmaṇa* II.8.9.6 makes it clear that *Brahman* is that Tree. The Supalāśavṛkṣa mentioned in *Ṛgveda*[29] is identified with *Brahman* in *Śatapatha Brāhmaṇa*, I.3.3.9, VI.6.3.7 and VII.1.1.5.

Again, in *Ṛgveda* I.164.20[30] (the verse re-appears *in toto* in *Muṇḍaka Upaniṣad* III.1.1) and in I.164.22[31] reference is made to the Self, the same Tree to which the contrasted aspects of the Supreme Being as *jīva* and *Brahman* are differently related. The *Mahābhārata* (Aśvamedha-Parva XXV.20-22 and XV.12-15) has a full description of the Brahmavṛkṣa. Viṣṇusahasranāma[32] also counts Nyagrodha, Udumbara and Aśvattha as names of Bhagavān Viṣṇu.

---

26 *yasmāt paraṁ nāparam-asti kiñcid-yasmān-nāṇiyo na jyayo 'sti kaścit* ।
vṛkṣa iva stabdho divi tiṣṭhatyekas-tenedaṁ pūrṇaṁ puruṣeṇa sarvam ॥
– *ŚvUp* III.9, also *MahUp* XII.13

27 *kiṁ svid-vanaṁ ka u sa vṛkṣa āsa yato dyāvā-pṛthivī niṣṭatakṣuḥ* ।
santasthāne ajare itaūti ahāni pūrvīruṣaso jaranta ॥ – *ṚVS* X.31.7

28 *kiṁ svid-vanaṁ ka u sa vṛkṣa āsa, yato dyāvā-pṛthivī niṣṭatakṣūh* ।
manīṣiṇo manasā pṛcchated u tad-yad-adhyatiṣṭhad-bhuvanāni dhārayan ॥
– Ibid. X.81.4

29 *yasminvṛkṣe supalāśe devaiḥ saṁ-pibate yamaḥ* ।
atrā no viśpatiḥ pitā puraṇān anu venati । – Ibid. X.135.1

30 *dvā suparṇā sayujā sakhāyā samānaṁ vṛkṣaṁ pari-ṣasvajāte* ।
tayor-anyaḥ pippalaṁ svādvattyanaśnannanyo abhi-cākaśīti ॥
– Ibid. I.164.20, also *MuṇUp* III.1.1

31 *yasminvṛkṣe madhvadaḥ suparṇā niviśante suvate cādhi viśve* ।
tasyedāhuḥ pippalaṁ svādvagre tannonnaśadyaḥ pitaraṁ na veda ॥
– *ṚVS* I.164.22

32 *nyagrodhodumbaro 'śvatthaṣ-cāṇurāndhraniṣūdaaḥ* । – *ViSaNā* 88

In the second conception/visualization, viz. the Saṁsāravṛkṣa (Tree of Life) is inverted, and has its roots up in the unmanifest, branching out in the manifest cosmos. *Kaṭha Upaniṣad* II.3.1[33] conceives it, *Śvetāśvatara Upaniṣad* VI.6[34] notices it and *Bhagavadgītā*[35] describes this Tree in detail. Śrī Śaṅkara also very eloquently comments on the Saṁsāravṛkṣa in both the contexts. In fact, *Brahman* being the material cause of the *jagat*, the tree is after all the same and he, who has known *Brahman* in essence, like Sage Triśaṅku, is conscious that he is the mover of the world tree as the inherent *Ātmā*, who is the cause of its manifestation, sustenance, as well as dissolution.

Eleventh Anuvāka:
Śiṣyānuśāsanam (Antaraṅga-sādhanā)

The last section of Śīkṣāvallī concludes with an exhortation by the teacher to his students. Although the instructions appear like a convocation address on the eve of their returning home as *snātakas* (graduates), after the completion of their studies, instructing them how to conduct themselves in the world, *Śāṅkara-bhāṣyam* does not think so.

---

33 *urdhvamūlo 'vākśākha eṣo 'śvatthaḥ sanātanaḥ* |
tadeva śukraṁ tad-brahma tad-evāmṛtam-ucyate |
tasmin-llokāḥ śritāḥ sarve tad-u nānyeti kaścana ||
etad-vai-tat | – *KaUp* II.3.1

34 *sa vṛkṣakālākṛtibhiḥ paro 'nyo yasmāt prapañcaḥ parivartate 'yam* |
dharmāvahaṁ pāpanudaṁ bhageśaṁ jñātvā 'tmasthamamṛtaṁ viśvadhāma ||
– *ŚvUp* VI.6

35 *ūrdhva-mūlam-adhaḥ-sākham-aśvatthaṁ prāhur-avyayam* |
chandāṁsi yasya parṇāni yas-taṁ veda sa vedavit || – *BhGī* XV.1

adhaścordhvaṁ prasṛtās-tasya śākhā guṇapravṛddhā viṣayapravālāḥ |
adhaś-ca mūlānyanusantatāni karmānubandhīni manuṣyaloke ||
– Ibid. XV.2

na rūpam-asyeha tathopalabhyate nānto na cadir-na ca sam-pratiṣṭhā |
aśvattham-enaṁ suvirūḍha-mūlam asaṅga-śastreṇa dṛdhena chittvā ||
– Ibid. XV.3

It happens to be in the form of instructions from a teacher to his students. The importance of truthfulness, righteousness, Vedic study, and respect to parents, teachers and guests are emphasized here. One should follow the way of life led by the noble ones. Charity must be given, and that too with the right attitude. In situations of conflict, one should follow the path of cultured people who are facing the same or similar situations. This is the injunction of scriptures. One should follow this for the well-being of all.

Only after all these preparations are done meticulously, the *śiṣya* is gently led to the study of *brahma-vidyā* that is introduced in the next *vallī*.

वेदमनूच्याचार्योऽन्तेवासिनमनुशास्ति । सत्यं वद । धर्मं चर । स्वाध्यायान्मा प्रमदः । आचार्याय प्रियं धनमाहृत्य प्रजातन्तुं मा व्यवच्छेत्सीः । सत्यान्न प्रमदितव्यम् । धर्मान्न प्रमदितव्यम् । कुशलान्न प्रमदितव्यम् । भूत्यै न प्रमदितव्यम् । स्वाध्यायप्रवचनाभ्यां न प्रमदितव्यम् । देवपितृकार्याभ्यां न प्रमदितव्यम् । मातृदेवो भव । पितृदेवो भव । आचार्यदेवो भव । अतिथिदेवो भव ।

vedam-anūcyācāryo 'ntevāsinam-anuśāsti । satyaṁ vada । dharmaṁ cara । svādhyāyān-mā pramadaḥ । ācāryāya priyaṁ dhanamāhṛtya prajātantuṁ mā vyavacchetsīḥ । satyān-na pramaditavyaṁ । dharmān-na pramaditavyam । kuśalān-na pramaditavyam । bhūtyai na pramaditavyam । svādhyāya-pravacanābhyāṁ na pramaditavyam । deva-pitṛkāryābhyāṁ na pramaditavyam । mātṛdevo bhava । pitṛdevo bhava । ācāryadevo bhava । atithidevo bhava । – I.11

Having[xxxvi] taught the Vedas, the teacher[xxxvii] instructs the students thus, "Speak the truth; follow the prescribed conduct;[xxxviii] be not complacent[xxxix] in the recitation/study of the Vedas. (At the time of departure from your preceptor) offering decent wealth to the teacher, may you not break the family-lineage.[xl] May you not neglect the truth.[xli] May you not neglect performance of prescribed duties. May you not neglect

> (your own) well-being.[xlii] May you not neglect propitious activities. May you not neglect the study and teaching of the Vedas.[xliii] May you not neglect the worship of gods and forefathers.[xliv] May your mother[xlv] be a god to you. May your father be a god to you. May your teacher be a god to you. May your guest be a god to you."

In order to unfold *brahmajñāna* (knowledge of the spiritual reality), which is the ultimate teaching of the Upaniṣads, the whole personality of a person must be regenerated through appropriate discipline undergone in one or more human lives. Good work and noble conduct must precede before knowledge is attained, even before a suitable birth is taken. Those whose conduct has been auspicious, says *Chāndogya Upaniṣad* V.10.7, will quickly attain some good birth, whereas those whose life has been of wrongdoings will immediately result in inferior birth. Good conduct is therefore an absolute necessity of spiritual life at all stages. A person, whose mind is not purified, is not capable of acquiring *ātmajñāna*, says Yājñavalkya, just as a mirror smeared with dirt cannot reflect an image. *Brahmasūtra*[36] makes it explicit that the performance of Vedic rites, whether undertaken with the motive of reaping future rewards, or done as a course of spiritual duty with no desire for fruits, will be crippled to produce the desired effect, if the agent of the action is not moral and pure. In this *anuvāka* therefore the ideals of character are formulated in a gentle and humane tone for edification of the daily conduct of a *brahmacārī*. In *Muṇḍaka*,[37]

---

36 *ānarthakyam-iti cen-na, tad-apekṣatvāt* I –*BrSū* III.1.10

37 *satyena labhyas-tapasā hyeṣa ātmā, samyag-jñānena brahmacaryeṇa nityam* I
antaḥ-śarīre jyotirmayo hi śubhro, yaṁ paśyanti yatayaḥ kṣīṇadoṣāḥ II
– *MuṇUp* III.1.5

satyam-eva jayati nānṛtaṁ, satyena panthā vitato devayānaḥ I
yenākramantyuṛṣayo hyāptakāmā, yatra tat-satyasya paramaṁ nidhānam II
– Ibid. III.1.6

Kena[38] and *Bṛhadāraṇyaka*[39] also truth is identified with *dharma*.

यान्यनवद्यानि कर्माणि । तानि सेवितव्यानि । नो इतराणि । यान्यस्माकꣳ सुचरितानि । तानि त्वयोपास्यानि । नो इतराणि । ये के चास्मच्छ्रेयाꣳसो ब्राह्मणाः । तेषां त्वयाऽऽसने न प्रश्वसितव्यम् ।

yānyanavadyāni karmāṇi । *tāni sevitavyāni* । *no itarāṇi* । *yānyasmākaṁ sucaritāni* । *tāni tvayopasyāni* । *no itarāṇi*। *ye ke cāsmacchreyāṁso brāhmaṇāḥ* । *teṣāṁ tvayā "sane na praśvasitavyam* । – I.11

Those actions that are irreproachable[xlvi] should be followed with diligence; not those that are their contrary. You must be intent on our good and righteous actions, and never on the contrary. When those people who are more distinguished and cultured than us are in session for religious enquiry, may you not even breathe[xlvii] a word.

श्रद्धया देयम् । अश्रद्धयाऽदेयम् । श्रिया देयम् । ह्रिया देयम् । भिया देयम् । संविदा देयम् ।

śraddhayā deyam । *aśraddhayā 'deyam* । *śriyā deyam* । *hriyā deyam* । *bhiyā deyam* । *saṁvidā deyam* । – I.11

Charity should be given with reverence[xlviii] (towards the receiver). Charity should not be given with disrespect. Charity should be given in plenty. Charity should be given with modesty. Charity should be given with fear. Charity should be given with fellow-feeling.[xlix]

अथ यदि ते कर्मविचिकित्सा वा वृत्तविचिकित्सा वा स्यात् । ये तत्र ब्राह्मणाः सम्मर्शिनः । युक्ता आयुक्ताः । अलूक्षा धर्मकामाः स्युः । यथा ते तत्र वर्तेरन् । तथा तत्र वर्तेथाः ।

---

38 *tasyai tapo damaḥ karmeti pratiṣṭhā vedāḥ sarvaṅgāni satyam-āyatanam* । – *KeUp* IV.8

39 *yo vai sa dharmaḥ satyaṁ vai tat, tasmāt satyaṁ vadantam āhur-dharmaṁ vadati-iti* । *dharmaṁ vā vadantaṁ satyaṁ vadati-iti-etad-hi-eva-etad-ubhayaṁ bhavati* । – *BṛUp* I.4.14

atha yadi te karmavicikitsā vā vṛttavicikitsā vā syāt । *ye tatra brāhmaṇāḥ sammarśinaḥ* । *yuktā āyuktāḥ* । *alūkṣā dharmakāmāḥ syuḥ* । *yathā te tatra varteran* । *tathā tatra vartethāḥ* । – I.11

If there arise any uncertainty/doubt regarding a course of action, or a doubt regarding the conduct in life, you would rule yourself exactly in the same manner as the brāhmaṇas (cultured people) who are[l] discriminating, experienced, impartial, considerate and committed to *dharma*. May you act in that situation in such a manner as those (cultured people) would act about such matters.

अथाभ्याख्यातेषु । ये तत्र ब्राह्मणाः सम्मर्शिनः । युक्ता आयुक्ताः । अलूक्षा धर्मकामाः स्युः । यथा ते तेषु वर्तेरन् । तथा तेषु वर्तेथाः ।

athābhyākhyāteṣu । *ye tatra brāhmaṇāḥ sammarśinaḥ* । *yuktā āyuktāḥ* । *alūkṣā dharmakāmāḥ syuḥ* । *yathā te teṣu varteran* । *tathā teṣu vartethāḥ* । – I.11

Now with regard to those who are falsely accused.[li] Conduct yourself on the model of those cautious, experienced, impartial, and considerate and committed to *dharma*. With respect to men accused by their fellows, may you be, as those (cultured people) would be towards them.

एष आदेशः । एष उपदेशः । एषा वेदोपनिषत् । एतदनुशासनम् । एवमुपासितव्यम् । एवमुचैतदुपास्यम् ॥

eṣa ādeśaḥ । *eṣa upadeśaḥ* । *eṣā vedopaniṣat* । *etad anuśāsanam* । *evam upāsitavyam* । *evam u caitadupāsyam* । – I.11

This is the teaching/command (of Śruti). This is the advice (of Smṛti). This is the essence of the Vedas. This is the commandment. Life must be led in this manner; verily life must be led in this manner.

Twelfth Anuvāka: Uttara-Śāntimantraḥ

शं नो मित्रः शं वरुणः । शं नो भवत्वर्यमा । शं न इन्द्रो बृहस्पतिः । शं नो

विष्णुरुरुक्रमः । नमो ब्रह्मणे । नमस्ते वायो । त्वमेव प्रत्यक्षं ब्रह्मासि । त्वामेव प्रत्यक्षं ब्रह्मावादिषम् । ऋतमवादिषम् । सत्यमवादिषम् । तन्मामावीत् । तद्वक्तारमावीत् । आवीन्माम् । आवीद्वक्तारम् । ॐ शान्तिः शान्तिः शान्तिः ॥

śaṁ no mitraḥ śaṁ varuṇaḥ । śaṁ no bhavatvaryamā । śaṁ na indro bṛhaspatiḥ । śaṁ no viṣṇur-urukramaḥ । namo brahmaṇe । namaste vāyo । tvameva pratyakṣaṁ brahmāsi । tvāmeva pratyakṣaṁ brahmāvādiṣaṁ । ṛtam-avādiṣam । satyam-avādiṣam । tan-mām-āvīt । tad-vaktāram-āvīt । āvīn-mām । āvīd-vaktāram । oṁ śāntiḥ śāntiḥ śāntiḥ ॥ – I.12

May Mitra, the Sun deity be the source of auspiciousness to us. May Varuṇa, the Ocean deity be the source of auspiciousness to us. May Aryamā, the lord of the manes, be the source of auspiciousness to us. May Indra, the king of the *devatā*s and Bṛhaspati, the preceptor of the *devatā*s, be the source of auspiciousness to us. May Viṣṇu, the all-pervasive, sustainer of the creation be the source of auspiciousness to us. May Urukrama, Lord Vāmana be the source of auspiciousness to us. Salutations to Hiraṇyagarbha. O! Lord Vāyu! Salutations to you. You alone are the perceptible *Brahman*. I have declared you to be the perceptible *Brahman*. I have declared you to be the Righteousness/right understanding. I have declared you to be the Truth/truthfulness. That Truth protected me. That Truth protected the teacher. That Truth protected me. That Truth protected the teacher. May there be Peace, Peace, Peace.

The deities mentioned in this *anuvāka* were invoked at the outset to ward off all the obstacles on the path of the seeker of *brahmajñāna*. Various meditations were then prescribed to purify the mind of the student of *brahma-vidyā*. It is assumed that they have brought about the necessary result. It now remains for the student to offer gratitude to the gods who have helped in preparing the way; otherwise, the demerit of ingratitude may still prevent the aspirant from reaching the goal. This is the purpose of this *uttaraśānti*.

Endnotes

[i] The various gods and manes are believed to thwart the attempts of a seeker to gain self-knowledge. *Bṛhadāraṇyaka Upaniṣad* I.4.10 states that, as long as one has not known the reality of the Self, one is like an animal to the gods. Just as in the world many animals serve the man, similarly each man serves the *devatās*. One does not like loss of one animal, what to talk of loss of many animals. Therefore, the *devatās* do not appreciate man to know *Brahman*. *Mahābhārata* XIV.22.59 contains similar statement addressed to Arjuna. The ritualistic people are responsible for filling the *devaloka* with gods. They naturally do not like mortals surpassing them. Śrī Śaṅkara remarks in his commentary on this passage, "as men try to save animals from being seized by tigers, etc. similarly the gods seek to prevent men from attaining the knowledge of *Brahman*, lest they should cease to be their objects of enjoyment. Gods bestow faith and other necessary virtues upon those whom they wish to set free, and incline others whom they do not favour to sceptism and the like. Therefore, a seeker of *mokṣa* should worship and obey gods, and be fully of faith and loving adoration." The above peace invocations are meant to win the blessings of the gods and *Saguṇa Brahman*, i.e. Hiraṇyagrabha, to make the path of the seeker trouble-free and easy.

[ii] *Tvameva pratyakṣaṁ brahmāsi* – In *Bṛhadāraṇyaka Upaniṣad* III.7.2, Yājñavalkya makes it clear that Vāyu stands for *sūtram*. Elsewhere *sūtra* or *sutrātmā* is also known as Hiraṇyagarbha or Prajāpati – the first manifestation of *Brahman* conditioned by time and space. The conscious and unconscious activity of the entire universe, style as cosmic-mind and cosmic-life, is represented by *prāṇa* that has the counterpart in the individual consciousness and the vital activity. Hiraṇyagarbha is endowed with *icchāśakti*, *jñānaśakti* and *kriyāśakti* (power of desire, power of intelligence and power of action). He is eulogized as perceptible, because he can be felt physically.

[iii] *Oṁ* and the three *śānti*s – *Oṁ* is the sound symbol and representative of *Brahman*. It is uttered for securing all-round auspiciousness. The word peace is then uttered three times to ward-off all *ādhyātmika* (internal), *ādhibhautika* (external) and *ādhidaivika* (heavenly) obstacles.

iv This prayer for glory is the outcome of the longing for achieving moral and spiritual worth, and not mere adulation from people. *Yaśas* (good name and fame) is also a manifestation of *Īśvara* as declared in *Bhagavadgītā* by Bhagavān Kṛṣṇa.

v *Brahmavarcas* (Refulgence). Here the term *Brahman* has the sense of the Vedas and *varcas* denotes power or refulgence. The whole word therefore stands for the sanctity and pre-eminence that one achieves by a life devoted to the study of Vedas that contain the sacred knowledge and knowledge of the reality through *tapas*. As per the *Bhāṣyam*, this prayer is for the student alone, since the teacher has already achieved his/her aspiration.

vi The term *saṁhitā* means conjunction or union, especially the combination of letters according to euphonic rules. The philosophical observations presented in this *anuvāka* are based on this linguistic phenomenon. However, to distinguish the philosophical application from the linguistic usage, the term *mahā-saṁhitā*, the great conjunctions are given here. *Saṁhitā* in grammar is closely connected with the science of phonetics, about which the immediately preceding *anuvāka* has dealt with. The Vedic student, who has memorized the Veda, has to analyse the words and letters of the sentence, to derive the correct meaning. In order to recite the text with proper flow, he also has to combine the various sentence elements. During this process, which involves greater penetration and subtlety of thought, than the mere memorization of the Veda, the learner cannot fail to take note of the terminal letter of the first word, the initial letter of the second word, a third cementing element (euphonic augment) in some cases, and the whole act of uniting. For instance, in a combined group of juxtaposed words like *iṣe*(*t*) *tvorjetvā*, *e* in *iṣe* is the terminal letter (*pūrvarūpa*) of the first word *iṣe*, *t* is the initial letter (*uttararūpa*) of the second word *tva* and *t* inside the bracket is the cementing element (*sandhānam)* and the act of joining them in connected speech is the *sandhiḥ* (combination). These four factors of a *saṁhitā* are called *pūrvarūpa*, *uttararūpa*, *sandhānam* and *sandhiḥ*, respectively. This is a matter of common experience to the Vedic student. With the help of the principle underlying it, some greater relation that exists between objects of universal importance is adduced to assist him in subtle thinking at a cosmic level.

vii *Veda* here means one who meditates on, it is a verb. The original word *veda* from the root √*vid* (to know) has the secondary sense of *upāsanā* (devout meditation) here. *Upāsanā* (devotion) implies an uninterrupted flow of similar thought on an object, as prescribed by the scripture. The word *upāsanā*, when used in connection with the service of a king or *guru*, implies constant attention or intentness. This notion is implied in religious meditation also. *Brahmasūtra* IV.1.11 suggests that no rule regarding time and place need be observed by the *upāsaka*, except in so far as the choice is based on facility for meditation and agreeableness. It is, however, necessary that the aspirant should be seated (*BrSū* IV.1.7) while contemplating; as otherwise, the mind will wander away if the body is in motion. If more than one meditation is given in different texts having one main purport, suitable attributes may be combined. All meditations, except that on the *Paramātman*, are symbolic. The *upāsaka*, in the first case, meditates on a visible or visualized object outside his own innermost self, and exalts it as a great deity (*Brahman*) itself. Self-knowledge not being the objective of all symbolic meditations, the objects of such meditations may vary successively as in the *upāsanā* of *mahāsaṁhitā* given above; for, the spiritual effect generated by the first meditation is not cancelled by the second, rather enhanced. Moreover, in such *upāsanā*s, the result promised, such as objects of enjoyment, will accrue only if all the meditations are performed flawlessly and in order. On the other hand, the meditations laid down with the purpose of helping self-knowledge do not allow any shifting, after having made the choice, one has to adhere to it until the objective is gained, constantly repeating the same process. It is to be noted that the symbol should be invariably regarded as superior to what it actually is, e.g. *śāligrāme viṣṇuṁ dhyāyet*. The same meditation, for which rewards are specified, may be performed without any specific desire other than *cittaśuddhi* (purity of the mind) needed for self-knowledge.

viii *Medhā* (intellectual vigour) means intelligence and mental power, especially tenacious memory. The seeker of *brahma-vidyā* must have an attention span on a given subject matter, and be able to hold it uninterrupted. In fact, this power of holding a particular subject matter for a length of time without distraction is the essence of all disciplines of knowledge. The mind should have the capacity to abide in the subject matter, and cease to wander. Study of the

Vedas is an auxiliary means to the direct intuition of the Reality, and concentration is an aid to it. One who does not possess such mental discipline may not be able to hold the subject matter in his mind. Hence, this prayer is very appropriate at the outset.

ix *Amṛta* literally means immortality, or whatever that confers immortality. Here it stands for the Vedas that is the means to immortality.

x The Upaniṣads often declare the need of strength, physical, moral and spiritual, for obtaining our highest destiny. The word *vicarṣaṇa* is an altered form of *vicakṣaṇa*.

xi *Oṁ* is compared to a sheath of *Brahman*. Since there cannot be a sheath for *Brahman*, which includes all; here sheath means, place of obtainment. The expression suggests that the highest Reality is also the Reality of the self, and can be objectified only through a *pratīka* (a sound symbol) for the purpose of worship. All worship is symbolic, of them worship of *oṁ* is the greatest.

xii The Upaniṣads mainly speak of knowledge and freedom. Hence, wealth is sought to perform religious rites that neutralizes past *duritas*. Fulfilment of earthly or heavenly desires is not the purpose of the rites laid down in the *jñāna-kāṇḍa* (section of knowledge) to which the Upaniṣads belong, as the entire section of rituals preceding it has that one definite aim of obtaining rewards on the earth or in heaven.

xiii Let there be complete unity between you and me.

xiv It may refer to the various texts of the Vedas that are expressions of *Praṇava*, or as Śrī Acyutakṛṣnānanda Tīrtha (author of *Vanamālā*) suggests, the various divine forms such as Brahmā, Viṣṇu and the rest. The utterance of *Praṇava* is the best means of cleansing oneself of *durita*.

xv Just as one sees oneself clearly, when the surface of the mirror is clean, similarly knowledge arises for a person on exhaustion of sin. - *TUB* quoting from – *MaBhā*, Śanti-Parva 204.08; *Gar.Pu* I.237.6

xvi By the mention of the name Māhācamasya of the *ṛṣi*, it is hinted that during the meditation, grateful remembrance of the sage, who initiated the particular worship must also be deemed part of the ritual.

xvii The worlds are maintained by the sun by making it possible for the denizens of the worlds to function in due order. The moon magnifies the stars by its primacy among them. *Brahman* here stands for *Oṁkāra*, and it is said that the whole Veda is esteemed for this essential element; or because *Brahman* is its subject matter. By food, all creatures are increased and gladdened because they subsist on food.

xviii When the *upāsaka* has attained his union with Virāṭ because of devout meditation, all the gods pay him homage in that capacity.

xix The *Puruṣa*, being an unextended Conscious entity, is bereft of all spatial suggestion, yet the instrument through which He can be known, according to the Upaniṣad, is the mind, since we get to know everything through mind alone.

xx *Indrayoniḥ* in the text is made out to be *susumnā*. Sāyaṇācārya clearly points out by saying that the *susumnā* lies through the nipple-like growth hanging down from the middle of the hard palate. The Upaniṣad states that it lies quite close to it. It is like pointing a finger to the tip of the branch of a tree, to show an invisible star. The *susumnā* is closed in the case of a common person, but a person adept in meditation, can open the path as stated in the Upaniṣad, and can gain union with the deity. By the discipline mentioned here, the whole body is made rhythmic, breath is regulated, and perfect calmness is brought over the whole personality.

xxi Similar expressions are found in *Chāndogya Upaniṣad* III.14.1 and VIII.6.1, *Kaṭha Upaniṣad* II.3.16 and *Bhagavadgītā* VIII.13.

xxii In *Bhagavadgītā* VIII.13, it is stated that he who departs from the body uttering *oṁ*, attains the highest goal. According to the present seer, the dying *upāsaka* utters the four *vyāhṛtis* and is united with *Brahman* that is characterized as *mahaḥ*, that has the other three *vyāhṛtis* as members. His union with *Brahman* is stated as abiding in fire, air, sun and *mahaḥ*. In fact, he gains cosmic consciousness as the cosmic *Puruṣa*.

xxiii He becomes the spirit behind all conscious and unconscious cosmic functions.

xxiv Only when the mind ceases from its pre-occupation with the sense-objects and turns to *Brahman*, it can enjoy itself, for *Brahman* is the source of all happiness which the mind experiences even in sense contact.

xxv *Prāṇa* comprises *prāṇa, vyāna, apāna, udāna* and *samāna*. Of these, *prāṇa* is that function of all vital airs that causes breathing out, *vyāna* sustains life when breath is arrested, *apāna* functions while breathing in/out and evacuating, *udāna* holds the joints and effects the departure of the subtle body from the body at death, *samāna* circulates in the body and digests food.

xxvi *Bhagavadgītā* XVII.24 says that with the utterance of the word *oṁ*, sacrifices, gifts and penance enjoined by the scriptural rule are always begun. There are scriptural words to the effect that all undertakings that start with *oṁ* become fruitful. Few examples are cited here from Vedic rituals showing how *oṁ* is employed in various ways.

xxvii Invocations: The original word *śāstra* is specially applied to the verses recited by the Hotā and his assistant as an accompaniment to the *graha*s at the Soma libation. They are recited either audibly or inaudibly. As opposed to the *śāstra* there is *stoma* which is sung.

xxviii Response, etc.: *Pratigara* denotes the responsive call of the Adhvaryu to the address of the Hotā, while singing. It is an encouragement given to the latter when he has sung part of the hymn, and it will be taken as an indication to proceed.

xxix Sets the sacrifice, etc. – urges the *ṛtvik*, i.e. the performing-priest, to begin the ritual, e.g. *oṁ prokṣa* (now, you sprinkle).

xxx Authorizes, etc. – While performing the fire-ritual called Agnihotra, the Adhvaryu has to take a portion of the milk from the milk vessel, and pour into the *agnihotra-havanī*. He asks the sacrificer – "Shall I take out the oblation?" The latter permits by uttering *oṁ*.

xxxi Two roots, √*vac* and √*vah*, with prefix *pra* give the future participle *pravakṣyan*. As the former means "to recite" and the latter "to convey", the passage would bear two interpretations: (i) A brāhmaṇa, when he is about to recite the Veda, says *oṁ*. (ii) A knower of *Brahman* about to take his pupil to *Brahman* imparts *oṁ* (as a means). Truly, with the help of it, he attains *Brahman*.

xxxii The expression *svādhyāya-pravacane ca* is repeated twelve times to emphasize that learning and teaching of the Vedas should never be missed even while engaged in the acquisition of the virtues and discharge of the duties enjoined above. It is repeated to inspire special regard for study and teaching of the Vedas. The highest good depends on the study of the Vedas. *Taittirīya Āraṇayaka* II.12 commands to recite the Veda without fail, standing or walking, or sitting or lying down, so that one may become and remain pure. Even the *sannyāsīs*, who are above the injunctions of the ritualistic part of the Veda, are to study repeatedly important portions of it. The study of the Veda cannot be properly undertaken without the person having value for truthfulness and austerity. Hence, the study of the Vedas and its imparting are emphasized as the obligatory duties, other qualities subserving them.

xxxiii The exalted spiritual state that he has attained is known even to the gods who pay homage to him.

xxxiv Refers to the deity in the Sun. Cf. *Chāndogya Upaniṣad* III.19.1.

xxxv *Draviṇa* means both wealth and power, just as wealth alleviates worldly suffering, so the power of *brahmajñāna* dispels all sorrow.

xxxvi Some commentators consider this *anuvāka* as a parting advice given to the graduating students by the teacher and compare it to a brief convocation address. It may not be so. *Anuvacana* (recitation) is only for the purpose of memorizing the Vedas. The injunction to study the Vedas includes also the inquiry into, and the understanding of the text, so that the disciple may put into practice what he has learnt, on entering the next stage of life. Śrī Śaṅkara therefore interprets *anuśāsti* in the text as *anu* after having caused the pupil to learn merely the text, the teacher teaches *śāsti*, the meaning. The disciple is not to depart from the teacher's *gurukulam* until the meaning also is grasped thoroughly with his help. Therefore, these admonitions are to be taken as a practical advice given after memorizing the text of the Vedas, and before commencing the enquiry into the meaning. On the completion of that, the pupil may leave the teacher.

xxxvii Preceptor (*ācārya*), literally means he who knows and teaches *ācāra* (established rules of conduct) (*MaSm* II.143.170). He invests the student with sacrificial thread and instructs him in the Vedas, in the rules of the Vedic rituals and in the mysteries of the Vedas.

xxxviii The term *dharma* here stands for prescribed duties with reference to oneself, to others and to gods.

xxxix At a time when books were unknown, memorizing what has been taught was very necessary for learning. Forgetting what one has learnt before is therefore condemned as equal to slaying a brāhmaṇa. The necessity of learning is repeatedly stressed, since knowledge in youth is wisdom in age. Vedic learning has also been emphasized in ninth *anuvāka*, suitably named *svādhyāya-praśaṁsā*. The *ṛṣi*s always held that learning is the eye of the mind. They never allowed gliding away from recollection of what has been once studied.

xl Refers to *vidyāvaṁśa* (succession of disciples) also, if the disciple chooses to be a *naiṣṭhika-brahmacārī*.

xli Truthfulness is insisted on a second time, to rule out utterance of falsehood even in forgetfulness. In *Praśna Upaniṣad* VI.1, the sixth student Sukeśā while asking Ācārya Pippalāda about the *ṣoḍaṣa-kalā-puruṣa* says, "He who tells a lie perishes up to the root". Also, "That pure world of Brahmā belongs to only them, in whom rest no deceit, falsehood or guile." (*PrUp* I.16.). In *Muṇḍaka Upaniṣad* III.1.5-6, *Kena Upaniṣad* IV.8 and *Bṛhadāraṇyaka Upaniṣad* I.4.14 truth is identified with *dharma*.

xlii Acts tending to self-preservation and welfare must be secured by religious and secular means.

xliii The repetition is to warn against the omission of leaning the Vedas and teaching the same to others.

xliv Worship and adoration of gods, and offering of *śrāddha* (post-funeral rites) to the manes.

xlv To respect our parents is the first law of nature; and it is insisted in all codes of morality. *Uśanḥ Saṁhitā* I.33-37 says, "Let a son be devoted to the service of the parents as long as they live. If they are satisfied with his virtue, he gets the reward of all religious deeds. There is no god equal to the mother, no guide at par with the father, there is no complete exoneration from a man's obligations to them, let him do for them daily what is agreeable, and let him not engage himself in any religious rite without their permission, the sole exception being what would lead to liberation." The mention of mother first shows that she is entitled to greater honour than the rest (father, *ācārya*, *atithi*).

xlvi *Yogavāsiṣṭha* lays down that, what is not consistent with reason should not be accepted even if Brahmā were to tell it. No human being is absolutely and perpetually free of blemish. Love or admiration of one's role model should not prompt one to copy his imperfections. The transgressions of great men are like the eclipse of the sun and the moon; we look up to them only when eclipse has passed. One should remember Paraśurāma's obedience to his father, and not his slaying of the mother, and not his desertion of his parents; Yājñavalkya's obtaining of *Śukla-Yajurveda* through austerity, and not his offending the co-disciples.

xlvii Politeness is the art of rendering to everyone, without effort, that which is socially his due. A youth ought not to interrupt when elders who are full of wisdom and experience assemble to enquire into and deliberate on weighty matters. He should wait upon them with obedience and eagerness to learn. The alternative meaning could be he should render them service and hospitality.

xlviii *Śraddhā* here means reverence and/or empathy and religious zeal. Devotion, adoration, oblation, rituals and prayer become complete and free of blemish, only if they are performed with *śraddhā*. Sureśvarācārya in the *vārttikā* says, "let him give with *śraddhā* even to those who do not deserve it". The same idea is expressed by Bhagavān Kṛṣṇa in *Bhagavadgītā* XVII.20-22. According to *Mahānārāyaṇa Upaniṣad* 63, *śraddhā* is acquired by penance. *Ṛgveda* X.151 is a complete hymn on *śraddhā*.

xlix *Saṁvid* is explained by Śaṅkara as friendliness; the word literally means harmony or agreement in opinion. A person should not give a gift to another, if he disagrees with the recipient about the purpose for which he seeks the gift. Śrī Kṛṣṇa refused the hospitality of Duryodhana since his attitude was not agreement with the purpose of the meeting.

l Who are – Briefly it means approved authorities. The Upaniṣadic seers hardly discuss ethical theories, because ethics is not an end in itself in their view. The perfection they sought and knew is beyond ethics, although through it. They held that individuality is only provisional, and the ego should be annihilated. The objective worth of an action therefore is not an absolute standard for judging ethical values; they interpret all action subjectively, that is, in terms of the self-denial and sacrifice which is involved in them. But attempts to fix the moral standard and the grounds of morality having reference only to individual preference or satisfaction, or one's own unguided reasoning and ephemeral ideals, have only failed. In fact, moral character has its basis in a multitude of specific habits formed in the light of the experience of those who are better than oneself. This point is emphasized in the text and is worth reflecting on deeply.

li Falsely accused – One must not be quick to judge a person, hearing others accusing him wrongly. One should observe what respectable elders do in regard to such persons, and behave similarly. *Yājñavalkya* III.263 says that, by falsely accusing another, a person incurs *pāpa* as a liar, and in addition, takes on himself the *pāpa* of the victim.

Gratitude: My acknowledgement and profuse gratitude to Swami Swahanada's *Taittirīyopaniṣad*, whose explanations I have used as Endnotes in this *vallī*. – Author

6

Brahmānandavallī

Introduction to Brahmānandavallī

SAGUṆA-VIDYĀ was the theme of the previous *vallī*. In this *vallī* as well as the next, *nirguṇa-vidyā* (knowledge of *Brahman*) is explained. Brahmānandavallī consists of nine *anuvāka*s (sections). It teaches the knowledge of *Nirguṇa-Brahman* that alone can destroy *avidyā*, the root cause of bondage. The concise opening sentence of the first section, "The knower of *Brahman* attains the highest", lays down that the knowledge of *Brahman* is the means to freedom. After defining *Brahman* as the Existence, Consciousness and Infinite, the Upaniṣad proceeds to show in this section that *Brahman* is identical (not similar) with the Self.

An account of the *annamaya*, *prāṇamaya*, *manomaya*, *vijñānamaya* and *ānandamaya* is given in five *anuvāka*s. Mistakes are committed at each level. The fifth section teaches that, as distinguished from these, there is *Brahman-Ātmā*, which is the basis[1] (*adhiṣṭhānam*) of all these.

The sixth *anuvāka* raises an important question, whether *Brahman* exists or not. It also raises further question, whether the knower of *Brahman*, as well as an ignorant person attains *Brahman*.

The Upaniṣad answers in the same section the existence of *Brahman* as the cause of the universe, consisting of things with forms and without forms. Further, reasons for the existence of *Brahman* are given in the seventh *anuvāka*. *Brahman*, it is said, exists as the source of all joy enjoyed by all beings, as the cause

---

1 *brahma puccham pratiṣṭhā* । – *TaiUp* II.5

of all vital and organic functions of the *jīva*, and as the cause of fear and fearlessness for the ignorant and wise man respectively.

The eighth *anuvāka* that contains a calculus of joy, describes *Brahman* as happiness par excellence, of which the worldly happiness enjoyed by all creatures is only a fraction. Worldly happiness increases a hundredfold, as one ascends the different classes of celestial beings mentioned in this section. A wise person, who is free from any desire, enjoys the highest joy that is *brahmajñāna*. It is also stated in this *anuvāka* that, one who knows *Brahman* as non-dual, i.e. as the same both in the human being and in the sun, attains it by differentiating from the non-self.

The concluding (ninth) *anuvāka* of the Brahmānandavallī states that he who has known *Brahman*, who remains as *Brahman* is no more tormented by right and wrong actions committed by him, since he does not consider himself as the doer any more.

The invocation beginning with *śaṁ no mitraḥ śaṁ varuṇaḥ* was recited (at the beginning of Śīkṣāvallī) to avert the obstacles to the acquisition of knowledge. Now the same invocation is being recited, as well as *sa ha nāvavatu*, for averting the obstacles to the acquisition of knowledge of *Brahman* that is going to be stated.

Śāntimantraḥ

ॐ । शं नो॑ मि॒त्रः शं वरु॑णः । शं नो॑ भवत्वर्य॒मा । शं न॒ इन्द्रो॒ बृह॒स्पतिः॑ । शं नो॑ विष्णु॒रुरु॒क्रमः॑ । नमो॒ ब्रह्म॑णे । नम॑स्ते वायो । त्वमे॒व प्र॒त्यक्षं॒ ब्रह्मा॑सि । त्वमे॑व प्र॒त्यक्षं॒ ब्रह्म॑ वदिष्यामि । ऋ॒तं व॑दिष्यामि । स॒त्यं व॑दिष्यामि । तन्माम॑वतु । तद्व॒क्तार॑मवतु । अव॑तु॒ माम् । अव॑तु व॒क्तार॒म् । ॐ शान्तिः॒ शान्तिः॒ शान्तिः॑ ॥

oṁ śaṁ no mitraḥ śaṁ varuṇaḥ । *śaṁ no bhavatvaryamā* ।
śaṁ na indro bṛhaspatiḥ । *śaṁ no viṣṇur-urukramaḥ* । *namo brahmaṇe* । *namaste vāyo* । *tvameva pratyakṣaṁ brahmāsi* ।
tvameva pratyakṣaṁ brahma vadiṣyāmi । *ṛtaṁ vadiṣyāmi* ।
satyaṁ vadiṣyāmi । *tan-mām avatu* । *tad vaktāram avatu* ।
avatu mām । *avatu vaktāram* । *oṁ śāntiḥ śāntiḥ śāntiḥ* । – I.1

May Mitra be the source of auspiciousness to us. May Varuṇa be the source of auspiciousness to us. May Aryamā be the source of auspiciousness to us. May Indra and Bṛhaspati be the source of auspiciousness to us. May Viṣṇu, the all-pervasive, sustainer of the creation be auspicious to us. May Urukrama, the Lord Vāmana be auspicious to us. Prostrations to *Brahman* (Hiraṇyagarbha). O Lord Vāyu! Prostrations to you. You are the perceptible *Brahman*. I declare you to be the perceptible *Brahman*. I declare you as the right understanding. I declare you as the Truth. May that Truth protect me. May that Truth protect my teacher. May that Truth protect me. May it protect the Teacher. *Oṁ*. May there be Peace, Peace, Peace.

Śāntimantraḥ: Prayer for Mutual Goodwill and Avoidance of Disagreement

सह नाववतु । सह नौ भुनक्तु । सह वीर्यं करवावहै । तेजस्वि नावधीतमस्तु ।
मा विद्विषावहै । ॐ शान्तिः शान्तिः शान्तिः ॥

sa ha nāvavatu । *sa ha nau bhunaktu* । *saha vīryaṁ karavāvahai* । *tejasvi nāvadhītamastu* । *mā vidviṣāvahai* । *oṁ śāntiḥ śāntiḥ śāntiḥ* ।

May He[i] (*Īśvara*) protect both of us (teacher and student). May He nourish both of us. May we together acquire the capacity (to study and understand the scriptures). May what is studied, be brilliant. May there not be disagreement between both of us. May there be Peace, Peace, Peace.

The second chapter, Brahmānandavallī, opens with the profound declaration: "He who knows *Brahman*, gains the Infinite. *Brahman* is Existence, Consciousness and Infinite." This key statement reveals in a flash, with aphoristic brevity, the quintessence of the entire philosophy of the Upaniṣads.

First Anuvāka: Svarūpa-lakṣaṇa of Brahman

Ātmā Equated with Brahman

ॐ ब्रह्मविदाप्नोति परम् । तदेषाभ्युक्ता ।

oṁ brahmavidāpnoti param । tadeṣā 'bhyuktā ।

Svarūpa-lakṣaṇa of Brahman

सत्यं ज्ञानमनन्तं ब्रह्म । यो वेद निहितं गुहायां परमे व्योमन् । सोऽश्नुते सर्वान् कामान् सह । ब्रह्मणा विपश्चितेति ।

satyaṁ-jñānam-anantaṁ brahma । yo veda nihitaṁ guhāyāṁ parame vyoman । so 'śnute sarvān kāmān saha । brahmaṇā vipaściteti ।

Ātmā Equated with Brahman

तस्माद्वा एतस्मादात्मन आकाशः सम्भूतः ।

tasmād vā etasmād-ātmana ākāśaḥ saṁbhūtaḥ ।

Cosmology

आकाशाद्वायुः । वायोरग्निः अग्नेरापः । अद्भ्यः पृथिवी । पृथिव्या ओषधयः । ओषधीभ्योऽन्नम् । अन्नात्पुरुषः ।

ākāśad vāyuḥ । vāyor-agniḥ । agner-āpaḥ । ādbhyaḥ pṛthivī । pṛthivyā oṣadhayaḥ । oṣadhībhyo 'nnam । annāt puruṣaḥ ।

Composition of the Annamaya-kośa

स वा एष पुरुषोऽन्नरसमयः ।

sa vā eṣa puruṣo 'nnarasamayaḥ ।

Contemplation of the Annamaya-kośa

तस्येदमेव शिरः । अयं दक्षिणः पक्षः । अयमुत्तरः पक्षः । अयमात्मा । इदं पुच्छं प्रतिष्ठा ।

tasyedam-eva śiraḥ । ayaṁ dakṣiṇapakṣaḥ । ayam-uttarapakṣaḥ । ayamātmā । idaṁ puchhaṁ pratiṣṭhā ।

A verse on the unity of Virāṭ and the Annamaya

तदप्येष श्लोको भवति ॥

tadapyeṣa śloko bhavati । – II.1

> The knower of *Brahman* attains the ultimate.[ii] With reference to that there is a verse – "*Brahman* is Existence, Consciousness and Infinite."[iii] He who knows Him as available in the intellect which is lodged in the great space in the heart (intellect),[iv] has all his desire fulfilled[v] at once, as *Brahman* the omniscient.
>
> From that very *Ātman*[vi] (which has been referred to) came the space, from space emerged the air, from air was born fire, from fire was created water, from water sprang forth the earth, from the earth were born the herbs, from herbs was produced food, from food the human being came to existence. That person is indeed a modification[vii] of the essence of food.[viii] This indeed is his head; this is his right wing[ix] (side); this is left wing (side); this is his trunk; and this is the hind part forming the support and foundation. There is, besides, this stanza explaining it.

The entire purport of the chapter is summed up in the sentence, "The knower of *Brahman* attains the highest", occurring in the Brāhmaṇa portion. It is not possible for anything finite to become infinite. Therefore, the *āpnoti* or *prāpnoti* or *bhavati* is in terms of knowledge.[x] And this pithy statement is briefly explained by the *Ṛg-mantra* quoted by the Upaniṣad itself with the words – *tad-eṣābhyuktā*. In this, *Brahman* is defined as Existence, Consciousness and Infinite. This is to be recognized as oneself. By this, once attains total fulfilment, being one with *Brahman*.

Since the meaning of that very statement has to be elaborately ascertained again, the succeeding text, *tasmād vā etasmād*, etc. is introduced as a sort of gloss to it. The object of the whole *vallī* (chapter) is laid down in the first sentence. The sequel elaborately explains the central idea.

Cosmology in Taittirīya:
The Five-Elemental Model and Their Sequence

The first *anuvāka* gives an elaborate exposition beginning with the creation. From *Brahman*, the Self comes the creation in order of the five elements, subtle to gross, followed by plants, food and human beings. It is a model.

Methodology of Teaching by Adhyāropa-Apavāda Nyāya

It is to be noted here that when Vedānta introduces the creation, it is called *adhyāropa* (superimposition). The purport of the Upaniṣad is not to teach the origin of creation. It is rather to explain the truth of the *jagat*, that it is *Brahman* indeed. The intention of the Upaniṣad is to shift our attention from the creation (i.e. the effect) to *Brahman* (i.e. the cause). As the vision is shifted, the effect is dismissed, since it does not exist separate from the cause. This dismissal is called *apavāda* (negation).

However, this shift cannot take place in one stroke. One cannot turn the attention from the grossest effect to the subtlest cause, all of a sudden. Hence, the Upaniṣad takes us gradually through stages. This is known as *pañca-kośa-viveka*. The method used here by the Śruti is known as *śākhā-candra-nyāya*,[xi] which is pointed out by Śaṅkara. One *kośa* has been spoken of as the self of the another only relatively, i.e. without reference to the absolute truth. In reality, all *kośa*s are apparent aspects of the one real Self.

Thus, what was gone by until now is *adhyāropa*, now *apavāda* is going to begin.

Second Anuvāka

A Verse on the Unity of Virāṭ and the Annamaya

अन्नाद्वै प्रजाः प्रजायन्ते । याः काश्च पृथिवीꣳश्रिताः । अथो अन्नेनैव जीवन्ति ।
अथैनदपियन्त्यन्ततः । अन्नꣳ हि भूतानां ज्येष्ठम् । तस्मात्सर्वौषधमुच्यते ।
सर्वं वै तेऽन्नमाप्नुवन्ति । येऽन्नं ब्रह्मोपासते । अन्नꣳ हि भूतानां ज्येष्ठम् ।
तस्मात्सर्वौषधमुच्यते । अन्नाद्भूतानि जायन्ते । जातान्यन्नेन वर्धन्ते ।
अद्यतेऽत्ति च भूतानि । तस्मादन्नं तदुच्यत इति ।

annād vai prajāḥ prajāyante । yāḥ kāśca pṛthivīm̐ śritāḥ । atho annenaiva jīvanti । athainadapi yantyantataḥ । annam̐ hi bhūtānāṁ jyeṣṭham । tasmātsarvauṣadham-ucyate । sarvaṁ vai te 'nnam-āpnuvanti । ye 'nnaṁ brahmopāsate । annam̐ hi bhūtānāṁ jyeṣṭham । tasmāt sarvauṣadham-ucyate । annād-bhūtāni jāyante । jātānyannena vardhante । adyate 'tti ca bhūtāni । tasmād-annaṁ taducyata iti । – II.2.1

All living beings[xii] that rest on the earth, truly are born of food. Besides, they live on food; and they go back to food finally. Indeed food is the first and foremost among all creatures; hence, it is considered the medicine for all. Those who worship food as *Brahman*,[xiii] acquire all the food. For food was born before all beings, hence it is called the medicine for all. All living beings are born from food, being born they grow by food. Since it is eaten and it eats the creatures, food is called *annam*.[xiv]

The Prāṇamaya-kośa

The Composition of Prāṇamaya-kośa

तस्माद्वा एतस्मादन्नरसमयात् । अन्योऽन्तर आत्मा प्राणमय । तेनैष पूर्णः ।

tasmād-vā etasmād-annarasamayāt । anyo 'ntara ātmā prāṇamayaḥ । tenaiṣa pūrṇaḥ ।

Contemplation of the Prāṇamaya

स वा एष पुरुषविध एव । तस्य पुरुषविधताम् । अन्वयं पुरुषविधः । तस्य प्राण एव शिरः । व्यानो दक्षिणः पक्षः । अपान उत्तरः पक्षः । आकाश आत्मा । पृथिवी पुच्छं प्रतिष्ठा ।

sa vā eṣa puruṣavidha eva । tasya puruṣa vidhatām । anvayaṁ puruṣavidhaḥ । tasya prāṇa eva śiraḥ । vyāno dakṣiṇaḥ pakṣaḥ । apāna uttaraḥ pakṣaḥ । ākāśa ātmā । pṛthivī pucchaṁ pratiṣṭhā ।

A Verse

तदप्येष श्लोको भवति ॥

tadapyeṣa śloko bhavati । – II.2

Verily, other than that one (*annamaya*), which consists of the essence of food, and contained by it, is this Self, consisting of *prāṇa* by which this *annamaya* is filled. Truly this one (*prāṇamaya*) also is exactly of the form of a person. That (*annamaya*) being in the shape of a person, this one (*prāṇamaya*) also accordingly, is of the form of a person. *Prāṇa*[xv] indeed is his head, *vyāna* is his right wing, *apāna* is his left wing, *samāna* is his trunk, and *ākāśa* is the self, the earth is support and foundation. Further, there is the following verse about it.

Third Anuvāka

The Verse

प्राणं देवा अनु प्राणन्ति । मनुष्याः पशवश्च ये । प्राणो हि भूतानामायुः । तस्मात्सर्वायुषमुच्यते । सर्वमेव त आयुर्यन्ति । ये प्राणं ब्रह्मोपासते । प्राणो हि भूतानामायुः । तस्मात्सर्वायुषमुच्यत इति । तस्यैष एव शारीर आत्मा । यः पूर्वस्य ।

prāṇaṁ devā anu prāṇanti । manuṣyāḥ paśavaśca ye । prāṇo hi bhūtānām āyuḥ । tasmāt sarvāyuṣam-ucyate । sarvam-eva ta āyur-yanti । ye prāṇaṁ brahmopāsate । prāṇo hi bhūtānām-āyuḥ । tasmāt-sarvāyuṣam-ucyata iti । tasyaiṣa eva śārīra ātmā । yaḥ pūrvasya ।

From Prāṇamaya to Manomaya

तस्माद्वा एतस्मात्प्राणमयात् । अन्योऽन्तर आत्मा मनोमयः । तेनैष पूर्णः ।

tasmād vā etasmāt-prāṇamayāt । anyo 'ntara ātmā manomayaḥ । tenaiṣa pūrṇaḥ ।

Contemplation of the Manomaya

स वा एष पुरुषविध एव । तस्य पुरुषविधताम् । अन्वयं पुरुषविधः । तस्य यजुरेव शिरः । ऋग् दक्षिणः पक्षः । सामोत्तरः पक्षः । आदेश आत्मा । अथर्वाङ्गिरसः पुच्छं प्रतिष्ठा ।

sa vā eṣa puruṣavidha eva । tasya puruṣavidhatām । anvayaṁ puruṣavidhaḥ । tasya yajureva śiraḥ । ṛg dakṣiṇaḥ pakṣaḥ । sāmottaraḥ pakṣaḥ । ādeśa ātmā । atharvāṅgirasaḥ pucchaṁ pratiṣṭhā ।

A Verse

तदप्येष श्लोको भवति ॥

tadapyeṣa śloko bhavati । – II.3

All the senses[xvi] depend upon *prāṇa* for their life. All the human beings and animals that are there act similarly, since the life of all creatures depend on *prāṇa*. Therefore, it is regarded as the universal life (*sarvāyuṣam*). Those who worship *prāṇa* as *Brahman* definitely attain the full span of life. Since *prāṇa* is the life of all creatures it is called the entire duration of life (*sarvāyuṣam*). The embodied Self of the former (*annamaya*) one is, verily, this one (*prāṇamaya*).[xvii]

Of the preceding (physical) one, this one, indeed, is the embodied self. Other than that Self consisting of this *prāṇa*, there is another internal Self constituted by the mind (*manas*)[xviii] (*manomaya*) by which this *prāṇamaya* Self is filled. This one (*manomaya*) also is of a human shape. The human shape of this (mental body – *manomaya*) takes after the human shape of that (vital body – *prāṇamya*). Of that (*manomaya*), *Yajus*[xix] is his head, *Ṛk* is his right wing, *Sāma* is his left wing, the injunctive[xx] part of the Vedas (the Brāhmaṇas) is his trunk and *Atharvaveda*[xxi] is his support and foundation. With reference to this, there is a verse.

Fourth Anuvāka

The Verse

Brahman is beyond Speech and Mind

यतो वाचो निवर्तन्ते । अप्राप्य मनसा सह । आनन्दं ब्रह्मणो विद्वान् ।

yato vāco nivartante । *aprāpya manasā saha* । *ānandaṁ brahmaṇo vidvān* ।

Fearlessness, the Fruit of Contemplation

न बिभेति कदाचनेति ।

na bibheti kadācaneti ।

The Outcome of the Study of Manomaya

तस्यैष एव शारीर आत्मा । यः पूर्वस्य ।

tasyaiṣa eva śārīra ātmā । yaḥ pūrvasya ।

From Manomaya to Vijñānamayakośa

तस्माद्वा एतस्मान्मनोमयात् । अन्योऽन्तर आत्मा विज्ञानमयः । तेनैष पूर्णः ।

tasmād vā etsmān-manomayāt । anyo'ntara ātmā vijñānamayaḥ । tenaiṣa pūrṇaḥ ।

Contemplation of the Vijñānamaya

स वा एष पुरुषविध एव । तस्य पुरुषविधताम् । अन्वयं पुरुषविधः । तस्य श्रद्धैव शिरः । ऋतं दक्षिणः पक्षः । सत्यमुत्तरः पक्षः । योग आत्मा । महः पुच्छं प्रतिष्ठा ।

sa vā eṣa puruṣavidha eva । tasya puruṣavidhatām । anvayaṁ puruṣavidhaḥ । tasya śrddhaiva śiraḥ । ṛtaṁ dakṣiṇaḥ pakṣaḥ । satyam-uttaraḥ pakṣaḥ । yoga ātmā । mahaḥ pucchaṁ pratiṣṭhā ।

A Verse

तदप्येष श्लोको भवति ॥

tadapyeṣa śloko bhavati । – II.4

"That[xxii] from which all speech come back along with the mind, being unable to reach it, he who knows that *Brahman*, is no more afraid of anything ever."

The embodied Self of the former (*manomaya*) is verily this one (*vijñānamayaḥ*).[xxiii] Other than the Self, which consists of *manas*, there is another inner Self which consists of *vijñāna*,[xxiv] (intelligence), by which this *manomaya* is filled. This one (*vijñānamayaḥ*) also is of human shape, in accordance with the other one's (*manomaya*) human shape. *Śraddhā* indeed is his head, righteousness[xxv] is his right wing/side; Truth is his left wing/side, *yoga* is the self/trunk and (the principle called) *mahat* (*mahat-tattvam*, meaning the first-born: Hiraṇyagarbha) is his support and foundation. Pertaining to this also there is this verse.

Fifth Anuvāka

The Verse

Contemplation of Vijñāna as Hiraṇyagarbha

विज्ञानं यज्ञं तनुते । कर्माणि तनुतेऽपि च । विज्ञानं देवाः सर्वे । ब्रह्म ज्येष्ठमुपासते । विज्ञानं ब्रह्म चेद्वेद । तस्माच्चेन्न प्रमाद्यति । शरीरे पाप्मनो हित्वा । सर्वान् कामान् समश्नुत इति ।

vijñānaṁ yajñāṁ tanute । *karmāṇi tanute 'pi ca* । *vijñānaṁ devāḥ sarve* । *brahma jyeṣṭham-upāsate* । *vijñānaṁ brahma ced-veda* । *tasmāc-cen-na pramādyati* । *śarīre pāpmano hitvā* । *sarvān kāmān samaśnuta iti* । – II.5

The agent (the *jīva* as the *kartā*)[xxvi] possessing intelligence performs *yajña* and accomplishes various deeds. All gods worship *vijñāna* as *Brahman* (Hiranyagarbha), the eldest. If one contemplates *vijñāna* as *Brahman* and never becomes complacent about it, one lays aside all wrongdoings in the body and attains all desires.

Outcome of Study of Vijñānamaya

तस्यैष एव शारीर आत्मा । यः पूर्वस्य ।

tasyaiṣa eva śārīra ātmā । *yaḥ pūrvasya* ।

The nature of Ānandamaya Self
The Ānandamaya is not Brahman

तस्माद्वा एतस्माद्विज्ञानमयात्। अन्योऽन्तर आत्माऽऽनन्दमयः । तेनैष पूर्णः ।

tasmād vā etasmād-vijñānamayāt । *anyo'ntara ātmā "nandamayaḥ* । *tenaiṣa pūrṇaḥ* ।

Contemplation of the Ānandamaya

स वा एष पुरुषविध एव । तस्य पुरुषविधताम् । अन्वयं पुरुषविधः । तस्य प्रियमेव शिरः । मोदो दक्षिणः पक्षः । प्रमोद उत्तरः पक्षः । आनन्द आत्मा । ब्रह्म पुच्छं प्रतिष्ठा ।

sa vā eṣa puruṣavidha eva । *tasya puruṣavidhatām* । *anvayaṁ puruṣavidhaḥ* । *tasya priyam-eva śiraḥ* । *modo dakṣiṇaḥ pakṣaḥ* । *pramoda uttaraḥ pakṣaḥ* । *ānanda ātmā* । *brahma puccham pratiṣṭhā* ।

A Verse

तदप्येष श्लोको भवति ।

tadapyeṣa śloko bhavati । – II.5

This one (*vijñānamaya*), indeed, is the embodied Self of the former one (*manomaya*). Within this *vijñānamaya* Self and apart, it is the Self consisting of *ānanda*[xxvii] by which the former (*vijñānamaya*) is filled. This one (*ānandamaya*) also is of the form of a person, according to that one's (*vijñānamaya*) being in the shape of a person. Happiness[xxviii] is his head, joy is his right wing, delight is his left wing, *ānanda* is his trunk and *Brahman* is his support/basis. On this, there is also this following verse.

Sixth Anuvāka

Brahman Is Introduced by Śruti
(Answer comes before the Question)

असन्नेव स भवति । असद्-ब्रह्मेति वेद चेत् । अस्ति ब्रह्मेति चेद्वेद । सन्तमेनं ततो विदुरिति ॥

asanneva sa bhavati । *asad-brahmeti veda cet* । *asti brahmeti ced-veda* । *santam-enam tato vidur-iti* ।

Brahman Is the Innermost Self

तस्यैष एव शारीर आत्मा । यः पूर्वस्य ।

tasyaiṣa eva śārīra ātmā । *yaḥ pūrvasya* ।

If a person takes *Brahman* to be non-existent, truly he is non-existent.[xxix] If he understands that *Brahman* is the existent entity, in consequence, the wise people will consider him to be wise. The Self embodied in that one (the *vijñānamaya* Self) is indeed this one (the *ānandamaya* Self).[xxx]

From the second section up to the sixth section, we get the analysis of five *kośa*s – *annamaya, prāṇamaya, manomaya, vijñānamaya* and *ānandamaya*. The limbs of each Self (*kośa*) are clearly pictured. This is to help the seeker shift his vision gradually from grosser to subtler levels. Each *kośa* is introduced as the Self. This is just to concur with common notion. Subsequently, it is negated and the next one is introduced. This is continued until the last. After the introduction of every *kośa*, the Upaniṣad quotes a *Ṛg-mantra*, revealing the identity of the individual *kośa* with the corresponding total. This serves two purposes: (a) at each level, both the microcosm and the macrocosm get negated leaving behind the non-dual basis; and (b) an average seeker can use this portion for the *upāsanā* of the macrocosm upon the microcosm. The description of the limbs also becomes useful. Finally, *Brahman* is revealed as the basis of *ānandamaya kośa* that means that *Brahman* is the basis of all.

The Questions of the Disciple

अथातोऽनुप्रश्नाः । उताविद्वानमुं लोकं प्रेत्य । कश्चन गच्छती ३ । आहो विद्वानमुं लोकं प्रेत्य । कश्चित्समश्नुता ३ उ ।

athāto 'nupraśnāḥ । utāvidvān-amuṁ lokaṁ pretya । kaścana gacchati 3 । āho vidvān-amuṁ lokaṁ pretya । kaścit-samaśnutā 3u ।

Now, the following questions arise in respect of what has been taught: "Does a person who has not known *Brahman* attain it, after having departed from this world? Whether a person who has known *Brahman*, departing from here, attains it?"

In the preceding *anuvāka*s, the five *kośa*s have been introduced for setting forth the knowledge of *Brahman*. *Brahman* has descended (as though) into human personality through space and other elements, and five sheaths. However, *Brahman* is the True Self of the enlightened, as well as of the ignorant. Hence, the questions arise. The plural *anupraśnāḥ* (questions) is explained by doubling the two main questions: (i) "does he reach?" and (ii) "or does he not?". The questions may also be formulated thus:

(i) does *Brahman* exist, and (ii) or not? *Brahman* being the same everywhere, (iii) if the ignorant fails to attain it, (iv) may it not be supposed that the wise may also be barred from attaining it. Will he who knows *Brahman* attain Him or not? The Upaniṣad answers the questions in the following *anuvāka*.

Brahman's Volition

सोऽकामयत । बहु स्यां प्रजायेयेति ।

so 'kāmayata । bahu syāṁ prajāyeyeti ।

Brahman's Volition to Manifest

स तपोऽतप्यत । स तपस्तप्त्वा । इदꣳ सर्वमसृजत । यदिदं किं च ।

sa tapo 'tapyata । sa tapas taptvā । idaṁ sarvam-asṛjata । yad-idaṁ kiṁ-ca ।

Brahman entering the Universe. Entering means Manifestation

तत्सृष्ट्वा । तदेवानुप्राविशत् ।

tat sṛṣṭvā । tad-evānuprāviśat ।

Brahman Manifests External Objects

तदनुप्रविश्य । सच्च त्यच्चाभवत् । निरुक्तं चानिरुक्तं च । निलयनं चानिलयनं च । विज्ञानं चाविज्ञानं च । सत्यं चानृतं च सत्यमभवत् । यदिदं किं च । तत्सत्यमित्याचक्षते ।

tad-anu-praviśya । sac-ca tyaccābhavat । niruktaṁ cāniruktaṁ ca । nilayanaṁ cānilayaṁ ca । vijñānaṁ cāvijñānaṁ ca । satyaṁ cānṛtaṁ ca satyam-abhavat । yad-idaṁ kiṁ-ca । tat-satyam-ityācakṣate ।

A Verse

तदप्येष श्लोको भवति ॥

tadapyeṣa śloko bhavati । – II.6

(i) He, the *Ātmā*, desired,[xxxi] "May I become many, let Me procreate Myself." (ii) He contemplated[xxxii] over Himself.

Having contemplated, (iii) He projected all this, whatever there is here. Having brought it forth, indeed He entered into it.[xxxiii] Having entered it, He became the form-ones[xxxiv] and formless-ones, the defined[xxxv] and undefined, the founded and the foundationless, the living and non-living, the real and the unreal; whatever else there is, He became the entire Reality. For that reason, sages declare that all this is real. Regarding that, there is also this verse.

Seventh Anuvāka

The Verse

Brahman, the Self-cause

असद् वा इदमग्र आसीत् । ततो वै सदजायत । तदात्मानꣳ स्वयमकुरुत । तस्मात् तत्सुकृतमुच्यत इति । यद् वै तत्सुकृतम् ।

asad vā idam agra āsīt । tato vai sad-ajāyata । tad-ātmānaṁ svayam-akuruta । tasmāt tat-sukṛtam-ucyata iti । yad vai tat-sukṛtam ।

"In the beginning[xxxvi] this was indeed unmanifest. From that (unmanifest), indeed the manifest came. That (*Brahman*) created itself by itself. Therefore it is called self-made,[xxxvii] or well-made."

Brahman, the Source of Limitless Joy

रसो वै सः । रसꣳ ह्येवायं लब्ध्वाऽऽनन्दी भवति ।

raso vai saḥ । rasaṁ hyevāyaṁ labdhvā ''nandī bhavati ।

Brahman Is the Source of All Joy

को ह्येवान्यात् कः प्राण्यात् । यदेष आकाश आनन्दो न स्यात् । एष ह्येवानन्दयाति ।

ko hyevānyāt kaḥ prāṇyāt । yad-eṣa ākāśa ānando na syāt । eṣa hyevānandayāti ।

He truly is the flavour,[xxxviii] which is the essence of existence. Surely, by grasping the flavour, this one, the individual soul, becomes blessed. Who indeed would breathe,[xxxix] who would remain alive, if this *Ānanda* were not in the space! Indeed, it is He and He alone that causes the blessedness.

True Knowledge Leads to Fearlessness

यदा ह्येवैष एतस्मिन्नदृश्येऽनात्म्येऽनिरुक्तेऽनिलयनेऽभयं प्रतिष्ठां विन्दते । अथ सोऽभयं गतो भवति ।

yadā hyevaiṣa etasminnadṛśye 'nātmye 'nirukte 'nilayane 'bhayaṁ pratiṣṭhāṁ vindate । *atha so 'bhyaṁ gato bhavati* ।

Sense of Duality Causes Fear

यदा ह्येवैष एतस्मिन्नुदरमन्तरं कुरुते । अथ तस्य भयं भवति ।

yadā hyevaiṣa etasminn-ud-aram-antaraṁ kurute । *atha tasya bhayaṁ bhavati* ।

Duality is the Result of Avidyā

तत्त्वेव भयं विदुषोऽमन्वानस्य । तदप्येष श्लोको भवति ॥

tat-tveva bhayaṁ viduṣo 'manvānasya । *tadapyeṣa śloko bhavati* ।　　–II.7

Now, the individual *jīva* becomes fearless[xl] only when it obtains a firm and peaceful ground in that invisible, selfless, unutterable, supportless Reality. Whenever the self assumes even a smallest division[xli] in that state of identity, then he has fear. That is why even a wise man has fear when he is not reflective. With reference to this, there is this verse.

The answers are in the seventh *anuvāka*. From the following portions, up to the end of the seventh *anuvāka*, the last of the three questions is answered. Seven points are given in favour of *Brahman*'s existence.

1. Any creation must have an intelligent cause. Being the intelligent cause of the entire universe, *Brahman*'s existence cannot be denied.

2. Having created all the beings, *Brahman* entered them as the very experience. Hence, the existence of the very experiencer reveals the existence of *Brahman*.
3. Also being the material cause of the universe, *Brahman*'s existence cannot be denied. The very existence of everything, sentient or insentient, manifest or unmanifest, reveals the existence of the *Brahman*.
4. As a *Ṛg-mantra* mentions, *Brahman* is the one which manifests itself as the world. It is *su-kṛta*, the self-creator and self-created. Who can deny such a *Brahman*?
5. *Brahman* is enjoyed by wise men alone, who do not have any other source of joy. Thus, as *rasa*, *Brahman*'s existence is clearly available in wise men.
6. *Prāṇa* is activating the body. However, *prāṇa* is inert by itself. Hence, it requires some other conscious principle for its function. This conscious principle is *Brahman*, whose existence is evident at every moment as one breathes in and out.
7. The fearlessness that a wise person enjoys does not come from worldly security. He is fearless because he is established in *Brahman*, the basis of all. Thus, *Brahman*'s existence is evident in the fearlessness of a wise person.

   The very same *Brahman* appears as the dualistic world for the ignorant one, causing limitation and fear. Thus, *Brahman*'s existence is evident even in the fear of the ignorant one.

Eighth Anuvāka

Brahman's Existence as the Source of Fear

Brahman as the Ruler of the Universe

भीषाऽस्माद्वातः पवते । भीषोदेति सूर्यः । भीषाऽस्मादग्निश्चेन्द्रश्च ।
मृत्युर्धावति पञ्चम इति ॥

bhīṣā 'smād vātaḥ pavate । *bhīṣodeti sūryaḥ* । *bhīṣā 'smād-aganiścendraśca* । *mṛtyur-dhāvati pañcama iti* । – II.8

Out of fear of Him,[xlii] the Wind blows, because of His fear, the Sun rises, because of His fear, Agni, Indra, and Death the fifth one, move fast.

Ānanda-Mīmāṁsā in Taittirīya

A gradation of higher and higher stages of happiness is presented towards the end of this *vallī* (chapter), taking a complete worthy human being – "a noble youth, in the prime of his age, most swift and alert, perfectly whole and resolute, most vigorous in health, laden with all the riches and of good learning – as the basic unit of this calculus. The acme is reached in *Brahman*, the source of *ānanda*, beyond which there is nothing higher to aspire. The happiness of the *Brahman-Ātmā* is perceivable on the perfection of desirelessness (*akāmahatattvam*). It is enjoyed and experienced by one who knows *Brahman*. That is the only happiness from which all happiness that we experience in the world." That is the uniqueness of this Upaniṣad. It shines in a class by itself.

Now, the Upaniṣad sums up. "The *ānanda* in the individual human being and the *ānanda* in the highest being are one and the same. The gradation of happiness is only in the manifestation because of the gradation in the quietude of the mind. The one who recognizes the true nature of *ānanda* becomes dissociated from all the *kośa*s and becomes established in *ānanda*." (By this statement, the first two questions are indirectly answered. There is no question of anyone attaining *Brahman*. It is one's own nature. Still, we say that the ignorant person does not attain *Brahman* because, he disowns *Brahman*. The wise person attains *Brahman*, as it were, because he owns up *Brahman* as himself.)

Ānanda-Mīmāṁsā

सैषाऽऽनन्दस्य मीमाꣳसा भवति ।

saiṣā 'nandasya mīmāṁṣā bhavati ।

Brahman's ānanda to be comprehended through human joy

The Unit of Human-ānanda

i) युवा स्यात्साधु युवाऽध्यायकः । आशिष्ठो दृढिष्ठो बलिष्ठः । तस्येयं पृथिवी सर्वा वित्तस्य पूर्णा स्यात् । स एको मानुष आनन्दः ।

yuvā syāt sādhu yūvā 'dhyāyakaḥ । *āśiṣṭho dṛḍhiṣṭho baliṣṭhaḥ*। *tasyeyaṁ pṛthivī sarvā vittasya pūrṇā syāt* । *sa eko mānuṣa ānandaḥ* ।

Now this is an assessment of *ānanda*.[xliii] Suppose there is a youth, a noble youth, in the prime of age, most swift[xliv] and alert, perfectly whole and resolute, most vigorous, and of good learning, and that to him belongs the entire earth laden with all riches. Consider that this constitute one unit of human joy.

The Unit of Manuṣya-Gandharva-ānanda

ii) ते ये शतं मानुषा आनन्दाः । स एको मनुष्यगन्धर्वाणामानन्दः ।

te ye śataṁ mānuṣā ānandāḥ । *sa eko manuṣya-gandharvāṇām-ānandaḥ* ।

Freedom from desire is the pre-eminent condition of ānanda

श्रोत्रियस्य चाकामहतस्य ।

śrotriyasya cākamahatasya ।

One hundred such units of human joy make a single unit of joy, which a human-*gandharva* possesses. A sage full of revelation, and free from all desires[xlv] also possesses the same joy.

The Unit of Deva-Gandharva-ānanda[2]

iii) ते ये शतं मनुष्यगन्धर्वाणामानन्दाः । स एको देवगन्धर्वाणामानन्दः ।

te ye śataṁ manuṣya-gandharvāṇām-ānandaḥ । *sa eko deva-gandharvāṇām-ānandaḥ* ।

Freedom from desire is the pre-eminent condition of ānanda

श्रोत्रियस्य चाकामहतस्य ।

śrotriyasya cākāmahatasya ।

One hundred such units of joy that a human-*gandharva* possesses make one unit joy of heavenly-*gandharva*. A sage full of revelation, and free from all desires also possesses the same joy.

The Unit of Pitṛs-ānanda

iv) ते ये शतं देवगन्धर्वाणामानन्दाः । स एकः पितृणां चिरलोकलोकानामानन्दः ।

te ye śataṁ deva-gandharvāṇām-ānandāḥ । *sa ekaḥ pitṛṇāṁ ciraloka-lokānām ānandaḥ* ।

Freedom from desire is the pre-eminent condition of ānanda

श्रोत्रियस्य चाकामहतस्य ।

śrotriyasya cākāmahatasya ।

One hundred such units of joy that a heavenly-*gandharva* possesses make one unit joy of the manes, who inhabit the long-enduring world. A sage full of revelation, and free from all desires also possesses the same joy.

The Unit of Ājāna Deva-ānanda

v) ते ये शतं पितृणां चिरलोकलोकानामानन्दाः । स एक आजानजानां देवानामानन्दः ।

---

2 Reference of *devagandharva* is in *Ṛgveda*. The *ṛṣi* as well as the *devatā* of *Ṛgveda* X.139 comprising six *ṛcā* is Viśvāvasu Devagandharva. Hence, it is considered as *ātmastuti*.

te ye śataṁ pitṛṇāṁ ciraloka-lokānām ānandāḥ । *sa eka ājānajānāṁ devānām ānandaḥ* ।

Freedom from desire is the pre-eminent condition of ānanda

श्रोत्रियस्य चाकामहतस्य ।

śrotriyasya cākāmahatasya ।

One hundred such units of joy that the manes inhabiting the long-enduring world possess make one unit joy of the gods who are so by birth, in the Ājāna heaven. A sage full of revelation, and free from all desires also possesses the same joy.

The Unit of Karma-deva-ānanda

vi) ते ये शतमाजानजानां देवानामानन्दाः । स एकः कर्मदेवानां देवानामानन्दः ।
ये कर्मणा देवानपियन्ति ।

te ye śatam-ājānajānāṁ devānām ānandāḥ । *sa ekaḥ karma-devānāṁ devānām-ānandaḥ* । *ye karmaṇā devānapiyanti* ।

Freedom from desire is the pre-eminent condition of ānanda

श्रोत्रियस्य चाकामहतस्य ।

śrotriyasya cākāmahatasya ।

One hundred such units of joy that the gods, who are so by birth in the Ājāna heaven, make the joy of those who have become gods by virtue of their deeds. For, it also happens that a man attains godhood by his own deeds. A sage full of revelation and free from all desires also possesses the same joy.

The Unit of Deva-ānanda

vii) ते ये शतं कर्मदेवानां देवानामानन्दाः । स एको देवानामानन्दः ।

te ye śataṁ karma-devānāṁ devānām ānandāḥ । *sa eko devānam ānandāḥ* ।

Freedom from desire is the pre-eminent condition of ānanda

श्रोत्रियस्य चाकामहतस्य ।

śrotriyasya cākāmahatasya ।

One hundred such units of joy of the gods, who have attained heaven due to their good deeds, make one unit of joy of highest gods. A sage full of revelation and free from all desires also possesses the same joy.

The ānanda of Indra

viii) ते ये शतं देवानामानन्दाः । स एक इन्द्रस्यानन्दः ।

te ye śataṁ devānām ānandaḥ । *sa eka indrasyānandaḥ* ।

Freedom from desire is the pre-eminent condition of ānanda

श्रोत्रियस्य चाकामहतस्य ।

śrotriyasya cākāmahatasya ।

One hundred such units of joy of the highest gods make the joy of Indra. A sage full of revelation, and free from all desires also possesses the same joy.

The ānanda of Bṛhaspati

ix) ते ये शतमिन्द्रस्यानन्दाः । स एको बृहस्पतेरानन्दः ।

te ye śatam indrasyānandāḥ । *sa eko bṛhaspater-ānandaḥ* ।

Freedom from desire is the pre-eminent condition of ānanda

श्रोत्रियस्य चाकामहतस्य ।

śrotriyasya cākāmahatasya ।

One hundred such units of joy of Indra make one unit of joy of Bṛhaspati. A sage full of revelation, and free from all desires also possesses the same joy.

The ānanda of Prajāpati

x) ते ये शतं बृहस्पतेरानन्दाः । स एक प्रजापतेरानन्दः ।

te ye śataṁ bṛahaspeter-ānandaḥ । *sa eka prajāpater-ānandaḥ* ।

Freedom from desire is the pre-eminent condition of ānanda

श्रोत्रियस्य चाकामहतस्य ।

śrotriyasya cākāmahatasya ।

One hundred such units of joy of Bṛhaspati make one unit of joy of Prajāpati. A sage full of revelation, and free from all desires also possesses the same joy.

The ānanda of Hiraṇyagarbha

xi) ते ये शतं प्रजापतेरानन्दाः । स एको ब्रह्मण आनन्दः ।

te ye śataṁ prajāpaterānandāḥ । *sa eko brāhmaṇa ānandaḥ* ।

Freedom from desire is the pre-eminent condition of ānanda

श्रोत्रियस्य चाकामहतस्य ।

śrotriyasya cākāmahatasya ।

One hundred such units of joy of Prajāpati make the *ānanda* of *Brahman* (*Saguṇa-Brahman*, i.e. Hiraṇyagarbha). A sage full of revelation and free from all desires also possesses the same joy.

Ānanda is One and Non-dual

स यश्चायं पुरुषे । यश्चासावादित्ये । स एकः ।

sa yaścāyaṁ puruṣe । *yaścāsāvāditye* । *sa ekaḥ* ।

To Know Brahman Is to Attain Him

स य एवंवित् । अस्माल्लोकात् प्रेत्य । एतमन्नमयमात्मानमुपसङ्क्रामति । एतं प्राणमयमात्मानमुपसङ्क्रामति । एतं मनोमयमात्मानमुपसङ्क्रामति । एतं विज्ञानमयमात्मानमुपसङ्क्रामति । एतमानन्दमयमात्मानमुपसङ्क्रामति ।

sa ya evaṁ-vit । *asmāllokāt pretya* । *etaṁ-annamayam-ātmānam-upasaṅkrāmati* । *etaṁ-prāṇamayam-ātmānam-upasaṅkrāmati* । *etaṁ manomayam-ātmānam-upsaṅkrāmati* । *etaṁ-vijñānamayam-ātmānam-upsaṅkrāmati* । *etaṁ-*

ānanadamayam-ātmānam-upasaṅkrāmati ।

A Verse

तदप्येष श्लोको भवति ॥

tadapyeṣa śloko bhavati । – II.8

This *ānanda,*[xlvi] which is in the human being and in the sun, is the same. He who comprehends fully as stated above, after departing from this world, transcends the *annamaya, prāṇamaya, manomaya, vijñānamaya* and *ānandamaya* Self. With reference to this, there is also this verse.

Ninth Anuvāka

Brahman is beyond Speech and Mind

यतो वाचो निवर्तन्ते । अप्राप्य मनसा सह ।

yato vāco nivartante । *aprāpya manasā saha* ।

The wise has no source of fear

आनन्दं ब्रह्मणो विद्वान् । न बिभेति कुतश्चनेति ।

ānandaṁ brahmaṇo vidvān । *na bibheti kutaścaneti* ।

The wise has no conflict of right and wrong since he is neither kartā nor bhoktā

एतꣳ ह वाव न तपति । किमहꣳ साधु नाकरवम् । किमहं पापमकरवमिति ।

etaꣳ ha vāva na tapati । *kim ahaꣳ sādhu nākaravam* । *kim-ahaṁ pāpam-akaravam iti* ।

The wise derives strength from right and wrong

स य एवं विद्वानेते आत्मानꣳ स्पृणुते । उभे ह्येवैष एते आत्मानꣳ स्पृणुते । य एवं वेद । इत्युपनिषत् ॥

sa ya evaṁ vidvān-ete ātmānaꣳ spṛṇute । *ubhe hyevaiṣa ete ātmanaꣳ spṛṇute* । *ya evaṁ veda* । *ityupaniṣad* । – II.9

That, from which the speech along with the mind come

back, unable to reach it; knowing the *ānanda* of that *Brahman*, a person is free from the cause of fear. Indeed, the very thought,[xlvii] "why did I not do good deeds?, why did I do wrong deeds?" do not torment him anymore. He, who understands thus in the above manner, redeems himself from both. Such is the secret knowledge.

In the ninth and last section, the glory of a wise person is pointed out with the support of an *Ṛg-mantra* quotation. Knowing himself to be the whole, the wise person has no source of fear. He is not tormented by the thoughts of the past omissions or commissions. For him, anything good or bad is non-different from himself. They do not stand separate to threaten him. He is the non-dual *Brahman*. Further, it proclaims that this Reality is the origin, ground and goal of the world of experience, thus establishing the fundamental identity of this intimate world with the ultimate Reality.

Śāntimantraḥ

सह नाववतु । सह नौ भुनक्तु । सह वीर्यं करवावहै । तेजस्वि नावधीतमस्तु । मा विद्विषावहै ॥ ॐ शान्तिः शान्तिः शान्तिः ॥

sa ha nāvavatu । *sa ha nau bhunaktu* । *saha vīryaṁ karavāvahai* । *tejasvi nāvadhītam astu* । *mā vidviṣāvahai* । *oṁ śāntiḥ śāntiḥ śāntiḥ* ।

Endnotes

i *Brahman* is the subject matter of this chapter. Great intellect is required to understand the subtle truth taught in the Upaniṣads. The teacher and the taught must be free from any kind of disagreement towards each other. No disagreement should spring between them due to either defects in the imparting, or receiving of instruction, or by entering into futile disputes. Perfect mutual amity alone ensures efficient teaching and thorough understanding.

ii The purpose (*prayojanam* or *phalam*) of *brahma-vidyā* is laid down in this statement.

iii Existence, Consciousness, Infinite – Two types of definitions of *Brahman* are given in Śruti: (i) by stating its essential qualities known as *svarūpa-lakṣaṇa*, and (ii) by marking its incidental attributes known as *taṭastha-lakṣaṇa*. The three predicates *satyam-jñānam-anantam* given here are the *svarūpa-lakṣaṇa* of *Brahman*. Existence, Consciousness and Limitlessness reveal the intrinsic nature of *Brahman* and not its attributes.

Etymologically too, *Brahman* (from the root √*bṛh* = *bṛdhau* = to grow without limit) gives this significance. The definition of *Brahman* as Saccidānanda made familiar in later history of Vedāntic thought, may be traced to this famous sentence. *Satyam* may be taken as equivalent to *sat*. Śrī Śaṅkara deems *sat* and *satyam* as well as *cit* and *jñānam* as equivalents. Nor is there any difficulty in equating *anantam* with *ānanda*. It is clearly stated in *Chāndogya Upaniṣad* VII.23 that infinite alone is happiness; and there is no happiness in the finite.

iv *Guhā* (cave) stands for the mind or intellect, because the three factors, knower, knowledge and the object of knowledge, merge from its operation. *Paramavyoma* (highest space) may be construed either independently or as qualifying the term cave; its position allows both ways. When construed paralleling it would read, "in the cave of the intellect and in the remotest space (i.e. *avyākṛta ākāśa* or the Unmanifest) virtually *Brahman*, the cause of the universe in whom all objects were hidden waiting for manifestation." Śaṅkara contends that, it is more appropriate to take the "highest space" as qualifying the cave of the intellect, the reason being that the purpose of the passage is immediate knowledge of *Brahman*, and that therefore the latter meaning alone would fit in with that context. Hence, the "highest space" should refer to the space in the heart, the seat of intellect (*buddhi*), where *Brahman* is intuited as the immediate Self-witnessing the modifications of *buddhi*.

v Not all desires can be fulfilled at once, physically. It can only be fulfilled by the knowledge that all that is here is me.

vi Here, as in *Bṛhadāraṇyaka Upaniṣad* I.4.1-4 and in *Aitareya Upaniṣad* I.1-3, *Ātmā* is spoken of as the First Principle from which the whole universe has emanated; and in that sense, it is equated with *Brahman*. We also get in this section, a general description of manifestation of the universe. *Ātmā* is determined as the First Principle for it is the basis of all that we perceive. From this Principle of Consciousness, which is also Existence and Limitlessness, first emanates space, embodying the subtle rudiment of matter known as space along with time. From the space come forms that are more distinct and becomes the relative phenomena. The quality of sound is associated with space as reception of sound demands space, air is cognized with the quality of touch added; fire is cognized with the quality of form added, water springs up from fire with its specific quality of taste; and finally the last constituent earth is evolved with the quality of smell included.

vii *Mayaṭ* here means *vikāre* (modification).

viii *Annam* stands for food or matter. Matter is what is used up by the energy. Even a common person can understand *Brahman* when he is told that this body is the *Puruṣa* or *Brahman*. The various limbs of the body are compared to the limbs of a bird, and its support is stressed to lead the mind to inner truths. All creatures have originated from *Brahman*; for it is the basis of all. However, a human being is specially cited because he alone is competent to know *Brahman*. The analogy of a bird is given to apply also to the other *kośa*s that are like the physical body. Only when the body is conceived in the shape of a bird, can we speak of a tail and a support; and only when each *kośa* is pictured as endowed with this support, the last *kośa* can be spoken of having its ground in *Brahman*. This is the significance of bird analogy.

ix *Pakṣaḥ* is interpreted as "wing" by Ānanda Giri and Śaṅkarānanda.

x The Tenth Man story frequently used by the Vedānta *ācāryas* to explain a point finds a reference in *Śāṅkarabhāṣyam* here.

xi The idea of something subtle that is difficult to comprehend is explained with the help of something more tangible. The second day waxing moon is not easily visible in the evening after sunset to the inexperienced eyes. The sight is facilitated through the branch of a tree nearby. This analogy is known as *śākhā-candra-nyāya*, which is used by Śruti to drive home the point.

xii All organisms are produced from inorganic matter; they subsist on it, and dissolve into it after some time. There is thus a fundamental unity in Nature with a deep significance. Nature or Virāṭ, constitute the *samaṣṭi-sthūla-śarīra*, of inorganic matter, strikes our mind at the first thought. It called *Anna-Brahman* here, or the Infinity's aspect of utility. The Upaniṣad takes this fact to lead the enquiring mind, step-by-step further, and more complete truths. The idea contained in the clause is repeated again for explaining the derivation of *annam*.

xiii Here Śruti advises us to reflect on one's own physical body as *Brahman*. This physical body is also called Self, because it is the first object which the common mind mistakes for one's true self or *Ātmā*. By this *upāsanā* of the *annamaya* Self, the aspirant takes his stand on the physical body. This meditation directs the mind to a fruitful enquiry into the Self.

xiv Here is an instance of etymological method of driving home subtler truths. The idea is stressed that the Cosmic Being who is manifest in the form of food or matter, exists as both the consumer and the consumed. It is the highest Principle, *Brahman*, that assumes the multiplicity and diversity of the aspects by being immanent in all beings, essentially invisible and yet manifesting. In the form of *annam*, the Cosmic Being outgrows His own nature, says Puruṣasūktam-2 and that very idea is reproduced in *Muṇḍaka Upaniṣad* I.1.8 that states "Through knowledge *Brahman* swells, and from that *annam* is born". *Bṛhadāraṇyaka Upaniṣad* I.4.6 says – *idaṁ sarvam-annaṁ ca-eva annādaśca* (This Universe is verily – the food, and consumer of food). *Praśna Upaniṣad* I.14 says *anna vai prajāpatiḥ* (food is indeed the Lord of all beings).

xv *Prāṇa* etc. – These various modifications of the vital energy are here made to correspond to the members of the physical body, *ākāśa* and *pṛthivī* in the text stand for *samāna* and *udāna*; for in this context no other interpretation can be appropriate.

xvi Personifications of Cosmic forces and the *indriyas* (sensory organs) are called *devatās*. They exist and function against the background of and supported by Cosmic Life called *sūtrātmā* or *prāṇa*. A particular being is said to be alive only so long as the vital air function in him. The word *sarvāyuṣam* is repeated twice in two sense; first in the sense of universal life, because all creatures remain alive in the universal life-force; second in the sense of complete span of life which in the case of man, according to the Vedas, is 100 years. Under whatever attribute an *upāsaka* meditates on *Brahman*, that same attributes he obtains if he so wishes. A person, who meditates on *prāṇa* as Universal Life (*sarvāyuṣam*), attains the allotted full life (*sarvāyuṣam*), *prāṇa* being the *sūtrātmā*.

xvii In the series of sheaths (as though sheath) of Self, the Self consisting of *prāṇa* is the second. Life is not confined to the physical body alone, rather extends to the other Self also. The second and succeeding sheaths are not like the first one, for they are subtle and they fill the first one like heat filling a metal piece put on fire. Therefore, each of them forms a homogeneous whole indistinguishable into parts unlike the physical body which contains all the others. Thus, here is a subtler and more spiritual conception of the Self. When a spiritual aspirant becomes deeply convinced that the *prāṇamaya* Self is the cause and support of the physical Self, the importance of the latter diminished and finally it becomes a shadow of the true Self, for there cannot be more than one Self in a person. An alternative interpretation of the passage is this: The *Ātmā-Brahman* Reality, which is the Self of the former (the *annamaya* Self), is the Self of this (the *prāṇamaya* Self) also. This view emphasizes that all *kośa*s (sheaths) are unreal. It is only in a relative sense that one Self is spoken of as the embodied Self of another.

xviii The internal organ of perception and cognition is called *manas*. Here it is employed to denote all its powers also – internal and external senses, memory, understanding and the rest. The *manomaya* Self is subtler and higher than the *praṇāmaya* Self, and is the basis of the functioning of the latter, either through conscious impulses, or through subconscious modifications called *saṁskāra*s. Just as the life-force (*praṇā*) is functioning in every cell of the body, the principle of *manas* is also pervading throughout the body, this fact may be assumed from the possibility of receiving sensations from every part of the organism. The same symmetrical allotment of parts is followed here also as before. The importance of *Yajus* is evident, and so it is given the position of the head. This allotment has no basis except that of the assertion of the Śruti. *Yajus* and the rest refer to a species of speech, which has its origin in the *vṛtti*, mode of function of the mind that can be repeated verbatim. The holy verses and passages of the Vedas are nothing but the pure intelligence of *Brahman* limited by the factor of *vṛtti*s assuming that form. That is how the Vedas are eternal; that is why the Vedas are identified with *Ātman* in some Śruti. By accepting the words of the Vedas as the expression of mental acts, their repetition becomes possible. The Vedas being one with the *Ātmā* (intelligence), they can shed light on truths hidden from the sense, which it will not be possible if they are mere sounds devoid of the background of intelligence. The *manomaya* Self of the spiritual aspirant consists of wisdom; it is *vedātmā*, say Śrī Śaṅkara.

xix *Yajus* means a kind of *mantra*s in which the number of letters and quarters, and length (of lines) are not restricted. The word *Yajus* denotes (prose) sentences. It is the head because of its pre-eminence, and the pre-eminence is owing to its subserving a fire-ritual directly, for an oblation is offered with a *Yajur-mantra* uttered along with a *svāhā*, etc.

xx *Ādeśa* here means the Brāhmaṇa portion of the Vedas, since (in consonance with the etymological meaning of *ādeśa* – command) the Brāhmaṇa portion enjoins all that has to be inculcated.

xxi *Atharvāṅgirasaḥ* – the Mantra and the Brāhmaṇa portions seen by Ṛsi Atharvāṅgiras; are *puccham pratiṣṭhā* since they are chiefly concerned with rites performed for acquiring peace, prosperity, etc. which bring about stability.

xxii This fourth *anuvāka* offers some difficulty in interpretation. In the place where the *manomaya* Self is described, a statement that the *ānanda* of *Brahman* is inconceivable and ineffable and is capable of removing all fear is inappropriate. Moreover, the same verse is found in its proper place in ninth *anuvāka*. Śaṅkarānanda explains that the passage is intended to show that *Brahman* as described here is the cause of *manomaya*, which is now in question, and it required to be described. Ānanda Giri, finding that Śaṅkara has omitted to comment on it assuming it explicit (*spaṣṭam*), states that *Brahman* here denotes *manas*, and ventures the following on it, nor its own modifications, which are also called *manas*. Hence, *manas* transcends word and mind.

xxiii *Prāṇamaya* Self and *manomaya* Self are related to each other as body and soul. In reality, the ultimate Self is the Self of each Self, just as the basis of an unreal serpent is indeed a rope.

xxiv The fourth in the series of Selfs is the *vijñānamaya* Self. The term *vijñāna* is used to denote the faculty of discernment or judgement, and in that sense, it is synonymous with *buddhi*. *Buddhi* (determinate knowledge) is only one of the functions of the mind, the others being mind, memory and ego (*manas, citta* and *ahaṅkāra*). Here *vijñāna* is used in the sense of *jñānātmā* used in *Kaṭha Upaniṣad* I.3.9-10 and 13. It is the subject who feels as "I" familiarly called the *jīva*. It is the principle of Ego permeated by the semblance of Consciousness, and forming the centre of agency (*kartṛtvam*) and experience (*bhoktṛtvam*). It is because of the fact that the *vijñānamaya* is coexistent with *manomaya* and *manomaya* permeates thoroughly the *prāṇamaya*, which again fills *annamaya*, that a person has the notion regarding his body. "I am a person." While *manomaya* is modification of the mind, *vijñānamaya* is the owner of such states or modifications.

xxv *Ṛtam* and *Satyam* – "Keeping the senses steady is considered *yoga*." (*Kaṭha Upaniṣad* II.3.11.) Just as the various members of the body function properly only when they united to the trunk, so also the attitude of *śraddhā* and other moral excellences, which the *upāsaka* has to cultivate, if he has to act efficiently and fruitfully, come only when they are based on steadying the senses or *yoga*. *Mahat* stands for the cosmic intellect or Hiraṇyagarbha, the source of all individual egos. Hiraṇyagarbha is the sum total of egos. He is the Universal Ego. Hence, *mahat* is the support of *vijñāna*.

xxvi *Vijñānam*, as has been pointed out stands for the individual *jīva*, who is the doer (*kartā*) and experiencer (*bhoktā*) of all actions. Truly, the doership (*kartṛtvam*) and experience (*bhoktṛtvam*) belong to the *vijñānamaya* Self; however, it is mistakenly attributed to the Consciousness that is the witness (*sākṣī*). Vedic rituals like *jyotiṣṭoma* and all *karma*s in general, which a person performs, are done by the *vijñānamaya* Self, through the various other Selves, which are, but its instruments. What is micro-cosmically known as the individual Self is macro-cosmically Hiraṇyagarbha or *mahat* or *sūtrātmā* – the Cosmic Ego, centred in cosmic understanding or *vijñāna*. This Hiraṇyagarbha or *Vijñāna-Brahman* is spoken of as the eldest because, He is the first manifestations of the Ultimate Reality in the realm of causal relations and so He is the cause of all subsequent activity. By contemplating on Him, the gods have attained their eminence. *Vijñāna* is proximate to *Brahman-Ātmā* Reality. There is a true similarity between the Individual Ego or the *vijñānamaya* Self, and Cosmic Ego or Hiraṇyagarbha inasmuch as both are agents and enjoyers, the one being an individual and the other being Total. The latter may therefore, be contemplated in terms of the former; that is, one may meditate, "I, the *vijñānamaya* Self, am the *Vijñānamaya Brahman* or Hiraṇyagarbha in essence". By constantly practising this type of contemplation zealously, the aspirant's mind will not wander away to the other outer sheaths, which are only the vehicles of the *vijñānamaya* Self. Moreover, he will be cleansed of all impurities, for the root of all impurities is the ignorance that the body is the Self, and the attachments and aversions that follow in its wake. He who is firm in the idea that "I am *vijñāna* and *vijñāna* alone", and so devoted to the contemplation of *Brahman* in the *upādhi* of intelligence, hardly feels that he is an individual acting and enjoying and suffering like the common person, and at death he will be united with Hiraṇyagarbha. There he will enjoy all desires by his mere will. The immediate result of the meditation on the *vijñānamaya* Self is the knowledge that *manomaya* Self too is only a wrapping and as such an instrument of the still interior Self.

xxvii The fifth and the last in the group of Selfs is the *ānandamaya* Self. It has been stated that the *vijñānamaya* is proximate to the real *Ātmā*, but *Ātmā* the Consciousness is not an agent. Even when one has withdrawn the notion of Selfhood from the external sheaths and fixed it on the *vijñānamaya* Self, the idea of agency or ego is not eliminated from one's consciousness. The core of the *vijñānamaya* Self is the notion of agency (*kartṛtvam*). So here, the *ānandamaya* is thought, still inward to that. The *ānandamaya* is the true Self, without the notion of agency, but conditioned by the internal organ modified as joy, etc. which are the result of knowledge and action. Even here, the Self is not free from all trappings, because there is the thin *upādhi* of intelligence transformed as joy, etc. – hence *ānandamaya* too is an effect, the happiness resulting from thought and action. Agency (*kartṛtvam*) and action (*karma*) are correlates. All actions are performed for the pleasure of an enjoyer, i.e. actions have their ground in the feeling of present of prospective joy, which an agent entertains. Just as action and joy are cause and effect, so also agency (*kartṛtvam*) and enjoyership (*bhoktṛtvam*) have the same relationship. Hence, it is stated that the *ānandamaya* Self is inner to the *vijñānamaya*

Self, and distinct from it. Joy is not a localized, the whole personality is pervaded by it, and so the *ānandamaya* Self is taken to pervade all the other Self; one filling the other. Joy again is a positive state and is of various degrees. The joy that is experienced by the individual agent is only a fraction of *Brahman*. Even the worldly joy is not entirely different from the *ānanda* of *Brahman*; it is either a reflection or a bit of the bliss of reality. *Ānanda* is an entity in itself, and the very being of Self, this is evident from the fact that the individual soul is the highest and dearest object of love. All other objects have value only for the sake of the individual Self, *Bṛhadāraṇyaka* II.4.5. The individual Self in its essence is *ānanda*, but the *ānanda* aspect is revealed only when the mind is in tranquil state, which may be inferred from dispassion, patience, generosity and other similar virtues. However, when the Self-alone is the object of love, and so in truth Bliss itself, by dwelling in each body it becomes divided and so becomes limited. Hence, the *ānandamaya* Self cannot be *Brahman* itself whose *ānanda* is not subject to any condition whatsoever. *Chāndogya Upaniṣad* VII.23.1 states "That which is Infinite alone is happiness". So here, the Upaniṣad without mentioning any reward for the contemplation of *ānandamaya* Self, as it has done in the case of the other Selfs, directly states that *Brahman* is its support and foundation.

xxviii The *ānandamaya* Self is also of human shape because it fills the previous *kośa* completely. The three distinctions of joy noted here as *priya, moda* and *pramoda* relate respectively to the perception, obtainment and enjoyment of a desired object. They are only the reflections of *pramoda* in the *sāttvika* state of the mind. The support and foundation of the *ānandamaya* Self is *Brahman*. The *ānandamaya* Self expresses itself in various degrees in different beings; and it is experienced as *priya, moda* and *pramoda* by the same being according to the various conditioning factors; but *Brahman*, who is the unparallel *ānanda*, is the basis of it as that of the others. It is for conducting the individual being who is engrossed in sense objects inward and further inward until he knows his innermost Self, namely the non-dual *Brahman*, that the five sheaths (as though sheaths) have been described. It may be noted that Śrī Śaṅkara deems that the true Self of a person is *Brahman*, and that all the five *kośa*s are but unreal appearance of the True Self. The *vijñānamaya* and *ānandamaya* together form the individual *jīva* as the agent (*kartā*) and the enjoyer (*bhoktā*), while the other sheaths form merely its instruments. This is just what is demanded by non-dualism through the testimony of reason and scripture. Rāmānujācārya and other teachers inclined in this way, take the *ānandamaya* to be *Brahman*, and the individual *jīva*s to be distinct and separate from it. Both the positions are reasoned out in the respective commentaries on the Ānandamaya-adhikaraṇa of *Brahmasūtra* 1.1.12-19.

xxix Śruti now establishes by the method of doubt and enquiry that *Brahman* spoken of as *sat* at the beginning of the chapter is an existing Reality. He who refuses to accept *Brahman* is as good as a non-entity, for thereby he loses the most precious thing in his life and drifts without any objective. To live without knowing one's real nature is as good as non-existence. The nature of such a person is described in *Bhagavadgītā* XVI.9 as *naṣṭātmānaḥ*. *Brahman* is the anchor of all living beings.

xxx The last Self, *ānandamaya*, stands in relation of the *Ātmā* of *vijñānanmaya* Self, since each *kośa* is said to be completely fill the preceding one.

xxxi In this passage, we get a sublime statement of creation as an act of the Divine volition. The creation of the cosmos from *Brahman* as described in the second *anuvāka* places beyond doubt the existence of *Brahman*; for the universe, which we experience is an existence, and it cannot therefore spring from non-existence. However, even an insentient primordial substance can be the first cause of subsequent evolution, as the Sāṁkhyas and the scientists may have it. The Upaniṣadic view is contrary. It is declared in the above sentence that the Divine will is what is behind the projected universe. The root *kam* in *akāmayata* (desired) is used in the same sense in *Ṛgveda Saṁhitā* X.129.4 (Nāsadīya-Sūktam) where *kāma* means volition/will. Unlike however, the *kāma* of creatures, the will of *Brahman* is one with Himself, because there is nothing besides Him and He does not need the help of accessories to manifest His will. What is meant by the act of His will is only the manifestation of the multiplicity and variety of the phenomenal universe, which is already present in Him as a possibility, by His own power of denomination and appearance, technically called *nāma-rūpa-vyākaraṇa*. These two oft-quoted cosmological passages (*so 'kāmayata । bahu syāṁ prajāyeya* and *sa tapo 'tapyata* । *sa tapas taptvā* ।) of *Taittirīya Upaniṣad* establish that *Brahman* is the intelligent as well as the material cause (*abhinna-nimitta-upādāna-kāraṇa*) of the universe.

xxxii The word *tapas* here denotes contemplation. The meaning of *tapas* in this context is the Lord's resolve about the design of the universe.

xxxiii It should not be supposed that the Lord enters into the created objects as a person having built a house enters it, this is impossible because the Lord is without any spatial relation whatever. He is all and the Whole; and the whole can never be contained by the part. The allegory is meant to point out the Truth of the Universe. The Universe is but the manifestation of the Consciousness.

xxxiv *Sat* and *tyat* are translated as what is manifest, gross and what is unmanifest, subtle respectively.

xxxv *Brahman* being the basis of all, He is immanent even in contradictories. Whatever there is, perceived, intuited, or imagined, all that is Him. The whole universe is Real as *Brahman*. This passage clearly shows that ontologically, the universe is never a non-existent like square-circle or human-horn. Understanding this world as non-different from *Brahman* is the correction of an error in perception. It is not possible to correct the erroneous perception of a snake in a rope without the knowledge of the identity between the superimposed snake and actual rope. Similarly, it is not possible to know that *Brahman* is the only Reality, and there is identity between the world and *Brahman*, without a proper means of knowledge. By stating that all this is *Brahman*, the above *anuvāka* serves this purpose most appropriately. Knowledge of *Brahman* is not an act of contemplation in which one object is replaced by another. It is a total comprehension in which the consciousness is deepened and widened and made to work at all levels. That is why while commenting on *Brahmasūtra* II.2.29 – *vaidharmācca na svapnādivat*, Śaṅkara says, *jāgaritopalabdhaṁ vastu na kasyacid-api-avasthāyāṁ bādhyate* (the objects experienced in waking state are not sublated under any state).

xxxvi *Agre* – It does not denote the beginning of any age, rather the first in order. Creation is an eternal flow in an ever-present now, of which empirical experience is not possible. What is presented here is not an agnostic conception of a primal non-existent, as some modern philosophers would think. *Chāndogya Upaniṣad* VI.2.1-2 (*sad eva saumya idam agra āsīt* | and *katham asataḥ sat jāyeta*?) makes that amply clear. Unmanifest cannot be equated with non-existence like a human-horn or a square-circle. *Ṛgveda Saṁhitā* X.129 (Nāsadīya-Sūktam) places *Brahman* above being (*sat*) and non-being (*asat*). The separation of Self and not-Self is the beginning of creation, therefore the Absolute is first said to have assumed of its own accord a self. The individual should too find firm peace only in the selfless, i.e. non-dual invisible Reality. Being and non-Being, *Saguṇa* and *Nirguṇa*, are correlate aspects of that one Supreme Identity. Non-Being is the permissive principle, or the first cause, of Being from which the universe issues. The ultimate Reality is at times negatively characterized in other religious traditions also. *Śūnya* (void) is one among the 1,000 appellations of Viṣṇu.

xxxvii *Brahman* being the cause par excellence is called *sukṛta*. The word *svakṛta* is blurred into *sukṛta* and two meanings are ascribed to it in these forms. Being the first cause *Brahman* is *svakṛta* or Svayambhū. *Sukṛta* is the good or meritorious act, which brings about desired effects. Actions have power to produce their respective fruits only through the great common cause, *Brahman*.

xxxviii *Rasa* causes satisfaction. Without *rasa*, the world will be devoid of taste or flavour. If the Lord were not *Rasa*, none would be attracted to Him. While annotating the third verse of *Bhāgavata Purāṇa*, Viśwanātha Chakravartin argues thus; in Brahmānandavallī of *Taittirīya Upaniṣad*, the *kośa*s from *annamaya* to *ānandamaya* are set forth in an ascending order of superiority, culminating in *Brahman*, who is the foundation, and then *rasa* is identified with Him; so in that series, *rasa* occupies the apex.

xxxix The joy and zest of life are here ascribed to the presence of *ānanda* at the core of existence. The prime motive of every living creature is the attainment of joy and happiness.

xl The individual *jīva* becomes fearless. We get here an incisive analysis of the emotion of fear and its remedy. The basis of fear is the feeling of otherness as stated in *Bṛhadāraṇyaka Upaniṣad* I.4.2 – *so 'bibhet* (he was frightened). However, fear departs without leaving a trace, when a person recognizes his own self as the all. Fearlessness is the characteristic trait of one who has known the Truth. Even for a wise person, the moment he becomes unreflective – makes a distinction in the Self as subject and object – there is unrest in him. The slightest objectification of the Self brings with it fear. As long as one considers *Brahman* as an object of knowledge, and not one's own self, one is exposed to fear. Here we get the answer to the question: *Brahman* being the common cause, will the ignorant along with the wise reach it? The ignorant will not reach it, and even the knower of *Brahman*, if he finds separated from it. The completely featureless and transcendent aspect of Reality alone gives ultimate rest and unshakable peace to the wandering *jīva*. That is what is emphasized by the string of negative description of *Brahman*.

xli The words in the text are differently construed: (i) *ut* + *aram antaraṁ kurute* | *aram* = *alam* = little, *antaram* = difference, *utkurute* = *udbhavayati* = creates (as per Bhaṭṭabhāskara); and (ii) or *u* + *daram* (little), *antaraṁ kurute*.

xlii It is observed that only when one is under pressure of necessity or fear of a master that one works incessantly and with precision. The great cosmic forces follow their law ceaselessly without least error. In fact, the will of the Lord is expressed in the Laws of Nature, hence they cannot be otherwise at any time. The very same idea is emphasized in *Kaṭha Upaniṣad* II.3.3 and in ch. X (Vibhūti-Yoga) of *Bhagavadgītā*. The Upaniṣad does not however conceive of a wrathful *Īśvara*. *Brahman* is the cause of fear as well as fearlessness. It has been already noted in the seventh *anuvāka* that one becomes fearless and tranquil when one finds his firm support in *Īśvara*. Fear springs up only when one is unthinking, when one perceives a distinction between one's self and *Īśvara*.

xliii *Bṛhadāraṇyaka Upaniṣad* IV.3.33 has given at great length a similar hierarchy of *ānanda* leading up to the *Ānanda* that is *Brahman*. Upaniṣads clarify that *Brahman* is not a Being full of *Ānanda*, rather it is *Ānanda* itself, admitting of no enhancement. That *ānanda* of *Brahman*, the Upaniṣad states, is not totally beyond the comprehension of a common person; for even the worldly joy, which he cherishes, is only a fraction of the *ānanda* of *Brahman*. Through a calculus, this is vividly brought out in this *anuvāka*. The human happiness, say of wise and healthy world-sovereign, is a trillionth part of the *ānanda* of Brahmā. Human and divine *gandharvas*, *pitṛs*, *ājānadevas*, *karmadevas*, *devas*, Indra, Bṛhaspati and Prajāpati have hundred billion, a ten-thousand billion and a million billion times more joy than the best person. From this calculus it cannot however be said that joy multiplied a given time will make divine joy. For Śruti clearly states that the joy of Brahmā is experienced by a person only in whom there is no trace of cravings and who is full of revelation and is free from impurities. Therefore, it should be understood that even the joy of Brahmā, the creator, cannot be the *ānanda* which is the Absolute Reality. Some interpret *ānanda* that is the highest denomination in the scale is actually *Brahman* itself.

xliv The three superlative adjectives – *āśiṣṭhaḥ, dṛḍhiṣthaḥ, baliṣṭhaḥ* – convey that pleasure of a fit body, happiness of good health and the joy of power. The *gandharva*s are a class of heavenly beings mentioned from *Ṛgveda* downwards. Viśvāvasu is their leader. In the epics and Purāṇas, the *gandharva*s are characterized as celestial musicians. They form the orchestra at the banquet of gods, and together with *apsarā*s, they belong to the heaven of Indra. They constitute one of the classes into which higher creation is divided. *Manuṣya-gandharva*s are those heavenly singers who possess human features, the term may refer also to those men who have ascended to the state of *gandharva*s. Viśvāvasu and the rest belong to the class of divine-*gandharva*s. Ājāna, according to Bhaṭṭabhāskara, means the repeated epochs of Manu, (*manvantara*) and the gods who are born in each of these *yuga*s as the attendants of higher gods are therefore called *ājāna-deva*s. Indra is the chief of gods, and Bṛhaspati is his preceptor. Prajāpati is explained as the Lord of creatures by some, and as Hiraṇyagarbha by others. If the latter meaning is accepted, Brahmā, immediately following, will refer to Brahmā the Supreme.

xlv The inference is freedom from desire is the pre-eminent condition of *ānanda*. Other two factors being same to the extent one is free from desires, to that extent is his experience of unsullied *ānanda*.

xlvi The word Āditya is rendered as Sun. It literally means that Being who exists from the beginning. The *upāsaka* who has been engaged in the contemplation of the various *kośa*s, transcends all of them and established himself in the *ānanda* of *Brahman*. The passage in question is generally translated thus, "He who is in the person here, and he who is in the sun is the same". The same expression is available in *Īśāvāsya Upaniṣad* 16 and many other places in the Upaniṣads. If *saḥ* is understood as *ānandaḥ*, immediately proceeding, as it does and as it has been translated here, the meaning given above would legitimately follow.

xlvii Ethics is about relation between the individual *jīva* and his social environment. It fixeṣ the norm for individual behaviour in the light of social and individual happiness. One, who has surpassed individuality, needs no moral rules to bind him to good life. He requires no conscious effort to be perfect. He transcends the realm of dos and don'ts, and he is no more impelled by any external standard. This is what is emphasized in the above passage.

Gratitude: My acknowledgement and profuse gratitude to Swami Swahanada's *Taittirīyopaniṣad*, whose explanations I have used as Endnotes in this *vallī*. – Author

7

Bhṛguvallī

Dialogue as a Method in Presenting the Knowledge

ŚĪKṢĀVALLĪ dealt with rituals and contemplations as a preparatory step to acquire *brahma-vidyā*; but they are comparatively remote and indirect means (*bahiraṅga-sādhanā*) to acquire *brahma-vidyā*. *Brahma-vidyā* was exhaustively dealt with in Brahmānandavallī. Enquiry (*vicāra*), which is a more proximate means to *brahma-vidyā*, was not treated in Śīkṣāvallī. In this chapter, method of *vicāra* as well as some other important topics, connected with this teaching is taught. With a view to extol *brahma-vidyā*, Śruti starts with a story, presented in the form of a dialogue between Bhṛgu and his father, Varuṇa. This is to point out that *brahma-vidyā* can be acquired only from a *guru* by properly approaching and seeking the wisdom from him. Even if he is one's father, one must request for this knowledge. This aspect is seconded in *Chāndogya Upaniṣad*, where Śvetaketu has to seek this knowledge from his father Uddālaka.

There are ten *anuvāka*s (sections) in Bhṛguvallī. The opening section of this chapter gives the *taṭastha-lakṣaṇa* of *Brahman*, as that, from which the universe comes into being, by which it is sustained, and unto which it finally goes back.

How Bhṛgu, the disciple, was able to arrive at *Brahman-Ātmā* as the cause of the creation, sustenance and resolution of the universe because of his systematic enquiry into *anna*, *prāṇa*, *manas*, *vijñāna* and *ānanda*, is stated in sections two to six (*pañcakośāntas-sthita-brahmanirūpaṇam*). The Upaniṣad declares in the sixth section that anyone who knows *Brahman* in the manner in which Bhṛgu did becomes firmly established in *Brahman*; he becomes *Brahman*.

Sections seven to nine (*anna-brahmopāsanam*) explain certain meditations on food that were not dealt with earlier in the Upaniṣad.

The tenth section (*brahmānandānubhavaḥ*) concludes with an account of a *jīvan-mukta*. The knower of *Brahman* who remains as *Brahman*, who has known the oneness of all things, proclaims his non-dual experience for the benefit of spiritual aspirants.

Śāntimantraḥ

ॐ स ह नाववतु । स ह नौ भुनक्तु । सह वीर्यं करवावहै । तेजस्वि नावधीतमस्तु । मा विद्विषावहै ॥ ॐ शान्तिः शान्तिः शान्तिः ॥

oṁ sa ha nāvavatu । sa ha nau bhunaktu । saha vīryaṁ karavāvahai । tejasvi nāvadhītam astu । mā vidviṣāvahai । oṁ śāntiḥ śāntiḥ śāntiḥ ।

May He (*Īśvara*) protect both of us (teacher and student). May He nourish both of us. May we together acquire the capacity (to study and understand the scriptures). May what is studied, be brilliant. May there not be disagreement between both of us. May there be peace, peace, peace.

Bhṛguvallī unfolds a scene, in which the son Bhṛgu approaches his father Varuṇa repeatedly in quest of the truth. The father, with all the paternal care, love and understanding, leads the son systematically through a thorough study of human personality, which according to this Upaniṣad is made up of as though five sheaths (*kośa*s) – the physical, the physiological, the mental, the intellectual and the experiential. The *kośa*s are not real, one makes mistake at each *kośa*, considering it to be the *Ātmā*.

First Anuvāka: Taṭastha-lakṣaṇa of Brahman

Brahman as Jagat-kāraṇam

भृगुर्वै वारुणिः । वरुणं पितरमुपससार । अधीहि भगवो ब्रह्मेति । तस्मा एतत् प्रोवाच ।

bhṛgur-vai vāruṇiḥ । varuṇaṁ pitaram-upasasāra । adhīhi bhagavo brahmeti । tasmā etat provāca ।

Gateways to the knowledge of Brahman

अन्नं प्राणं चक्षुः श्रोत्रं मनो वाचमिति । तꣳ होवाच ।

annaṁ prāṇaṁ cakṣuḥ śrotraṁ mano vācam iti । taṁ hovāca ।

Taṭastha-lakṣaṇa of Brahman

यतो वा इमानि भूतानि जायन्ते । येन जातानि जीवन्ति । यत् प्रयन्त्यभिसंविशन्ति । तद् विजिज्ञासस्व । तद् ब्रह्मेति ।

yato vā imāni bhūtāni jāyante । yena jātāni jīvanti । yat prayantyabhisaṁviśanti । tad vijijñāsasva । tad brahmeti ।

Vicāra (Enquiry)

स तपोऽतप्यत । स तपस्तप्त्वा ॥

sa tapo 'tapyata । sa tapas-taptvā । – III.1

The famous Bhṛgu,[i] who was Vāruṇi, approached his father Varuṇa requesting, "Revered Sir! Please teach me *Brahman*". Varuṇa taught him food, *prāṇa*, sight, hearing, mind and speech as means of knowledge of *Brahman*.[ii] He added, "From whom all this is born, having been born by whom all this is sustained, to whom all this goes back, understand that to be *Brahman*. Try to know[iii] that by *tapas* (enquiry). Bhṛgu contemplated.[iv] Having contemplated:

The translation of the first six *anuvāka*s is to be read together, as they are syntactically connected. Having given in the second *vallī* an account of the Absolute Reality, the cosmology and the reality of the universe, and the purpose of human life, the Upaniṣad now teaches with the help of a story, the means of attaining the purpose of life. The story of Varuṇa instructing his son about *Brahman* suggests what a great treasure *brahma-vidyā* is, and how the worthy son Bhṛgu was anxious to receive it as a paternal gift. We learn from *Praśna Upaniṣad*,[1] *Bṛhadāraṇyaka Upniṣad*,[2] *Śvetāśvatara Upaniṣad*,[3] *Maitrāyaṇī Upaniṣad*[4] and *Subāla Upaniṣad*[5] that the spiritual wisdom is to be imparted to none other than a son or a disciple, whose conduct and descent are well known, and who has served the *guru*, a term of at least one year with perfect self-control. The story makes it clear that even if one is a son, only if he has a true longing (*jijñāsā*) for it, and asks for it, he is instructed the knowledge. It is suggested by commentators that Bhṛgu is the famous founder of Bhārgava clan. A dialogue between Bhṛgu and Varuṇa is given in *Śatapatha Brāhmaṇa* II.6.1. The story also brings home to us the truth that the knowledge of *Brahman* is attained only through a proper teacher.

Pañcakośa-viveka as a Methodology of Teaching

Based on these clues, Bhṛgu conducts an enquiry. Shifting his vision form one *kośa* (*kośa iva kośa*) to another, he ultimately arrives at *Brahman*, which is the core of himself. Thus, the enquiry culminates in abiding in his true nature of *Ānanda*, which is identical with *Brahman*. Through this section, the importance of enquiry, i.e. *tapas* is emphasized. The teaching on the part of the *guru* and enquiry on the part of the *śiṣya* lead one to this knowledge.

---

1 *PrUp* I.2.

2 *BrUp* VI.3.12.

3 *ŚvUp* VI.22.

4 *MaiUp* VI.29.

5 *SubUp* 16.

Second Anuvāka: Anvaya-vyatireka method in arriving at the Truth

Annam as Brahman

अन्नं ब्रह्मेति व्यजानात् । अन्नाद्ध्येव खल्विमानि भूतानि जायन्ते । अन्नेन जातानि जीवन्ति । अन्नं प्रयन्त्यभिसंविशन्तीति ॥

annaṁ brahmeti vyajānāt । annāddhyeva khalvimāni bhūtāni jāyante । annena jātāni jīvanti । annaṁ prayantyabhisaṁviśantīti ।

Annam not exactly Brahman

तद्विज्ञाय । पुनरेव वरुणं पितरमुपससार । अधीहि भगवो ब्रह्मेति ।

tad-vijñāya । *punar-eva varuṇaṁ pitaram-upasasāra* । *adhīhi bhagavo brahmeti* ।

Vicāra continues

तꣳ होवाच । तपसा ब्रह्म विजिज्ञासस्व । तपो ब्रह्मेति । स तपोऽतप्यत । स तपस्तप्त्वा ॥

taṁ̐ hovāca । *tapasā brahma vijijñāsasva* । *tapo brahmeti* ।
sa tapo 'tapyata । *sa tapas-taptvā* । – III.2

He understood that food is *Brahman*; for, certainly, all living beings here are indeed born of food, having been born, they remain alive by food and on departing, they enter into food. Having contemplated thus, he again approached his father Varuṇa saying, "Revered Sir, Please teach me *Brahman*". "Seek to know *Brahman* by enquiry. Enquiry is *Brahman*." He contemplated, and having contemplated:

Finding that *annam* did not suit the definition of *Brahman* (*yato vā imāni bhūtāni jāyante*), the son returns to the father. At this stage, Varuṇa again suggests *tapas* (enquiry) as a means of knowing *Brahman*, for encouraging his son to persist in the method of deep reflection he had chosen, until he achieved his goal. The fact that Bhṛgu took "food" for *Brahman* also indicates that further *tapas* (enquiry) was required to make his vision subtle.

Third Anuvāka: Anvaya-vyatireka method in arriving at the Truth

Prāṇa is Brahman

प्राणो ब्रह्मेति व्यजानात् । प्राणाद्ध्येव खल्विमानि भूतानि जायन्ते । प्राणेन जातानि जीवन्ति । प्राणं प्रयन्त्यभिसंविशन्तीति ॥ तद्विज्ञाय । पुनरेव वरुणं पितरमुपससार । अधीहि भगवो ब्रह्मेति । तꣳ होवाच । तपसा ब्रह्म विजिज्ञासस्व । तपो ब्रह्मेति । स तपोऽतप्यत । स तपस्तप्त्वा ॥

prāṇo brahmeti vyajānāt । prāṇāddhyeva khalvimāni bhūtāni jāyante । prāṇena jātāni jīvanti । prāṇaṁ prayantyabhisaṁviśantīti । tad-vijñāya । punar-eva varuṇaṁ pitaram-upasasāra । adhīhi bhagavo brahmeti । taṁ hovāca । tapasā brahma vijijñāsasva । tapo brahmeti । sa tapo 'tapyata । sa tapas-taptvā । – III.3

He understood that *prāṇa* is *Brahman*; for, certainly, all living beings here are indeed born of *prāṇa*, having been born, they remain alive because of *prāṇa*, and on departing, they enter into *prāṇa*. Having contemplated thus, he again approached his father Varuṇa saying, "Revered Sir! Please teach me *Brahman*". "Seek to know *Brahman* by enquiry. Enquiry is *Brahman*." He contemplated, and having contemplated:

In this *anuvāka*, *annam* is dropped in favour of *prāṇa*. Just as food cannot be *Brahman* as it is subject to change, so also *prāṇa* cannot be *Brahman*. The material body is produced by the vital force, which is a higher category. In the absence of *prāṇa*, *annam*[6] decays. *Chāndogya Upaniṣad*[7] also states that without life this body will die. *Annam* or the gross universe is not *Brahman*, *prāṇa*, which is the aspect of the activity of the Cosmic Being, also cannot be *Brahman*, even though it appears to be such, by noticing that *apāna* brings about childbirth, the fivefold breath sustains it, and *udāna* causes death.

---

6 *BṛUp* V.12.1.

7 *ChāUp* VI.11.3.

Fourth Anuvāka:
Anvaya-vyatireka method in arriving at the Truth

Mind as Brahman

मनो ब्रह्मेति व्यजानात् । मनसो ह्येव खल्विमानि भूतानि जायन्ते । मनसा जातानि जीवन्ति । मनः प्रयन्त्यभिसंविशन्तीति । तद्विज्ञाय । पुनरेव वरुणं पितरमुपससार । अधीहि भगवो ब्रह्मेति । तꣳ होवाच । तपसा ब्रह्म विजिज्ञासस्व । तपो ब्रह्मेति । स तपोऽतप्यत । स तपस्तप्त्वा ॥

mano brahmeti vyajānāt । *manaso hyeva khalvimāni bhūtāni jāyante* । *manasā jātāni jīvanti* । *manaḥ prayantyabhisaṁviśantīti* । *tad-vijñāya* । *punar-eva varuṇaṁ pitaram-upasasāra* । *adhīhi bhagavo brahmeti* । *taṁ hovāca* । *tapasā brahma vijijñāsasva* । *tapo brahmeti* । *sa tapo 'tapyata* । *sa tapas-taptvā* । – III.4

He understood that *manas* is *Brahman*; for, certainly, all living beings here are indeed born of *manas*, having been born, they remain alive because of *manas*, and on departing, they enter into *manas*. Having contemplated thus, he again approached his father Varuṇa saying, "Revered Sir, Please teach me *Brahman*." "Seek to know *Brahman* by *tapas* (enquiry). Enquiry is *Brahman*." He contemplated and having contemplated:

By enquiry and contemplation, Bhṛgu next considers *manas* to be *Brahman*. Unlike *prāṇa*, which is inert, mind appears to be a conscious entity. It is the principle of knowing, and it represents the will-power of the Cosmic Being. The Universal mind has created the material universe. Even the individual life begins by the volition of the mind, as *Praśna Upaniṣad*[8] says, "the *prāṇa* comes into the physical body. Beings are sustained through life (*prāṇa*), by acting with the environment through mind (*manas*). Mind appears to be the principle of Consciousness, which is *Brahman*." Therefore, Bhṛgu accepted the mind to be *Brahman* since it appeared to have the features of *Brahman*. However,

8 *PrUp* III.3 and 10.

through enquiry, he soon discovered that the mind is not independent, it is just an organ of knowledge just as sight and the rest, and that its consciousness is only borrowed.

Fifth Anuvāka: Anvaya-vyatireka method in arriving at the Truth

Intellect as Brahman

विज्ञानं ब्रह्मेति व्यजानात् । विज्ञानाद्ध्येव खल्विमानि भूतानि जायन्ते ।
विज्ञानेन जातानि जीवन्ति । विज्ञानं प्रयन्त्यभिसंविशन्तीति । तद्विज्ञाय ।
पुनरेव वरुणं पितरमुपससार । अधीहि भगवो ब्रह्मेति । तꣳ होवाच । तपसा
ब्रह्म विजिज्ञासस्व । तपो ब्रह्मेति । स तपोऽतप्यत । स तपस्तप्त्वा ॥

vijñānaṁ brahmeti vyajānāt । vijñānād-hyeva khalvimāni bhūtāni jāyante । vijñānena jātāni jīvanti । vijñānaṁ prayantyabhisaṁviśantīti । tad-vijñāya । punar-eva varuṇaṁ pitaram-upasasāra । adhīhi bhagavo brahmeti । taṁ hovāca । tapasā brahma vijijñāsasva । tapo brahmeti । sa tapo 'tapyata । sa tapas-taptvā । – III.5

He understood that *vijñāna* is *Brahman*; for, certainly, all living beings here are indeed born of *vijñāna*, having been born, they remain alive because of *vijñāna*, and on departing, they enter into *vijñāna*. Having contemplated thus, he again approached his father Varuṇa saying, "Revered Sir! Please teach me *Brahman*." "Seek to know *Brahman* by *tapas* (enquiry). Enquiry is *Brahman*." He enquired, and having contemplated:

Vijñāna is *Brahman*. *Vijñāna* is the individual *jīva*, the self-conscious principle in a person. Mind is its organ. *Vijñāna* controls the mind, the senses, the body and initiates activity in them. This faculty, which is the centre of knowledge, still cannot be the cause of the entire universe. Therefore, Bhṛgu abandoned that too.

Sixth Anuvāka:
Anvaya-vyatireka method in arriving at the Truth

Ānanda as Brahman

आनन्दो ब्रह्मेति व्यजानात् । आनन्दाद्ध्येव खल्विमानि भूतानि जायन्ते । आनन्देन जातानि जीवन्ति । आनन्दं प्रयन्त्यभिसंविशन्तीति ।

ānando brahmeti vyajānāt । ānandāddhyeva khalvimāni bhūtāni jāyante । ānandena jātāni jīvanti । ānandaṁ prayantyabhisaṁviśantīti ।

Ānanda is the Self

सैषा भार्गवी वारुणी विद्या । परमे व्योमन्प्रतिष्ठिता ।

saiṣā bhārgavī vāruṇī vidyā । parame vyoman pratiṣṭhitā ।

Fruit of Self-knowledge

य एवं वेद प्रतितिष्ठति । अन्नवानन्नादो भवति । महान् भवति प्रजया पशुभिर्ब्रह्मवर्चसेन । महान् कीर्त्या ॥

ya evaṁ veda pratitiṣṭhati । annavān-annādo bhavati । mahān bhavati prajayā paśūbhir-brahmavarcasena । mahān kīrtyā । – III.6

He understood[v] that *Ānanda* is *Brahman*; for, certainly, all living beings here are indeed born of *Ānanda*, having been born, they remain alive because of *Ānanda*; and on departing, they enter into *ānanda*. This knowledge of Bhṛgu and Varuṇa is founded on the highest place; the knowledge is hidden in the space of the intellect. He, who knows this, becomes firmly established. He commands food,[vi] and obtains power to assimilate and enjoy it. He becomes great in progeny, in cattle, and in effulgence born of sacred wisdom. He becomes great through renown, stemming from righteous conduct.

Anna-Brahman-Upāsanā

In the next 7th, 8th, and 9th *anuvāka*s, three pairs of objects are taken for *upāsanā*. The seeker has to appreciate the mutual dependence in each of these pairs. This is to remember that the whole universe is interrelated. The first pair is *prāṇa* and the body; the second pair is water and fire; the third pair is the earth and space. Through these *upāsanā*s, one can attain plenty of food, progeny, cattle, etc. and finally, heaven.

These three *anuvāka*s also contain some disciplines to be followed with respect to food. The disciplines are in the form of respect for food, procurement of food, etc. Food is glorified here because it (as *annamaya-kośa*) serves as the first step in the enquiry of *Brahman*. These *upāsanā*s and disciplines can give worldly benefits if one wants them. However, if these are practised without any desire, they can prepare the mind for *brahma-vidyā*.

Seventh Anuvāka: Anna-Brahman-Upāsanā

Some Minor Upāsanā

अन्नं न निन्द्यात् । तद् व्रतम् ।

annaṁ na nindyāt । tad vratam ।

Contemplation of Prāṇa and Body

प्राणो वा अन्नम् । शरीरमन्नादम् । प्राणे शरीरं प्रतिष्ठितम् । शरीरे प्राणः प्रतिष्ठितः । तदेतदन्नमन्ने प्रतिष्ठितम् । स य एतदन्नमन्ने प्रतिष्ठितं वेद प्रतितिष्ठति । अन्नवानन्नादो भवति । महान् भवति प्रजया पशुभिर्ब्रह्मवर्चसेन । महान् कीर्त्या ॥

prāṇo vā annam । śarīram-annādam । prāṇe śarīraṁ pratiṣṭhitam । śarīre prāṇaḥ pratiṣṭhitaḥ । tad-etad-annam-anne pratiṣṭhitam । sa ya etad-annam-anne pratiṣṭhitaṁ veda pratitiṣṭhati । annavān-annādo bhavati । mahān bhavati prajayā paśubhir-brahmavarcasena । mahān kīrtyā । – III.7

One[vii] should not disrespect food. That should be observed as a sacred injunction. Life indeed is food. The body[viii] is the consumer of food. The body is set in life; life is set in the body. Therefore, food is established in food. He who knows and contemplates on food, which is established in food, becomes firmly established. He becomes an enjoyer of food, commanding plenty of food. He becomes great in progeny, in cattle, and in effulgence born of sacred wisdom. He becomes great for his righteous conduct.

Eighth Anuvāka: Anna-Brahman-Upāsanā

अन्नं न परिचक्षीत । तद् व्रतम् । आपो वा अन्नम् ।

annaṁ na paricakṣīta । tad vratam । āpo vā annam ।

Contemplation of Water and Fire

ज्योतिरन्नादम् । अप्सु ज्योतिः प्रतिष्ठितम् । ज्योतिष्यापः प्रतिष्ठिताः । तदेतदन्नमन्ने प्रतिष्ठितम् । स य एतदन्नमन्ने प्रतिष्ठितं वेद प्रतितिष्ठति । अन्नवानन्नादो भवति । महान् भवति प्रजया पशुभिर्ब्रह्मवर्चसेन । महान् कीर्त्या ॥

jyotirannādam । apsu jyotiḥ pratiṣṭhitam । jyotiṣyāpaḥ pratiṣṭhitāḥ । tad-etad-annam-anne pratiṣṭhitam । sa ya etad-annam-anne pratiṣṭhitaṁ veda pratitiṣṭhati । annavān-annādo bhavati । mahān bhavati prajayā paśubhir-brahmavarcasena । mahān kīrtyā । – III.8

One[ix] should not disregard food. That should be observed as a sacred injunction. Water[x] indeed is food. Fire is the eater of food. Fire is established in water, water is established in fire. So, food is established in food. Therefore, he who knows and contemplates on food, which is established in food, becomes firmly established. He becomes an enjoyer of food, commanding plenty of food. He becomes great with progeny, cattle and effulgence born of sacred wisdom. He becomes renowned for his righteous conduct.

Ninth Anuvāka: Anna-Brahman-Upāsanā

अन्नं बहु कुर्वीत । तद् व्रतम् ।

annaṁ bahu kurvīta । *tad vratam* ।

Contemplation of Earth and Space

पृथिवी वा अन्नम् । आकाशोऽन्नादः । पृथिव्यामाकाशः प्रतिष्ठितः । आकाशे पृथिवी प्रतिष्ठिता । तदेतदन्नमन्ने प्रतिष्ठितम् । स य एतदन्नमन्ने प्रतिष्ठितं वेद प्रतितिष्ठति । अन्नवानन्नादो भवति । महान् भवति प्रजया पशुभिर्ब्रह्मवर्चसेन । महान् कीर्त्या ॥

pṛthivī vā annam । *ākāśo 'nnādaḥ* । *pṛthivyam-ākaṣaḥ pratiṣṭhitaḥ* । *ākāśe pṛthivī pratiṣṭhitā* । *tad-etad-annam-anne pratiṣṭhitam* । *sa ya etad-annam-anne pratiṣṭhitaṁ veda pratitiṣṭhati* । *annavān-annādo bhavati* । *mahān bhavati prajayā paśubhir-brahmavarcasena* । *mahān kīrtyā* । – III.9

One should produce abundant food. Let that be observed as a sacred vow. The earth indeed is food.[xi] Space is the eater of food. Space is established in the earth, the earth is established in the space. Therefore, food is established in food. And, he who knows and contemplates on food, which is established in food, becomes firmly established. He becomes an enjoyer of food, commanding plenty of food. He becomes great with progeny, cattle, and effulgence born of sacred wisdom. He becomes renowned for his righteous conduct.

Tenth Anuvāka: Social Values (Bahiraṅga-Sādhanā) in Taittirīya

न कंचन वसतौ प्रत्याचक्षीत । तद् व्रतम् । तस्माद् यया कया च विधया बह्वन्नं प्राप्नुयात् । अराध्यस्मा अन्नमित्याचक्षते । एतद् वै मुखतोऽन्नꣳ राद्धम् । मुखतोऽस्मा अन्नꣳ राध्यते । एतद् वै मध्यतोऽन्नꣳ राद्धम् । मध्यतोऽस्मा अन्नꣳ राध्यते । एतद् वा अन्ततोऽन्नꣳ राद्धम् । अन्ततोऽस्मा अन्नꣳ राध्यते । य एवं वेद ॥

na kañcana vasatau pratyācakṣīta । *tad vratam* । *tasmād yayā kayā ca vidhayā bahvannaṁ prāpnuyāt* । *arādhyasmā annam-ityācakṣate* । *etad vai mukhato 'nnaṁ rāddham* । *mukhato*

'smā annaṁ rādhyate । *etad vai madhyato 'nnaṁ rāddham* । *madhyato 'smā annaṁ rādhyate* । *etad vā antato 'nnaṁ rāddham* । *antato 'smā annaṁ rādhyate* । *ya evaṁ veda* ।
– III.10

A spiritual seeker[xii] should not refuse anyone at his residence. Let this be observed as a sacred vow. He should therefore acquire abundant food by any means whatsoever. It is for the sake of this (guest), that food has been prepared, so declare (the householders). The food that is prepared and given in the best manner[xiii] returns to the giver in the best manner; what is offered in the medium fashion returns exactly so; food prepared and offered in the lowest fashion accrues to the giver in the lowest way. He, who knows this as stated, gets what he merits.

Contemplation of Brahman in a human

क्षेम इति वाचि । योगक्षेम इति प्राणापानयोः । कर्मेति हस्तयोः । गतिरिति पादयोः । विमुक्तिरिति पायौ । इति मानुषीः समाज्ञाः ॥

kṣema iti vāci । *yoga-kṣema iti prāṇāpānayoḥ* । *karmeti hastayoḥ* । *gatiriti pādayoḥ* । *vimuktir-iti pāyau* । *iti mānuṣīḥ samājñāḥ* ।

The contemplations[xiv] of *Brahman* associated with a human consist in meditation on *Brahman* as preservation in speech, as acquisition and preservation in *prāṇa* and *apāna*, as work in the hands, as motion in the feet and as evacuation in the anus.

Contemplation of Brahman in the Cosmic Being

अथ दैवीः । तृप्तिरिति वृष्टौ । बलमिति विद्युति ।

atha daivīḥ । *tṛptir-iti vṛṣṭau* । *balam-iti vidyuti* । – III.10

यश इति पशुषु । ज्योतिरिति नक्षत्रेषु । प्रजातिरमृतमानन्द इत्युपस्थे । सर्वमित्याकाशे ॥

yaśa iti paśuṣu । *jyotiriti nakṣatreṣu* । *prajātir-amṛtam-ānanda ityupasthe* । *sarvam-ityākāśe* । – III.10

The contemplation of *Brahman* as associated with the celestial consists in meditating on *Brahman* as satisfaction in the rain, as strength in the lightning, as fame in the cattle (wealth), as light in the stars, as procreation and pleasure in the procreative organ, and as everything in the space.

Contemplation of Brahman in Some Special Aspects

तत्प्रतिष्ठेत्युपासीत । प्रतिष्ठावान् भवति॥ तन्मह इत्युपासीत । महान् भवति । तन्मन इत्युपासीत । मानवान् भवति ।

tat pratiṣṭhetyupāsīta । *pratiṣṭhāvān bhavati* । *tan-maha ityupāsīta* । *mahān bhavati* । *tan-mana ityupāsīta* । *mānavān bhavati* । – III.10

तन्नम इत्युपासीत । नम्यन्तेऽस्मै कामाः । तद् ब्रह्मेत्युपासीत । ब्रह्मवान् भवति । तद् ब्रह्मणः परिमर इत्युपासीत । पर्येणं म्रियन्ते द्विषन्तः सपत्नाः । परियेऽप्रिया भ्रातृव्याः ॥

tan-nama ityupāsīta । *namyante 'smai kāmāḥ* । *tad brahmetyupāsīta* । *brahmavān bhavati* । *tad brahmaṇaḥ parimara ityupāsīta* । *paryeṇaṁ mriyante dviṣantaḥ sapatnāḥ* । *pariye 'priyā bhrātṛvyāḥ* ।

Should one meditate on That as the foundation of all, one becomes well-founded. Should one meditate on That as greatness, one becomes great. Should one meditate on That as mind, one becomes mindful. Should one meditate on That as salutation, all objects of desire bow before him. Should one meditate on That as *Saguṇa-Brahman*, or as the Veda, one becomes possessor of Vedic wisdom. Should one meditate on That as destructive power, his hating foes and enemies die around him.

The Self Equated with Brahman

स यश्चायं पुरुषे । यश्चासावादित्ये । स एकः ।

sa yaścāyaṁ puruṣe । *yaścāsāvāditye* । *sa ekaḥ* । – III.10

The Wise Sees Oneness in All

स य एवंवित् । अस्माल्लोकात् प्रेत्य। एतमन्नमयमात्मानमुपसङ्क्रम्य ।
एतं प्राणमयमात्मानमुपसङ्क्रम्य । एतं मनोमयमात्मानमुपसङ्क्रम्य ।
एतं विज्ञानमयमात्मानमुपसङ्क्रम्य । एतमानन्दमयमात्मानमुपसङ्क्रम्य ।
इमाँल्लोकान् कामान्नी कामरूप्यनुसञ्चरन् । एतत् साम गायन्नास्ते ।

sa ya evaṁ-vit । asmāl-lokāt pretya । etam-annamayam-ātmānam-upasaṁkramya । etaṁ-prāṇamayam-ātmānam-upasaṁkramya । etaṁ-manomayam-ātmānam-upasaṁkramya । etaṁ-vijñānamayam-ātmānam-upasaṁkramya । etaṁ-ānandamayam-ātmānam-upasaṁkramya । imāṁl-lokān kāmānnī kāmarūpyanusañcaran । etat sāma gāyannāste ।

Expression of a Jīvan-mukta

हा३वु हा३वु हा३वु ।

hā 3 vu hā 3 vu hā 3 vu ।

अहमन्नमहमन्नमहमन्नम् । अहमन्नादो२ऽहमन्नादो२ऽहमन्नादः । अह१ श्लोककृदह१ श्लोककृदह१ श्लोककृत् । अहमस्मि प्रथमजा ऋता ३ स्य । पूर्वं देवेभ्यो अमृतस्य ना ३ भायि । यो मा ददाति स इदेव मा३वाः । अहमन्नमन्नमदन्तमा ३द्मि । अहं विश्वं भुवनमभ्यभवाम् । सुवर्न ज्योतीः ।

aham-annam-aham-annam-aham-annam । aham-annādo 3 'ham-annādo 3 'ham-annādaḥ । ahaṁ ślokakṛd-ahaṁ ślokakṛd-ahaṁ ślokakṛt । aham-asmi prathamajā ṛtā 3 sya । pūrvaṁ devebhyo amṛtasya nā 3 bhāyi । yo mā dadāti sa ideva mā 3 vāḥ । aham-annam-annam-adantamā 3 dmi । ahaṁ viśvaṁ bhuvanam abhyabhavām । suvar na jyotīḥ ।

Self-knowledge Ensures Ānanda

य एवं वेद । इत्युपनिषत् ॥

ya evaṁ veda । ityupaniṣat । – III.10

And this one who is here in the person,[xv] and that one in the sun, are one and the same. He who knows thus, on departing

> from this world, transcends successively the Self consisting of *anna, prāṇa, manas, vijñāna* and *ānanda*, traverses[xvi] these worlds enjoying food at will, and assuming forms at will, and remains singing the following *sāman* – "Oh, wonderful![xvii] Oh, wonderful! Oh, wonderful! I am the food, I am the food, I am the food. I am the eater, I am the eater, I am the eater. I am the link, I am the link, I am the link. I am the first-born of the cosmic-order! I exist even prior to gods, and I am the centre and source of immortality! He who gives me away has protected me! I the food, eat him, who eats food all for himself! I have overcome the whole world! I am splendour like the sun. He, who knows this, has the results mentioned. Thus ends the sacred doctrine.

The last section, tenth *anuvāka,* begins with the glorification of *annadāna* (food distribution). If one serves others with plenty of food with due honour, he gets the same treatment wherever he goes. In ninth and eleventh *anuvāka*s of Śīkṣāvallī, certain disciplines were given to be followed by the *jijñāsu* (a seeker seeking *brahmajñānam*) as *antaraṅga-sādhanā* – personal values to be cultivated and developed with reference to one's own self. Here an aspect of *bahiraṅga-sādhanā* is given – a social value to be developed with reference to others while relating to them. The grossest form by means of distribution of food is emphasized. One could take this as *upalakṣaṇa* (example) for any kind of gift that one is capable of giving. And one can proceed to subtler forms such as providing emotional support to others who need it.

Then follow some *ādhyātmika upāsanā*s where *Brahman* is meditated as various faculties in the individual limbs. This is followed by some *ādhidaivika-upāsanā*s where *Brahman* is meditated as various powers in the phenomenal forces.

The last *upāsanā* is that of space, as identical with *Brahman.* Space is to be meditated as (i) the support of all, (ii) as the greatest of all, (iii) as intelligence of all, (iv) as prostration, (v) as the biggest of all, and (vi) as the agent of destruction. The fruit of these meditations will be in accordance with the type of meditation. As one meditates, so one becomes.

Coming to the conclusion, the Upaniṣad comes back to the wise person. One, who has recognized the essential identity between the individual and the total, transcends all the *kośa*s and becomes established in *Brahman*. He is free. He moves everywhere freely, eating whatever comes, assuming any form and singing the song of *Brahman:* "I am the food. I am the eater. I am the link. I am the first born as well as the centre of immortality. I protect those who distribute me (the food) to all. I destroy those who eat me (the food) without giving to anyone. I am the effulgence that occupies the universe like the effulgence of the sun."

With this glorification of the wise person, the Upaniṣad is concluded.

Śāntimantraḥ

सह नाववतु । सह नौभुनक्तु । सह वीर्यं करवावहै । तेजस्वि नावधीतमस्तु ।
मा विद्विषावहै ॥ ॐ शान्तिः शान्तिः शान्तिः ॥

sa ha nāvavatu । *sa ha nau bhunaktu* । *saha vīryam karavāvahai* । *tejasvi nāvadhītam astu* । *mā vidviṣāvahai* । *oṁ sāntiḥ śantiḥ śāntiḥ* ।

Endnotes

i It shows that Bhṛgu was a celebrated person. There was a great sage Maharṣi, Bhṛgu by name, the founder of a family (*gotra-pravartaka*). He was a celebrated person often referred to in the Mantra and Brāhmaṇa portions of the Veda. The descendants of Bhṛgu and Aṅgiras shall consecrate Fire addressing Him "I consecrate Thee, O Lord of sacrifices, for the sacrifice of the Bhṛgu and the Angiras" (*TaiBr* I.1.4).

ii Experienced teachers throw hints to the pupils and leave them to work out the problem by themselves. They never supply them with clear-cut and readymade answers, thereby keeping their spirit of enquiry kindled. Nevertheless, they are genuinely anxious to guide them systematically and correct possible errors. A great preceptor that Varuṇa was, he indicated the way to the knowledge of *Brahman* by suggesting him to go by logical method and find out the fallacy by himself. Food, vital air and mind, form the substance of the first three sheaths or Selfs. Sight, hearing and speech are here indicative of all the five sense-organs. Together they form the gateways to knowledge. The help of all these was summoned to push Bhṛgu's enquiry into *Brahman*. Sight, hearing and speech stand for *vijñānamaya*, which comes immediately after food, vital airs, and mind, in the order of the categories that Bhṛgu reflected upon as *Brahman* and found inadequate to merit the highest status of *Brahman*.

iii Enunciation, definition and examination are the well-known methods recognized in a rational enquiry into truth. *Brahman* has been enunciated as the Principle to be known through the means of food and the rest. In this passage, a definition of *Brahman* is given in the light of which, the tentative categories are to be examined by the seeker. *Kena Upaniṣad* I.1.4 also states that Principle that lies behind sense of hearing, mind, speech, *prāṇa*, sight is the Principle. These faculties although appear to be indicatory of *Brahman*; they absolutely depend on *Brahman* to function. These sensory organs as well as the material, out of which the subtle and physical body of a person is constituted are to be examined in the light of the definition of *Brahman* given by Varuṇa. The definition states that *Brahman* is that in which the universe has its origin, sustenance and dissolution. Such a definition of *Brahman* is also available in *Śvetāśvatara Upaniṣad* III.2, *Muṇḍaka Upaniṣad* II.2, *Brahmasūtra* I.1.2 and *Bhagavadgītā* VIII.18-19. The various categories suggested cannot square with the definition. The defining clause suggests that the *Brahman* alone is the cause of all, sustains all and in It all beings resolve. Varuṇa here exhorts his son to have an intense longing to know *Brahman*. To get oneself free from the bondage of transmigratory existence, through knowledge of *Brahman*, is the purpose of spiritual life. *Mumukṣā* and *jijñāsā* are but the same urge manifesting as cause and effect. When the will and desire are potent, the means and end will naturally follow.

iv This sentence *sa tapo'tapyata* is repeated five times at the end of five *anuvākas* in which we get the portrayal of Bhṛgu's attempt to rise from the points of error. It is an attempt, which, in other words, synchronizes with his progressive effort to arrive at *Brahman* by applying the definition supplied by his father to categories such as food, life force, sight, sense of hearing, mind and speech. The repetition is meant to serve as a powerful reminder that *tapas* (*vicāra* – enquiry) is the an effective means of knowing *Brahman*.

v Through observation and reasoning Bhṛgu found out that food is perishable, *prāṇa* is inert, mind is changeable, and the intelligence is limited and exposed to pleasure and pain. Hence, none of these can satisfy the definition of *Brahman* given by his father. Therefore, he came to the highest category, *Ānanda*, through enquiry and deep reflection. The term *Ānanda* here does not stand for the sheath (*ānandamaya-kośa*) designated by that name in the previous chapter (Brahmānandavallī), rather it is the *vastu* itself – *Ātmā-Brahman* depicted in *Chāndogya Upaniṣad* VII.23.1 as *Bhūmā – yo vai bhūmā tat sukham*. He who knows this *Ānanda*, which is the *Ātmā*, reaches the Ultimate, and he has nothing more to achieve. The *Ānanda* here cannot be a *kośa* because of three reasons:

a. Nothing higher than *Ānanda* mentioned in this context as in the previous ones, where *Brahman* is declared to be the basis.

b. The knowledge of this *Ānanda* is in the mind, called the highest heaven, according to the statement here, and it is only a reassertion of what has been said in the opening passage of the Brahmānandavallī while describing the result of *brahma-vidyā*.

c. It is stated again that *Ānanda* is the culmination of the enquiry and that he, who knows it, stands firmly grounded for he becomes *āptakāma* (perfect).

vi All living beings have food so long as they live, and they eat it too, but by this specific mention, the visible result of this knowledge is eulogized. The *upāsaka* will have plenty of food, a perfectly healthy body, and external and internal wealth.

vii An aspirant of *brahma-vidyā* should never condemn or speak ill of food, for the body built by food is the first gateway to know *Īśvara*. Food deserves from him respect as a *guru*. Manu says:

pūjayed-aśanaṁ nityam-adyāt-ca-etad-akutsayan ।
dṛṣṭvā hṛṣyet prasīdet ca pratinandet ca sarvaśaḥ ॥
– *MaSm* II.54

"Let him worship food daily, and partake of it without reviling it. Let him also feel happy and calm at its sight, and appreciate it in every way." The suggestion is that, the body that is the instrument for knowing *Īśvara*, should not be neglected. Even when one has ascended to the highest rung of knowledge, one should not neglect it willfully. The monk should be satisfied with the food that chance brings, and should never blame it even when it is modest. Every spiritual aspirant should foster this respect for food as a holy observance. As a matter of decorum, one may cease to blame food, but in order to render one's contemplation on food as *Brahman* effective, one has to take a religious vow not to condemn food even in mind.

viii The reciprocal support of *anna* and *prāṇa* is mentioned here for praising the importance of food as the support and the supported. Thereby it is recommended as an object of contemplation, an indirect means of knowing *Brahman*. *Prāṇa* in its cosmic aspect is the energy that manipulates the matter and creates manifold objects. Food or matter is only its expression; and as a cosmic force, *prāṇa* is co-present with matter. Even as a house and its various parts such a roof, wall, and the rest are not independent, so also the body and *prāṇa* are not mutually independent; both are in reality two aspects of food. No one can get the highest knowledge of *Brahman* without the aid of the body and *prāṇa*. Therefore, even the grossest part of our being deserves respect.

ix One should respect food by not rejecting what is offered, and by not casting out what one already has; for food represents the basic stuff of earthly life, and common need of all living beings. Sages consider those who cast into sea or fire large quantities of foodstuff – for economic, commercial, or political reasons – are worst offenders against Nature and *Īśvara*. Smṛti says:

sarveṣām-eva dānānam-annadānaṁ paraṁ smṛtām ।
sarveṣām-eva jantunāṁ yatastad jīvitaṁ param ॥

Sharing food with others is the highest charity, for food is the support of life.

x Food is ultimately produced with water, which pours as rain. So water is identified with food, being its cause. Sun gives rain through vapour produced by heat. Therefore, water and fire are reciprocally dependent. This mutual relation, similar to that of food and its eater, is given to praise food that may be worshipped by looking upon it as *Brahman*.

xi The earth may be looked upon as the food of space, as it is surrounded by the latter. Apparently, the earth is the support of space, which is around it. Therefore, here the reciprocal relation of food and its eater may be assumed. In the three *anuvāka*s (7-9) ending with this one (9th), "food" is conceived in a figurative sense. It is suggested that all the relations given may be thought of as cause and effect, or as the support and the supported. Thus, it is taught that, the complete phenomenal universe, and all its changes and movements can be reduced to some simple concept. Through reflection on this basic fact, the relation of all created things – from *prāṇa* to space, as food and consumer – the aspirant can rise to a higher unity in which this duality will be transcended. That unity is first emphasized by taking "food" in the broadest sense, and in the sequel sublimating it into spirit. To stress the sublimity of this conception of expanding *anna* to *Brahman*, at each step contemplation is formulated and proper results are promised to motivate the seekers.

xii Here is the root of the conception of *Nṛ-yajña* or the ritual duty that is enjoined upon a householder to his fellow beings. *Nṛ-yajña* is one among the five great *yajña*s that a householder has to do. *Śātātapa* says:

priyo yā yadi vā dveṣyaḥ mūrkhaḥ patita eva vā ।
saṁprāpto vaiśvadevānte so 'tithiḥ svarga-saṁkramaḥ ॥

Friend or foe, ignorant or fallen, he who comes just when a householder's daily Vaiśvadeva worship is over, is a guest; and when the guest is properly honoured, will cause the host to go to heaven.

Viṣṇu Purāṇa says:

hiraṇyagarbha-budhyā taṁ manyeta-abhyāgataṁ gṛhī

The householder should look upon the guest as a deity.

Śrīmad Bhāgavatam says:

gṛheṣu yeṣu-atithayo nārcitāḥ salilairapi ।
yadi niryānti te nūnaṁ pheruraja-gṛhopamāḥ ।
– VIII.16.7

When a guest leaves a home without being honoured even with water, that house can certainly be compared to the residence of a sovereign jackal.

Kaṭha Upaniṣad I.1.7-8 also warns against any neglect of hospitality. Therefore, it is laid down among the foremost duties of a householder, even if he were a seeker of *mokṣa*, to gather wealth by using all his power. *Bhagavadgītā* III.13 states that those who prepare food only for filling their stomach, are vile and they eat sin. Therefore, good householders declare that food has been cooked for others, gods, guests, etc.

xiii *Mukhataḥ, madhyataḥ* and *antataḥ* may also be interpreted as the *sāttvika, rājasika* and *tāmasika* mode of giving. This is elaborately explained in *Bhagavadgītā* XVII.20-22. An alternative explanation of the three words is that they denote the three periods of life, namely youth, middle age and old age. The principle underlying the announcement is that the gifts that a man makes return to him in this life itself, or in the next, exactly in the same way as he gives. If a man gives in youth, he gets in his youth. If he is charitable in middle age, he will not be in want in his middle age; gifts given in old age will accrue to the giver in old age.

xiv These *upāsanās* (contemplations) are formulated to help the average aspirant to accustom himself to meditations, which purify the mind. Speech, respiration, movement and nourishment are the fundamental facts of a human being as a living organism. The best use of speech, as well as of thought and knowledge implied by it, is to make it serve one's safety. Therefore, just as in the Vibhūti-Yoga of *Bhagavadgītā,* where certain prominent members or qualities are recommended for special reverence, similarly the aspirant is advised to meditate on *Brahman* as safety and the rest in regard to speech and like. The peculiar human gift of speech should be respectfully used for leading one to expressions of life, and the main purpose of life is progress and security is *yoga* and *kṣema*. The progress and security which aspirants seek should be centred on *Brahman*; that is to say, they should be made an occasion to remember *Īśvara* constantly.

Movement of hands and feet indicate life, and the presence of *Īśvara* makes life possible. Therefore, all movement of limbs should be thought of as inspired by *Īśvara* within. Evacuation is the completion of nourishment. The body that is the vehicle of life is sustained by food that is assimilated, so this process is here recommended to be taken as an indication to reflect on *Brahman* whose power underlies it. The satisfaction that people feel when abundant food is brought about by abundant rain should be meditated upon as coming from *Brahman*. The wonder caused by violent flashes of lightning and twinkling of the stars also are to be understood as the manifestation *Brahman* and are to be meditated as *Brahman*. The prosperity and prowess that the ancients possessed consisted of cattle. They too are *vibhūti* of *Brahman*. Even the function of the generative organ should be considered as a symbol for continuation of *dharma*; the race is perpetuated through procreation; through children, a person pays off his debt to his ancestors, and thereby he enables himself to attain relative immortality. Again, an aspirant is advised to meditate on *Brahman* under various attributes such as support, greatness, mind, reverence, Veda and destructive power. Whenever, one thinks of *Brahman*, one does so under some attribute or other. Here specific attributes are given for meditation. It is a general principle of *upāsanā* that, in whatever form under whichever attribute a person may worship *Brahman*, he becomes the possessor of such attributes and powers. However, if the meditation has no special desire behind it, the result will be spiritual elevation and mental purity.

xv The truth in the person and in the sun is identified here, because the Self of the knower is all. This passage *sa yaścāyaṁ puruṣe* । *yaścāsāvāditye* । *sa ekaḥ* । (10th *anuvāka*) and part of what follows is repeated from eighth *anuvākā* of Brahmānandavallī: *sa yaścāyaṁ puruṣe* । *yaścāsāvāditye* । *sa ekaḥ* ।

xvi This describes the state of one who has known *Brahman*, one gets all enjoyments and all forms at one's will; because one who knows becomes *Saccidānanda* and in that capacity enjoys all existences together. He is the truth in all. Being one with *Īśvara*, all forms and enjoyments that *Īśvara* has, becomes his. He traverses all worlds because he is omnipresent. Singing *sāma* therefore denotes proclaiming for the benefit of the world the unity of the Self with *Īśvara*. The passage also is interpreted as describing the behaviour of *jīvan-mukta* who eats dresses and moves at will, without being bound by any rule.

xvii The original passage is a Vedic stanza set to *sāma* tune. This accounts for the prolation of some vowels, interposition of additional letters, and interjections suitable to the mode of singing. The whole song is a transcription of the mystic experience of a sage who has known *Brahman*. It is his unspeakable wonder that although, he is the consciousness, he has become the material universe with its dualities. The repetition of each clause expresses the boundless joy and wonder that is experienced. The liberated *jīva* knows that he is one with Hiraṇyagarbha, who existed even before the gods and the universe, and that he is the source of immortality. He also becomes conscious that the whole universe as *anna* represents the Infinite's manifestation, and therefore he who gives food to the deserving helps the cosmic order. And he thereby chooses Grace; whereas he who does not give food to the needy and accumulates it for himself, becomes the prey of the destructive power of "food". In reality, food also is *Ātmā*; this is stressed by repeating thrice, "I am food". The experiencer of this transcendent Unity knows that he is the food as well as the eater, the Conscious Principle that forms the link between the two, and the Immortal that finally assimilates the entire universe, perceived as a duality before knowledge into himself, and remains as the ever self-luminous Light of Intelligence. This miraculous experience is again given here to disclose that whoever aspires to attain this goal shall have to perform *tapas* (enquiry) repeatedly like Bhṛgu, and then only he become the possessor of *Ānanda* of *Brahman*.

Gratitude: My acknowledgement and profuse gratitude to Swami Swahanada's *Taittirīyopaniṣad*, whose explanations I have used as Endnotes in this *vallī*. – Author

8

Vision of Advaita Vedānta in Taittirīya Upaniṣad

Vision of Advaita Vedānta

ESTABLISHING *Brahman* is the main subject matter of Vedānta; there are no two opinions about this. This becomes clear from the first *sūtra* of *Brahmasūtra – athāto brahma-jijñāsā*, and the second *sūtra – janmādyasya yataḥ*. However, there is dispute amongst the various philosophers with reference to the relationship between the *jīva* and *Brahman*. While Śaṅkara establishes the unity of the *jīva* and *Brahman*, the Dvaitin Madhvācārya considers the *jīva* and *Brahman* as two separate entities. Rāmānuja's Viśiṣṭādvaita considers the relationship between the *jīva* and *Brahman* as part and the whole. That is why Śaṅkara's presentation is known as Advaitavāda.

Besides this, there is considerable dispute between the *bhāṣyakāras* as to, whether *Brahman* is *saguṇa* or *nirguṇa*. While Śaṅkara established that *Brahman* is *nirguṇa*, Rāmānuja presents *Brahman* as *saguṇa*. Further, depending on the reality of the creation as described in the Upaniṣads, both *Sa-prapañca-Brahman* and *Niṣ-prapañca-Brahman* are mentioned in the Upaniṣads. Some Upaniṣads present *Brahman* as the creator of *jagat* and the created *jagat* as real. Elsewhere[1] *Brahman* as the only reality and this *jagat* is established as unreal. In the Śāṇḍilyavidyā section[2]

---

1 *vācārambhanaṁ vikāro nāmadheyaṁ mṛttiketyeva satyam* । – *ChāUp* VI.1.4

2 *sarvaṁ khalvidaṁ brahma, taj-jalān-iti* । – *ChāUp* III.14.1

of *Chāndogya Upaniṣad, Brahman* has been described as *tajjalān* as the creator, sustainer and dissolver of this creation. This is to be understood as the description of *Sa-prapañca-Brahman*. *Bṛhadāraṇyaka Upaniṣad* mentions *Niṣ-prapañca-Brahman*. Yājñavalkya explained *Niṣ-prapañca-Brahman* as *neti neti.*[3] As per the *niṣ-prapañca* view, *jagat* is not a reality, hence much less the *jagat* is *māyā* and *Brahman* is the creator. The same *niṣ-prapañca* concept of *Brahman* is endorsed in the *Bṛhadāraṇyaka Upaniṣad*[4] and *Kaṭha Upaniṣad*[5] as – *neha nānāsti kiñcana*. Thus, the views of Śaṅkara and Rāmāṇuja vary on these Upaniṣadic statements. Ācārya Śaṅkara has followed the *niṣ-prapañca* statements of the Upaniṣads and written his *bhāṣya*s. Based on the views of the Upaniṣads, *Bhagavadgītā* and *Brahmasūtra*, many philosophical contentions have evolved. Amongst all these, Śaṅkara's Advaita Vedānta vision stands tall.

The Advaita Vedānta Philosophy

Advaita philosophy means mainly Śaṅkara Bhagavatpāda's presentation of the Vedāntic vision. However, it must be remembered that this vision was established by previous *ācārya*s much before his arrival. The tradition of Advaita Vedānta is indeed ancient.

Therefore, the names of many *ācārya*s are mentioned in the tradition. By the following *śloka* the students of Advaita Vedānta express their devotion and respect to the *ācārya-paramparā*:

nārāyaṇaṁ padmabhuvaṁ vasiṣṭhaṁ,
śaktiṁ ca tat putra parāśaraṁ ca ।
vyāsaṁ śukaṁ gauḍapadaṁ mahāntaṁ,
govinda yogīndram-athāsya śiṣyam ॥

3 *BṛUp* II.3.6, IV.4.22, IV.5.15.

4 *manasā-eva-anudṛṣṭavyaṁ, neha nānāsti kiñcana* ।
mṛtyoḥ sa mṛtyum-āpnoti, ya iha nāneva paśyati ॥ – *BṛUp* IV.4.19

5 *manasā eva idam aptavyaṁ, neha nānāsti kiñcan* ।
mṛtyoḥ sa mṛtyuṁ gacchati, ya iha nāneva paśyati ॥ – *KaUp* II.1.11

śrī-śaṅkarācāryam-athāsya padmapādaṁ,
ca hastāmalakaṁ ca śiṣyam ।
taṁ toṭakaṁ vārtikakāram anyān,
asmad gurūn santatamānato 'smi ॥

Lord Nārāyaṇa is remembered as the first propounder of Advaita philosophy. From Nārāyaṇa comes Padmabhuva, followed by Vasiṣṭha, then Vasiṣṭha's son Śakti, followed by Śakti's son Parāśara, then his son Vyāsa, followed by his son Śuka, then Gauḍapāda, and then his disciple Govindapāda. These *ācārya*s are accepted as pre-Śaṅkara *ācārya*s of Advaita philosophy. Ācārya Śaṅkara is famous as the disciple of Govinda Bhagavatpāda. Amongst the disciples of Śaṅkara Bhagavatpāda, four are noteworthy – Padmapādācārya, Sureśvarācārya, Toṭakācārya and Hastāmalakācārya.

In the above *śloka*, the names of the *ācārya*s beginning from Nārāyaṇa to Śuka are Purāṇic and based on tradition, and no text authored by any one of them on Advaita Vedānta philosophy is available to us.

The earliest text on Advaita Vedānta philosophy available to us is *Māṇḍūkya-Kārikā* authored by Gauḍapāda. In fact, Gauḍapāda receives the distinction of the only pre-Śaṅkara *ācārya* of Advaita Vedānta, and his *Māṇḍūkya-Kārikā* became the foundation stone of the Advaitic philosophy of Śaṅkara. Gauḍapāda was the *guru* of Govindapāda, who was Śaṅkara's *guru*. No text authored by Govindapāda is available with us. Therefore, to study pre-Śaṅkara Advaita philosophy, *Māṇḍūkya-Kārikā* of Gauḍapāda becomes an invaluable text.

The philosophy of Ācārya Śaṅkara has been briefed in the following *śloka* attributed to him:

ślokārdhena pravakṣyāmi yad-uktaṁ granthakoṭibhiḥ ।
brahma satyaṁ jagan-mithyā jīvo brahmaiva nāparaḥ ॥

> In half of a *śloka* I state what has been stated by crores of texts; that is, *Brahman* alone is real and this *jagat* is *mithyā*, and the *jīva* is non-different from *Brahman*.

From this statement, the Advaita philosophy can be divided into three distinct areas of analysis – (i) *Brahman* is Real, (ii) *jagat* is *mithyā*, and (iii) relationship between the *jīva* and *Brahman*. We try below to analyse the above.

Brahman Alone Is Real

As per Śaṅkara's interpretation of the Vedānta-Śāstra, *Brahman* is the only reality – *satyam*. The word *Brahman* is derived from the Sanskrit root √*bṛhi*, meaning *vṛddhau*, meaning growing, and the suffix *man*, added to it, signifies an absence of limitation (in expanse). So, *Brahman* derivatively means, that which is limitlessly big. One has to understand that, the root meaning of the word *Brahman* indicates its *nitya-śuddha-buddha-mukta-satya-svabhāva* and its *sarvajñatvam* and *sarva-śaktimattvam*.[6] This *Brahman* is the intelligent and material cause of the *jagat*'s origin, existence and dissolution.

In explaining the meaning of the *sūtra* – *janmādyasya yataḥ* (*BrSū* I.1.2), Śaṅkara says, from that omniscient omnipotent cause has come this *jagat*, comprising various names and forms, various doers and enjoyers, dependent on specific time and space and result of their actions, of incomprehensible varied forms and is sustained and dissolved by Him. One has to remember here that, as per Śaṅkara, *Brahman* is represented from two points of view: (i) One is *vyāvahārika* (empirical) point of view, and (ii) the other is *pāramārthika* (absolute) point of view. From the *vyāvahārika* point of view, *Brahman* is regarded as the cause of this *jagat*'s origin, existence and dissolution, because this *jagat* indeed has

---

6 *asti tāvad brahma nitya-śuddha-buddha-mukta-svabhāvaṁ, sarvajñaṁ-śarva-śaktisamanviaṁ* । *brahma-śabdasya hi vyutpādamānasya nitya-suddhatvādayo 'rthāḥ pratiyante, bṛhater-dhātor-arthānugamāt* ।
– *BSSB* I.1.1.1

an empirical reality. However, from absolute point of view, since this *jagat* is *asat* or *mithyā*, the question of its origin, existence and dissolution does not arise, much less *Brahman* being its cause. Again, from *vyāvahārika* point of view, *Brahman* is *sarvajña*, *sarva-śaktimān*, of varied attributes and of *nitya-śuddha-buddha-mukta-svabhāva*. As per Śaṅkara, this description belongs to *Saguṇa-Brahman* or *Īśvara*. One can worship and meditate upon this *Īśvara*.[7] However, *Saguṇa-Brahman* has only a *vyāvahārika* reality. From *pāramārthika* point of view, one has to understand that *Brahman* is neither the cause of *jagat*, nor is omniscient or omnipotent. The origin of *jagat* is not the intrinsic feature (*svarūpa-lakṣaṇa*) of *Brahman*. This phenomenon is his incidental feature (*taṭastha-lakṣaṇa*). Therefore, from absolute point of view, *Brahman* is not the creator, sustainer or dissolver of this *jagat*. He is devoid of any form or attribute. From absolute point of view, *Brahman* is *Satyam-Jñānam-Anantam*.[8] This is the essential feature (*svarūpa-lakṣaṇa*) of *Brahman*.

Brahman does not have any kind of difference. Differences are of three kinds: (i) difference of one member of the same class (*sajātīya*), (ii) difference from another class (*vijātīya*), and (iii) internal differentiation (*svagata*). *Brahman* is free from any of these three differences – *sajātīya, vijātīya* or *svagata bheda*.[9] This undifferentiated *Brahman* without any kind of distinction is the only *Satyam* (Reality) and except Him, everything else is to be understood as *asat* (*vyāvahārika, prātibhāṣika* or *tuccham*) – unreal. However, one has to understand here that, although *Brahman* is devoid of any attribute, He is not *śūnya* (void).[10]

---

7 *paraṁ cet jñātavyam, aparaṁ cet prāptavyam* । – *KUSB* I.2.16

8 *TaiUp* II.1.

9 *tathā sadvastuno bhedatrayaṁ prāptaṁ nivāryate* । – *Pañ* II.22

10 *yat-tad-adreśyam-agrāhyam-agotram-avarṇam-acakṣuḥ-śrotraṁ tad-apāṇipādam* । *nityaṁ vibhuṁ sarvagataṁ susūkṣmaṁ tad-avyayaṁ yadbhūtayoniṁ pari-paśyanti dhirāḥ* ॥ – *MuṇUp* I.1.6
Here the term *nityam* negates any concept of *Brahman* being *śūnyam*.

Otherwise one can be caught by the Buddhist understanding. As per Śaṅkara, people of less intellect consider *Brahman* as *śūnya*. It is not possible for *bhāva* – something to come out of *abhāva* or *śūnya* (nothing). Therefore, one has to notice that Śaṅkara's establishment of an attributeless *Brahman* completely swallows Buddhist theory of *śūnyavāda*.

Doctrine of Jagat Being Mithyā

Śaṅkara has established the reality of this *jagat* as *mithyā*. However, by *mithyā* here, one is not to understand the reality of *jagat* as that of the reality of *vandhyā-putra* or *śaśa-śṛṅga*. Here, what is *mithyā* as per Śaṅkara needs to be made clear. That this *jagat* is not non-existent like the *vandhyā-putra* or *śaśa-śṛṅga* is clear from the fact that *jagat* is evident to us. However, this *jagat* is not *pāramārthika* or absolute real like *Ātmā* or *Brahman*, because it is subject to time, subject to change and can be negated, therefore *asat* (here *asat* means *vyāvahārika* reality). So *jagat* is not *sat* like *Brahman-Ātmā*, nor *asat* (here *asat* means *tuccham* – absolute non-existent) like the *vandhyā-putra*. Therefore, it is *anirvacanīya*, i.e. neither *sat* nor *asat*. This is what is meant by his – *jagat mithyā*. After this explanation, it becomes imperative to explain the Māyāvāda falsely attributed to Śaṅkara. That this *jagat* is because of *māyā* or *avidyā* has been presented in many places of his *bhāṣyam*. Śaṅkara is accused of being a Māyāvādī philosopher by others, has been criticized. Now let us discuss what is the essence of Śaṅkara's doctrine of *māyā*.

Doctrine of Māyā before Śaṅkara

According to Śaṅkara, this *jagat* is a creation of *māyā*. In the Vedas and Upaniṣads, the use of the word *māyā* is seen in many places. Generally, it has been used as mysterious power. The earliest reference to the word *māyā* is found in *Ṛgveda*, in the *mantra* – *indro māyābhiḥ pururūpa iyate*.[11] The *mantra* means – One

---

[11] *ṚVS* VI.47.18.

Indra appears as many, because of the power of *māyā*. Another Ṛgvedic *mantra* says:

> 'O! Mitra Varuṇa! Your power of *māyā* is residing in the space. By this power of *māyā*, the bright sun moves with its colourful rays. You cover the sun by the clouds and the rains, thereby sweetly drenching the earth with the rains. All this happens because of your power of *māyā*.[12]

In *Śvetāśvatara Upaniṣad*, *māyā* is described as *prakṛti*, and *Parameśvara* as *māyin* or *māyāvī*.[13] It further says that *māyā* is the *upādhi* of *Īśvara* and because of *māyā*, *Akṣara Paramātmā* creates this *jagat*.[14] In *Bhagavadgītā* also, in many places *māyā* is mentioned:

> My threefold *māyā* is indeed difficult to perceive. Only those who surrender to me can overcome this *māyā*.[15]

Further:

> Those whose intellect has been stolen by *māyā*, such evil people do not please me.[16]

In *Śrīmad Bhāgavatam*, *māyā*'s power has been accepted as the cause and destroyer of this *jagat*.[17] Thus *māyā* has been referred to in Śruti, Smṛti as well as the Purāṇas. Therefore, the doctrine of *māyā* is very ancient. However, Śaṅkara has given this the distinction of a philosophical doctrine. Therefore, by Māyāvāda,

---

12 *māyā vāṁ mitrāvaruṇā divi śritā sūryo jyotiścarati citramāyudham* ı
tamabhreṇa vṛṣṭyā gūhatho divi parjanya drapsā madhumanta īrate ıı
– *ṚVS* V.63.4

13 *māyāṁ tu prakṛtiṁ vidyāt, māyinaṁ tu maheśvaraṁ* ı – *ŚvUp* IV.10

14 *asmān māyī sṛjate viśvam-etat, tasminścānyo māyayā sanniruddhaḥ* ı
– Ibid. IV.9

15 *daivī hyeṣā guṇamayī mama māyā duratyayā* ı
mameva ye prapadyante māyām etāṁ taranti te ıı – *BhGī* VII.14

16 *na māṁ duṣkṛtino mūḍhāḥ prapadyante narādhamāḥ* ı
māyayāpahṛtajñānā āsuraṁ bhāvamāśritāḥ ıı – Ibid. 7.15

17 *eṣā māyā bhagavataḥ sargasthityantakāriṇī* – *BhāPu* XI.3.16

generally Śaṅkara's philosophy is understood. Let us now analyse Śaṅkara's doctrine of Māyā.

The notion of *māyā* is understood as the principle that shows the *Niṣ-prapañca-Brahman* as *Sa-prapañca*. The doctrine of *māyā* was not unknown to the Upaniṣads. It is already there, but naturally, it does not yet exhibit all the various features which, because of later elaboration and development, are associated with it in Śaṅkara's Advaita. It is true that the word *māyā* occurs rarely in the earlier Upaniṣads (than *Śvetāśvatara*); but it is found in literature considered older, though its meaning there may not be always be clearly determinable, and also in the Upaniṣads which are not very late.[18] Even in the earlier Upaniṣads where we do not find *māyā*, we have its equivalent *avidyā*.[19-20] There also statements in them such as – "where there is duality as it were (*iva*) one sees another"[21] – which clearly point out to the existence of idea in the Upaniṣads that the duality is unreal.

Śaṅkara's Māyāvāda

By *māyā*, Ācārya Śaṅkara means the power of *Parameśvara*.[22] Its other name is *avyakta*. Elsewhere, Śaṅkara has mentioned this as *avidyā*. Because of this *māyāśakti*, *jagat* is created. It is erroneous to contend that by referring both *Brahman* and *māyā* as two parallel realities, Śaṅkara's doctrine of Advaita is negated. Just as the burning power of fire is non-separable from the fire, *māyā* is not a parallel reality apart from *Brahman*;

---

18 *māyāṁ tu prakṛtiṁ vidyāt, māyinaṁ tu maheśvaraṁ* । – *ŚvUp* IV.10

19 *avidyāyam antare vartamānāḥ svayam dhīrāḥ paṇḍitaṁ manyamānāḥ* ।
dandramyamāṇāḥ pariyanti mūḍhā andhenaiva niyamānā yathā 'ndhāḥ ॥
– *KaUp* I.2.5

20 *avidyāyam antare vartamānāḥ svayam dhīrāḥ paṇḍitaṁ manyamānāḥ* ।
jaṅghanyamānāḥ pariyanti mūḍhā andhenaiva niyamānā yathā 'ndhāḥ ॥
– *MuṇUp* I.2.8

21 *yatra hi dvaitam iva bhavati, tad itara itaraṁ pasyati* । – *BṛUp* IV.5.15

22 *prakṛtim = vaiṣṇavīṁ = māyām = triguṇātmikāṁ* । – *BGSB* IV.6

rather *māyā* is completely dependent on *Brahman* (*brahmāśrayā-māyā*). Thus, by acknowledging the existence of *māyā*, the doctrine of Advaita is not negated. In *Vivekacūḍamaṇi*, Śaṅkara has described her as:

> *Māyā*, through which this world is born, is called *avyakta* (unmanifest), and is the power of the Lord. She is beginningless ignorance, of the nature of three *guṇas*, and superior to her effects. Her existence is to be inferred from her effects, by a person with a clear mind.[23]

Endowed with *māyā*, *Nirguṇa-Brahman* appears as *Saguṇa-Brahman* or *Īśvara*, and this *Īśvara* is the creator of this *jagat*. In the Advaita tradition, *māyā* is defined as *anirvacanīya* – categorically undefinable. It is neither *sat* (absolute real) nor *asat* (here non-existent). One cannot define *māyā* as *sat*, since once one gets to know *Brahman*, *māyā* and its creation ceases to exist (in his understanding) for the knower. For the knower of the truth, *Brahman* alone is Truth. However, although *māyā* is *asat*, it is not non-existent; because non-existent objects like *śaśa-śṛṅga* are not perceivable, whereas *māyā* and its products are objects of perception. Therefore, in Advaitic tradition it is described as *anirvacanīya* – categorically undefinable, this *māyā* is not different from *Brahman*, nor non-different. {Note, here the example of *agni* and its burning power (*guṇa-guṇī-sambandha*) is defeated.} Since *māyā*'s *svarūpa* is *anṛta*, and it being the cause of the *jagat* that is full of grief, it cannot be defined as non-different from *Brahman*. *Māyā* is not different from *Brahman*, just as the pot is not different from clay. If it is defined as different from *Brahman*, the doctrine of Advaita will be negated. And it is not a quality of *Brahman*, because *Brahman* is without any qualities. Again *māyā* cannot be both part of *Brahman* and separate from it at the same time.

---

23 *avyaktanāmī parameśaśaktiḥ, anadyavidyā triguṇātmaikā parā* ।
kāryānumeyā sudhiyaiva māyā, yayā jagat sarvamidaṁ prasūyate ॥
– *ViCū* 110

Therefore, it is *anirvacanīya*.[24] From the absolute (*pāramārthika*) point of view, *māyā* is non-existent, i.e. there is no such thing as *māyā* (just as from the gold's viewpoint there is no chain, or bangle, or ring; from water's point of view, there is no wave or ocean; from clay's point of view, there is no pot). However, as long as one is in the *saṁsāra*, in this empirical world, the effect of *māyā* is evident. Therefore, *māyā* has both the qualities of negation and existence. All the object of this *jagat* is of the nature of *anirvacanīya*. As per Śaṅkara, only that which is always unchangeable and unnegatable, that alone is *sat*, the absolute Reality.[25] Any object of the empirical world is not absolute real, since it is subject to change and subject to time. On the other hand, the objects of the world are not non-existent like *vandhyā-putra*, since a *vandhyā-putra* is not evident, whereas the evidence of the objects of the world is undeniable. Therefore, the objects of the world are neither *sat* nor *asat* (non-existent), they are *anirvacanīya*. Therefore, their cause *māyā* is also *anirvacanīya*.

Doctrine of Māyā Different from Śūnyavāda Buddhism

As per Śaṅkara, prior to knowing the oneness and non-difference between *Brahman* and *Ātmā*, all the empirical transaction whether Vedic or local appears real. *Jagat* is not *śūnya*. Without basing on the absolute, one cannot negate the non-absolute. *Brahman* is the *adhiṣṭhānam* – basis of this *jagat*. Without acknowledging the reality of this basis, to label everything as *śūnya* will negate the basis. And it is imperative to mention, where *jagat* has to be negated. Since *Brahman* is the basis of *jagat*, *jagat* is negated in *Brahman*, just as the pot is negated in the knowledge of the clay. Therefore, as per Śaṅkara's doctrine of *māyā*, even if *jagat* is *asat*, it is not *prātibhāṣika* like the dream nor void.

---

24 *san-nāpi-asannāpi-ubhayātmikā no, bhinnāpi abhinnāpi ubhayātmikā no* ।
sāṅgāpi-anaṅgā hi ubhayātmikā no, mahādbhūtā anirvacanīyarūpā ॥
– *ViCū* 111

25 *yad-viṣayā buddhiḥ na vyabhicarati, tat sat* ।
yad-viṣayā buddhiḥ vyabhicarati, tad-asat । – *BGSB* II.16

Doctrine of Māyā Different from Vijñānavāda Buddhism

Here, one has to remember that, as per Śaṅkara, the objects of the world are not *vijñāna* either. Śaṅkara's doctrine of *māyā* is completely different from Buddhist doctrine of *vijñāna*. Even though *jagat* is *mithyā* from *pāramārthika* point of view, it is not *vijñāna*. Due to the logic of *sahopālambana*, the Vijñanāvādī philosophers (of Yogācāra School) do not accept existence of any external reality. They accept the reality of the *vijñāna* alone. Śaṅkara, in his *Brahmasūtra-Śāṅkara-Bhāṣya* has negated the contention of the Vijñānavādīs by saying:

> One has to accept the existence of objects like the pot, cloth. We have the cognition of the external objects. The knowledge and the object of knowledge cannot be one and non-separable.

As per Śaṅkara, knowledge is *vastu-tantra*. Generally, there is no knowledge without the object of knowledge. Besides, the Vijñānavādī Buddhists consider *jagat* as non-existent, treat the experience of the waking world similar to the experience of the dream world, and consider *vijñāna* as the cause of the experience of the dream world as well as the waking world. However here, while explaining the *sūtra – vaidharmāt ca na svapnādivat*[26] of *Brahmasūtra*, Śaṅkara has clearly negated the contentions of the Vijñānavādī Buddhists. He states, the difference between the waking experience and dream experience is very clear. The dream state is negated by the waking state, but the waking state is not negated as such. Waking state can be negated only from the *pāramārthika* point of view. Even from the absolute point of view it may be *asat* (unreal), but has *vyāvahārika* (empirical) reality, whereas the dream state reality has only *prātibhāṣika* reality – "You see, therefore it is". If the external object is not there, one cannot say that the internal *vijñāna* is reflected as the external object. It is not possible to accept a Viṣṇumitra as a *vandhyā-putra*.

---

26 *BrSū* II.2.29.

Therefore, external objects are not *vijñāna*. Thus, while Śaṅkara accepts the empirical reality of *jagat*, he does not confer on it any *pāramārthikattvam* – absolute reality. In the field of empiricality, Śaṅkara is a Vastu-svātantrya-vādī (a realist). From *pāramārthikattvam* (absolute viewpoint) he is Advaitātmā-vādī, since he accepts the reality of *Brahman-Ātmā*.

Māyā of Śaṅkara Is not the Same as of Sāṁkhya's

Although Śaṅkara has defined *māyā* as *avyakta* in many[27] places, it is not the same *avyakta* or *prakṛti* as per Sāṁkhya. Because, in Sāṁkhya philosophy *prakṛti* is *satyam*, whereas in Śaṅkara's Advaita, *māyā* is *asat* or *mithyā*. As per Sāṁkhya, *prakṛti* has a special existence. However, as per Śaṅkara, *māyā* has no independent existence other than *Brahman*. Only because of our *ajñānam*, we consider *Īśvara*'s *māyāśakti* as *satyam* and *jagat* that is projected because of that *mayāśakti* as *satyam* (real). But when knowledge dawns, one gets to know the non-dual *Brahman*, and that (i) *Īśvarattvam*, (ii) His *māyāśakti*, and (iii) the projected *nāma-rūpa-jagat* because of that *māyāśakti*, is not real. Therefore, the difference between Śaṅkara's *māyā* and the *prakṛti* of Sāṁkhya is clear.

Another evidence of Śaṅkara treating *māyā* as the cause of error is seen in his *Kaṭhopaniṣad-Bhāṣyam*:

> *aho atigambhīrā duravagāhyā vicitrā māyā ca iyaṁ, yad ayaṁ sarvo jantuḥ paramārthataḥ paramārthasatatvo 'pi evaṁ bodhyamāno 'ham paramātmeti na gṛhṇāti* ।[28]

It becomes clear that the perception of *jagat* is in fact the perception of *ajñāna* or *avidyā* or *māyā*. The only truth is *Brahman*. Even if *jagat* enjoys an empirical reality, it is unreal from absolute viewpoint.

---

27 *avyaktanāmnī parameśaśaktir-anādi-avidyā triguṇātmikā parā* ।
kāryānumeyā sudhiyaiva māyā yayā jagat-sarvam idaṁ prasūyate ॥
– *ViCū* 110

28 *KUSB* I.3.12.

It now becomes necessary to explain three orders of reality as per Śaṅkara.

The Three Orders of Reality

Śaṅkara has used the three orders of reality in his explanation of Advaita-Vedānta: (i) *prātibhāṣika,* (ii) *vyāvahārika,* and (iii) *pāramārthika.* The appearance of the snake on the rope, or the objects seen in the dream state, which is negated in waking state belongs to *prātibhāṣika* (subjective) reality. Before knowledge of *Brahman-Ātmā,* whatever appears as real and wherein transaction is possible, is *vyāvahārika* (objective) reality. And *Nirguṇa-Brahman* or *Ātmā* that can never be negated is *pāramārthika* (absolute) reality (Table 8.1).

The Orders of Reality[29]

It may be noted here that the philosophy of the Mahāyāna Buddhism accepts two orders of reality. Nāgārjuna (CE 150–250) the founder of Śūnyavādī Mādhyamika School has accepted (i) *saṁvṛtti*[30] *satyam,* and (ii) *pāramārthika satyam.* As per Nāgārjuna, the *saṁsāra* is *saṁvṛtti satyam* and *nirvāṇa* is *pāramārthika satyam.*

The philosophy of Mahāyāna Yogācāra Buddhists (fourth century CE) – the Vijñānavādīs – describes three orders of reality: (i) *parikalpita,* (ii) *paratantra,* and (iii) *pariniṣpanna* that can be compared to Śaṅkara's (i) *prātibhāsika,* (ii) *vyāvāharika,* and (iii) *pāramārthika* realities respectively. As per Śaṅkara, *jagat* has some kind of reality that is neither *prātībhāsika,* nor *pāramārthika.*

---

[29] Personally I would like to believe that Śaṅkara's model of three orders of reality is a development of thought, and is better to understand the reality of this empirical *jagat.* The hunger that we experience and the food that we eat belong to the same order of reality. Diabetes and insulin also belong to the same order of reality, i.e. *vyāvahārika.*

[30] *Saṁvṛtti* is a Buddhist term used in the sense of *māyā* in Buddhist philosophy.

Table 8.1: Śaṅkara's Three Order of Reality

School of Thought	*Subjective Reality**	*Objective Reality†*	*Absolute Reality*
Śūnyavādī Mādhyamika School of Nāgārjuna (CE 150–250)	*Saṁvṛtti satyam* (*saṁsāra*)		*Pāramārthika satyam* (*nirvāṇa*)
Vijñānavādī Yogācāra School of Āryasaṅgha	*Parikalpita* (imaginary)	*Paratantra* (externally valid, dependent)	*Pariniṣpanna* (perfect knowledge said to be possessed by the Buddha
Śaṅkara (CE 788–820)	*Prātibhāsika* (ontologically *mithyā*, e.g. dream)	*Vyāvāharika* (ontologically *mithyā*, e.g. this world and all our transactions)	*Pāramārthika* (ontologically *satyam*, the only e.g. *Brahman-Ātmā*)

* You see, therefore it is.

† It is, therefore you see.

Therefore, while trying to understand the *mithyātvam* of *jagat* as per Śaṅkara, one should not lose sight of this *vyāvahārika* reality. That this *jagat* is not real is the purport of Śaṅkara's doctrine of *jagat-mithyā*.

Various Theories about the Reality of Jagat

To explain the existence of *jagat*, various schools propounded different theories. The famous theories are Asatkāryavāda and Satkāryavāda.

1. **Asatkāryavāda**, or theory of non-pre-existent effect, or the theory of origination, is held by the Vaiśeṣika School. It posits that the cause is one thing, the effect is another. Kaṇāda, propounder of Vaiśeṣika School, is an Asatkāryavādī. Vaiśeṣikas hold that a *kārya* does not exist before its creation. The effect is held to be non-existent before its production by the cause. Effect comes into being on the destruction of cause. The non-existent pot is created, and it stands alone, independently real.
2. **Satkāryavāda or Pariṇāmavāda**,[31] or the theory of transformation states that the effect exists in a latent state in the cause prior to its manifestation, i.e. the cause is continually transforming itself into effects. This theory again has two divisions:
   (a) *Prakṛti-pariṇāma-vāda* – held by Sāṁkhya School posits that the *jagat* is the transformation of *prakṛti*.
   (b) *Brahma-pariṇāma-vāda* – held by the Viśiṣṭādvaita School posits that *jagat* is the transformation of *Brahman*.

In view of the above, Śaṅkara's theory can be rightly called as Satkāraṇavāda. As per Śaṅkara, this *jagat* is the *vivarta* of

---

31 Śaṅkara's primary objective is to establish the Vivartavāda as against the Pariṇāmavāda of certain commentators on the *Brahmasūtra*, especially Bhartṛprapañca who preceded him.

Brahman, and not *pariṇāma* of *Brahman*. This is worth noting and mentioning here that, as per Rāmānuja (propounder of Viśiṣṭādvaita School), *jagat* is *pariṇāma* of *Brahman*. Here it becomes imperative to know the difference. As per Pariṇāmavāda – both the cause and effect are *sat*, and the cause becomes the effect. As per Vivartavāda – the effect is not real; the cause appears as the effect. This can be explained thus – when a nacre is mistaken for silver, it has not become silver; it is only a perception. Similarly,[32] Śaṅkara says, *Brahman* does not become this *jagat*, *Brahman* appears as this *jagat*, due to the power of *māyā*. The cause alone is real, and the effect is its *vivarta*. It may be mentioned here that the origin of this Vivartavāda is in the statement of *Chāndogya Upaniṣad*: *vācārambhaṇaṁ vikāro nāmadheyaṁ, mṛttiketyeva satyam*,[33] and not created/coined by Śaṅkara. In such an explanation of this *jagat* being a *vivarta* of *Brahman*, Advaita Vedānta is: (i) different from Nyāya that says – before the origin the effect is *asat*, and (ii) different from Sāṁkhya that says – before the origin the effect is *sat*. As per Advaita Vedānta, the effect is *anirvacanīya*. The cause alone is *sat* (absolute real), from which originates the *anirvacanīya* effect. *Vivarta* is the technical jargon for this *anirvacanīya* effect. In *Vedānta Paribhāṣā* of Dharmaraja Adhvarindra (seventeenth century), the difference between Pariṇāmavāda and Vivartavāda is given as:

> *pariṇāmo nāma upādāna samasattāka-kāryāpattiḥ* । *vivarto nāma upādāna-viṣama-sattāka-kāryāpattiḥ* ।[34]

> The effect that enjoys same order of reality is *pariṇāma*, and the effect that enjoys different order of reality is *vivarta*.

---

32 The example however does not belong to the same order of reality. In case of nacre appearing as silver is *prātibhāsika* reality, whereas, the *Brahman* appearing as the *jagat* is a *vyāvahārika* reality.

33 *ChāUp* VI.14.

34 *VePa*, Pratyakṣa Pariccheda, p. 83.

A simpler definition of *pariṇāma* (intrinsic change) is, *sva-svarūpa parityāgena rūpāntara āpattiḥ pariṇatiḥ* – as in the case of milk turning curd. Conversely, the definition of *vivarta* is, *sva-svarūpa aparityāgena rūpāntara āpattiḥ, vivarta iti* – as when a rope is mistaken for snake, or nacre for silver. Now *Brahman* and *jagat* belong to two different orders of reality. Whereas *Brahman* is *sat* (absolute real), *jagat* is *anirvacanīya*, being completely dependent on *Brahman*. Sadānanda Yogīndra Saraswatī (mid-fifteenth century) has said in his *Vedāntasāra*:

> *Vikāra* is the actual modification of a thing altering into another substance, whereas *vivarta* is only an apparent modification that really is not.[35]

Various Khyātis in Indian Philosophical Tradition

Khyāti means "error" or "erroneous knowledge". There are some theories of error (*khyāti*), which make different ontological assumptions with regard to the nature of the real and the unreal, and their interrelation.

There are mainly three types of theory of error in Indian philosophy:

1. *Sat-khyāti* – Theories where the object of error is real. Under this are *ātmakhyāti* (of Vijñānavādin Yogācāra Buddhists), *anyathā-khyāti* (of Nyāya), *akhyāti* (of Sāṁkhya and Prābhākara-Mīmāṁsā Schools), *viparīta-khyāti* (of Bhāṭṭa-Mīmāṁsā School) and *sat-khyāti* (of Viśiṣṭādvaita of Rāmānuja).

2. *Asat-khyāti* – Theories where the object of error is unreal. Under this are *asatkhyāti* (of Śūnyavādin Mādhyamika Buddhists) and *abhinava-anyathā-khyāti* (of Dvaita of Madhva).

---

35 *satattvataḥ-anyathāprathā vikāra ityudīritaḥ* ।
atattvataḥ-anyathāprathā vivarta ityudīritaḥ ॥ – *VeSā* 138, p. 81

3. *Anirvacanīya-khyāti* – Theory where the object of error is neither real nor unreal (of Advaita Vedānta).

Sat-khyāti

1. *Ātma-khyāti*

Ātma-khyāti or theory of apprehension of the subjective cognition. This is the theory of error held by the Kṣaṇika-Vijñānavādins (idealistic) of Yogācāra Buddhist School. As per this, the error is mistaking what is internal to be external. All determinate cognitions of objects are erroneous, as there are no external objects at all. What exists is only cognition, idea. The object of error is real, but not existing outside in space. It is real as a modification of the mind. The "this" of the externally perceivable rope is superimposed on the mentally present snake to form the erroneous judgement – "this is a snake". Their psychological explanation is this: it may so happen that owing to the past impression inhering in consciousness, there may be a simultaneous flow of the consciousness of the external "this" and internal "snake", in which case the two get mixed up.

2. *Anyathā-khyāti*

Anyathā-khyāti or theory of mis-apprehension. This theory of error is propounded by the Nyāya School. All error is knowing one thing for the other. The object of error exists, but not in the place where it is perceived. This School maintains that the object, apprehended or perceived, exists elsewhere, and recollection of the object produces the perception of the object, in contact with the visual organ. We have first a vague awareness of "this" with regard to the rope in front. Since the mind is not satisfied with "this" alone; it craves for a distinct perception. However, some defect in (i) the cognizer, (ii) his instruments of perception, or (iii) the environment debars this, at the same time that the similarity of the rope and the snake calls up the memory of the latter. This memory conjures up the visual perception of the snake, and so the "this" is apprehended as – "this is a snake".

Errors consist in wrongly synthesizing the "this" with the object (this is a snake) of error.

In *ātma-khyāti* and *anyathā-khyāti*, the idea of the object, reproduced in memory by association, produces the visual perception or cognition of the object. The Akhyāti-vādins do not accept this theory of the Anyathākhyāti-vādins; because they say that there remains a great difference between recollection (*smṛti*) and perception (*pratyakṣa*).

3. *Akhyāti*

Akhyāti, the theory of non-apprehension is held by the Sāṁkhya and Prābhākara-Mīmāṁsā Schools. The theory is named *akhyāti* because of the emphasis on non-apprehension as the chief element of errors. As per this, there is no such thing as erroneous knowledge, and all knowledge must be recognized as valid. In case of a so-called error, we do not really have a single cognition, but two, though we err by failing to recognize the difference between the two. The rope–snake experience consists of two cognitions: (i) one being the nature of memory (*smṛti*), and (ii) the other of the nature of "perception" (*anubhava*). For example, when an individual mistakes a rope for a snake, and makes a judgement that "this is a snake", the error lies in the non-apprehension of the non-relation between the perceived "this" (rope) and the remembered (*smṛti*) snake. There is no error in respect of the object that is seen, or in respect of the snake remembered. The error is in one's failure to realize that they are non-related as subject "this" and predicate "snake". Thus, error is due to non-perception of the difference, or non-relation.

According to Mīmāṁsaka Prabhākara Miśra (eighth century CE), knowledge can never contradict its logical nature and there is consequently no error. We simply overlook that there are two *jñānas*. Consequently, we fail to notice the separateness of their respective objects. It is a kind of non-observation. However, mere failure to know will not suffice to explain an error. Otherwise, error would occur in dreamless sleep that is also characterized by the absence of knowledge. An error according to Prabhākara is a partial or incomplete knowledge. There are two factors necessary to cause an error: positive and negative – (i) the partial knowledge of things presented, and (ii) the failure to note the distinction between them. Prabhākara takes up a different standpoint to explain error, since unlike his *guru* Kumārila Bhaṭṭa (eighth century CE), he cannot do so from a purely logical point of view. He regards all knowledge as a means to an end.

4. *Viparīta-khyāti*

Viparīta-khyāti, the theory of error propounded by the Bhāṭṭa-Mīmāṁsā School, which maintains that error arises when an object appears otherwise than what it is. The object of error is held to be real, and it is the identity of its appearance with its basis that is unreal. According to this School, error is not "a unit of knowledge, but a composite of two *jñāna*s". When we wrongly perceive a snake in place of a rope, what really happens is, we perceive "this" and also certain features of the snake which it possesses in common with a rope. The knowledge of those common features recalls to our mind, the impression of an experience, i.e. our past recollection of a snake. Perception is immediately followed by memory. Of these two *jñāna*s, the first is true as far as it goes. However, the second is not found in the given context. The former puts forward a claim to validity; the latter does not.

5. *Sat-khyāti*

Sat-khyāti also known as *yathārtha-khyāti,* theory of apprehension of the real, is held by Rāmānuja (CE 1017–1137) the propounder of Viśiṣṭādvaita. The aim of *sat-khyāti* is to show that *jñānam,* including the so-called error (*khyāti*) never deviates from reality (*sat*). As per this, the object of error (*khyāti*) is real (*sat*), which is qualified. Hence, all that is presented in experience is real. The arising error is explained by *pañcīkaraṇa* (the theory of quintuplication). The error (*mithyā-jñānam*) is unreal, not because it has an unreal object, but because it fails in life. When error is dispelled, the object is not negated, but only activity is arrested. Rāmānuja uses *pañcīkaraṇa*-theory to explain his theory of *sat-khyāti*. Depending upon the doctrine of *pañcīkaraṇa*, Rāmānuja and his followers have asserted that – "everything contains the elements of everything" – *pṛthivyādi-sarva-bhūtānāṁ sarvatra vidyamānatvāt*.

Asat-khyāti

1. *Asat-khyāti*

Asat-khyāti or theory of apprehension of the non-existent (*asat*) is held by of Śūnyavādin (nihilists) Mādhyamika Buddhists School of Nāgārjuna. It posits that the object of error is unreal – *asat* (non-existent), appears on the unreal – *asat* (non-existing) as real. The non-existing silver appears on the non-existing nacre. Error is the cognition of a non-existent (*asat*) object as being existent. There is no substrate whatever for the elusive cognitions and the sublation of these delusions is without limit, e.g. *śuktikā-rajata*.

2. *Abhinava-anyathā-khyāti*

The theory of "apprehension otherwise" is the Dvaita Vedānta theory of error. It is a combination of *asat-khyāti* (of Śūnyavādins) in that, the object of the erroneous cognition is held to be unreal, and of *anyathā-khyāti* (of Nyāya), in that the object of error appears as other than what is. Thus, what is seen in erroneous cognition is unreal, but is seen in a substrate, which is real.

Nani Lal Sen has given an elaborate account of fourteen kinds of theories of error (*khyāti*s) in his book, *A Critique of the Theories of Viparyaya* (1965). He defines and describes (i) *viśeṣa-khyāti*, (ii) *adhiṣṭhāna-khyāti*, (iii) *akhyāti*, (iv) *alaukika-khyāti*, (v) *prasiddhārtha-khyāti*, (vi) *anya-khyāti*, (vii) *sad-asad-khyāti*, (viii) *ātma-khyāti*, (ix) *asat-khyāti*, (x) *sat-khyāti*, (xi) *viveka-khyāti*,

(xii) *anyathā-khyāti*, (xiii) *anirvacanīya-khyāti*, and (xiv) *acintya-khyāti*.[36] However, it seems that these fourteen theories of *viparyaya* may be reduced to three main *khyātis* – *sat-khyāti*, *asat-khyāti* and *anirvacanīya-khyāti*.

Anirvacanīya-khyāti

To discuss *anirvacanīya-khyāti*, we will travel a little farther in time, to Maṇḍana Miśra, a predecessor or contemporary of Śaṅkara. One of the concepts – for its development, Maṇḍana's testimony is most important – is that of *anirvacanīya*, the inexpressibility of *māyā*/*avidyā* as, (i) existent, or (ii) non-existent; (i) as identical to *Brahman*, or (ii) different from *Brahman*. This concept, although not found in Śaṅkara, later became commonplace of Advaita Vedānta.

Anirvacanīya-khyāti, the theory that error is a cognition that can be expressed neither as existent, nor non-existent, was already known as a Vedānta-doctrine in Maṇḍana's (CE 768) as well as Śaṅkara's time. Maṇḍana was not its propagator. This doctrine of inexpressibility must have arisen in a grammatical tradition, and been taken over before Maṇḍana's time by the Vedānta tradition, or have arisen in the Vedānta and been taken over into Śabdabrahmavāda by Bhartṛhari (CE 480–540), or a predecessor.[37]

Śaṅkara refrained from calling *māyā* or *avidyā*, *sad-asad-anirvacanīya* because this would have been giving it too much reality. Since we know from *Vibhrama Viveka* (of Maṇḍana) that at least *avidyā*, if not *māyā*, was in currency thus (*sad-asad-anirvacanīya*) in Maṇḍana's time, his failure to do so cannot have been chance, it must have been a deliberate refusal. Maṇḍana's approach is more cosmological and theistic than that of later Vedāntins of his School.

---

36 Vide, *A Critique of the Theories of Viparyaya* (1965).

37 Cf. *Brahmasiddhi*.

Maṇḍana says, *avidyā* is not the essence of *Brahman*, nor another thing, not absolutely non-existent, nor existent. It is just for this reason that it is called *avidyā, māyā, mithyā-avabhāsa*. If it were the essence of anything, whether different or non-different from it, it would be ultimately real, and therefore not *avidyā*. If it were absolutely non-existent, it would not enter into practical activity anymore than a non-existent *kha-puṣpa* (a sky-flower). Therefore, it is inexpressible. This is but a logical development of the concept of two orders of reality – *saṁvṛtti* (practical), and *pariniṣpanna* (ultimate) – found in Mahāyāna Buddhism, corresponding to *vyavahāra* and *paramārtha* in Vedāntic terms. *Anirvacanīya* formulation is clearly a development of the two-truth theory. *Avidyā* has enough reality to cause bondage, yet not so absolute a reality as to prevent *mokṣa*.

Śaṅkara calls *māyā* a *śakti* of *Brahman* and identifies it with *prakṛti, nāma-rūpa* as the primordial substance of the world, and the like. However, Maṇḍana does not call *avidyā* a *śakti* of *Brahman*. To allow *Brahman* a multiplicity of powers, or even a single power, would threaten the non-duality of *Brahman*, and bring him close to a *bhedābheda* position that Maṇḍana rejects.

Śaṅkara explains *bhrānti-jñāna* as, when there is error of the snake on the rope, the subject of this error, that is the snake, is neither *sat* (*pāramārthika*) nor *asat* (*prātibhāsika* or *alīka*). It is *mithyā*. However, it may be noted that as per Rāmānuja, this *bhrānti-jñāna* (*jagat*) is *sat*. Whereas as per Śaṅkara, since the object of *bhrānti-jñāna* (*jagat*) is subsequently negated, it is not *sat*, and since it is perceivable (*jagat*), it is not *asat* (*prātibhāsika*). It (*jagat*) is *mithyā*. This doctrine of Śaṅkara about *bhrānti-jñāna* subsequently came to be known as *anirvacanīya-khyāti*.[38] Śaṅkara's concept of *māyā* and the *mithyāttvam* of *jagat* gel well with *anirvacanīya-khyāti*. As stated earlier in this topic, Śaṅkara has not used the term *anirvacanīya* explicitly in his *bhāṣyam*.

---

38 *ajñānaṁ tu sad-asadbhyam-anirvacanīyaṁ* . . . । – *VeSā* 34

Māyā, Avidyā,[39] Ajñāna, Prakṛti[40, 41, 42] and Adhyāsa are Synonyms[43]

One has to note here that in Śaṅkara's commentaries, *avidyā, māyā, ajñāna* and *adhyāsa* have been used as synonyms.[44] (In fact, the term *adhyāsa* was introduced by Śaṅkara, in his famous Adhyāsa-Bhāṣyam in his commentary on *Brahmasūtra*). Post-Śaṅkara, some Advaita Vedāntins, i.e. Vidyāraṇya (fourteenth century CE) in *Pañcadaśī*,[45] and subsequently Sadānanda[46] (mid-fifteenth century CE), in his *Vedāntasāra*,[47] have differentiated between *māyā* and *avidyā*. As per their explanations, *ajñāna* is of two types – *māyā* and *avidyā*. Whereas *māyā* is the *upādhi* of *Īśvara* who wields it, *avidyā* is the *upādhi* of the *jīva* who succumbs to its power. Whereas *māyā* is *śuddha-sattva*, *avidyā* is *aśuddha-sattva*. As per Śaṅkara, *jagat* is ontologically *mithyā*, and due to *ajñāna*, the error of *jagat* is perceived on *Brahman*. *Jagat* is *adhyastha* on *Brahman*. Śaṅkara has defined *adhyāsa* as *atasmin tad buddhiḥ* (to accept something as something that it is not). Sadānanda has defined *adhyāsa* or *adhyāropa* thus – *asarpabhūtāyaṁ rajjau sarpāropavat, vastūni avastu āropaḥ, adhyāropaḥ*,[48] meaning superimposition of the inert world on the non-dual *Brahman* that is Consciousness, is *adhyāropa*, just as a snake is superimposed on the rope that is indeed not a snake. Superimposition of

---

39 *BGSB* IX.10.

40 *BGSB* IV.6.

41 *BGSB* VII.4.

42 *BGSB* IX.10.

43 See Chart 8.

44 *tam etaṁ lakṣaṇam adhyāsaṁ paṇḍitā avidyā iti manyate* । – *BSSB*

45 *Pañ* I.16.

46 Sadānanda's *Vedāntasāra* based on *Māṇḍūkya Upaniṣad* and *Pañcadaśī*.

47 *VeSā* (*ajñānam vyaṣṭi-samaṣṭi* – 35, 41, *samaṣṭi-viśuddha-sattva-pradhāna* – 37, *vyaṣṭi malina-sattva-pradhāna* – 42, *ajñāna* – 43).

48 *VeSā* 32.

something seen earlier (*smṛti*) is superimposed on something else is *adhyāsa – smṛtirūpaḥ paratra pūrvadṛṣṭa-avabhāsaḥ;*[49] for example, mistaking the mother-of-pearl (nacre) to be silver. Similarly, the appearance of *jagat* on *Brahman* is *adhyāsa.*[50]

When we say that *jagat* is *adhyastha* on *Brahman*, one has to understand that *ajñāna* creates this error. This *ajñāna* is not absence[51] (*abhāva*) of *jñāna*. It is *jñāna-virodhī*. That is why it is possible to end it. To explain *ajñāna* further, it is stated that it has some kind of *bhāvarūpa-ajñāna,*[52] because through this *ajñāna* alone the Vedāntins have defined *jagat* as *prapañca*. Thus, *jagat* is not of the nature of *abhāva* (non-existent). However, one has to remember that it is not *sat* (absolute real) like *Brahman*; otherwise, the doctrine of Advaita will be negated. Actually, *ajñāna* is different from *sat* and *asat*, and is *anirvacanīya*. And this *ajñāna* is opposed (*virodha*) to *jñāna*, therefore, it can be ended. This *ajñāna* or *bhrānti* being other than *sāvayava, niravayava, sat, asat, sad-asat* is defined as *sarva-nyāya-virodhinī*[53] meaning this error is *nirālambā* and does not come under any logic. It collapses under enquiry, just as darkness cannot exist with the rising of the Sun. Sureśvara says: "The feature of *avidyā* is, it cannot stand

49 *Adhyāsa-Bhāṣyam – BSSB*

50 Not a very good comparison, since the example (*prātibhāsika*) and the exemplified (*vyāvahārika*) belong to two different orders of reality.

51 Knowing the six different applications of the negative particle of *nañ* is so important in this case: (i) *sādṛśye nañ*, (ii) *abhāve nañ*, (iii) *bhinne nañ*, (iv) *alpe nañ*, (v) *aprāśastye nañ*, and (vi) *virodhe nañ*.

These six applications of *nañ* have been beautifully given in a *śloka*:

tat sādṛśyam-abhāvaśca tad-anyatvaṁ tad-alpatā ।
aprāśastyaṁ virodhaśca nañarthāḥ ṣaṭ prakīrtitaḥ ॥

52 *ajñānaṁ tu sad-asadbhyām-anirvacanīyaṁ, triguṇātmakaṁ, jñāna-virodhī, bhāvarūpaṁ yat kiñcit iti* । – *VeSā* 34

53 *seyaṁ bhrāntir-nirālambā, sarva-nyāya-virodhinī, sahate na vicāraṁ sā, tamo yad vad divākaram* । – *NaiSi* III.66

enquiry, it cannot be known by any means, otherwise it would be an object."[54] Since *avidyā* has conflicting features such as *bādhā* (negation) and *pratīti* (projection), and since it is indescribable being *sad-asat*, *avidyā* is not subject to *pramāṇa* and cannot stand enquiry. We have to understand that *avidyā* has been endorsed by Śaṅkara to explain the origin of *jagat*.

It may be noted that *anirvacanīya-khyāti* was propounded by Sureśvara (disciple of Śaṅkara) after negating *anyathā-khyāti* of Nyāya. Later, it was followed by Padmapāda (also disciple of Śaṅkara) and forwarded by Śrīharṣa (CE 1169–1225) in his *Khaṇḍana-Khaṇḍa-Khādyam* and Citsukha (CE 1220), a follower of Śrīharṣa.[55]

Characteristics of Māyā or Avidyā

Śaṅkara brought about the following characteristics of *māyā* or *avidyā*:

- It is material and inert.
- It is *triguṇātmikā*[56, 57]
- It is an inherent power of *Brahman* (*vaiṣṇavī-śakti*)[58, 59] and non-different from it.
- It is beginningless (*anādi*).
- It is positive (*bhāvarūpa*) in nature, because it does exist until we are able to go beyond it.

---

54 *avidyayā avidyātvam idam eva tu lakṣaṇam* ।
yat pramāṇa-asahiṣṇutvam, anyathā vastu sā bhavet ॥ – *BUBV* 18

55 Śrīharṣa's *Khaṇḍana-Khaṇḍa-Khādyam* is a famous dialectical/polemical work on Advaita system. Citsukhācārya's (a follower of Śrīharṣa) *Bhāvadīpikā* is a commentary on *Khaṇḍana-Khaṇḍa-Khādyam*.

56 *BGSB* IV.6.

57 *BGSB* IX.10.

58 *BGSB* IV.6.

59 *BGSB* VII.14.

- It is categorically undefinable because it is neither real (*sat*) nor unreal (*tuccham*).
- It is an appearance (*vivarta*) and phenomenal (*vyāvahārika*), because it is responsible for the creation of the world.
- It is superimposed (*adhyāsa*) on the reality (the *vastu*, i.e. *Brahman*).
- It can be negated by right knowledge (*vijñāna-nirāsya*).
- Its locus is *Brahman*.

Māyā: A Statement of Fact

The inexplicable *māyā* is described as *aghaṭana ghaṭanā paṭīyasī*[60] – making the impossible possible. Under its spell, even an incarnation of the Lord appears to forget his superhuman resplendence and behaves like an ordinary mortal.[61] *Māyā* is responsible for the contradiction in our thinking and actions.

It is often contended that the doctrine of *māyā*, which denies the reality of right and wrong, is inconsistent with ethics. One can take shelter under *māyā* and trample all moral values. This is a distortion of the concept of *māyā*. As long as a person remains under the spell of *māyā*, right and wrong are real to him. As long as one sees a distinction between right and wrong, one must avoid the wrong and follow the right. Śaṅkara admits the reality of the relative world during the state of ignorance and stresses the fact that, in that state both right and wrong should be treated as real. Therefore, ethical laws must be obeyed. They form the foundation of the Vedāntic discipline. Only by pursuing the right and shunning wrong, one can ultimately go beyond the pairs of opposites. Likewise, social service, worship, prayer and the performance of various duties in the world are not in conflict with man's longing to get himself rid of *māyā* and attain *mokṣa* (freedom).

---

60 *Māyāpañcakam* attributed to Ādi Śaṅkara.

61 Think of Lord Rāma believing that there is such a thing as golden deer and chasing it.

Two Powers of Māyā: Āvaraṇa and Vikṣepa[62]

Īśvara's māyā that is *anirvacanīya*, from which this *anirvacanīya jagat* has come, has two powers – (i) *āvaraṇa-śakti* (veiling power), and (ii) *vikṣepa-śakti* (power of projection). By the veiling power, the basis is veiled, and by the power of projection, the *mithyā jagat* is projected.

Though *māyā* is indescribable and undefinable, its existence can be inferred from its effects, such as the projection or manifestation (*sṛṣṭi*), the preservation (*sthiti*) and the dissolution (*laya*), of the universe. *Māyā* carries on this work through two powers, known as the power of concealment (*āvaraṇa-śakti*) and the power of projection (*vikṣepa-śakti*). The former obscures the knowledge of the observer; it conceals, as it were, the true nature of *Brahman*. Although herself insignificant and unsubstantial, through an inscrutable power, it hides the Absolute Existence–Consciousness–Infinite, just as a patch of cloud conceals the effulgent solar disc. Just as the sun, in spite of this concealment, retains its brilliance intact, the Self or *Brahman* retains in full its nature of Consciousness, in spite of its concealment by *māyā*.

Āvaraṇa (Power of Projection) and Vikṣepa (Veiling Power)

When the true nature of *Brahman* is hidden by the power of *māyā*, there arises the condition of individuality (*jīvattvam*) and relative existence; just as when the real nature of a rope is concealed by darkness, there arises the possibility of its being mistaken for a snake or a stick or a fissure in the earth. Similarly, when the true nature of *Ātmā* becomes concealed by *māyā*, conditions are created for its appearance as a *jīva* (a finite being), endowed with the notion of being a doer or agent (*kartā*), and the experiencer (*bhoktā*) of pleasure and pain, love and hatred, and the other pairs of opposites; just as when a person's consciousness is obscured by the concealing-power of sleep, there arises the condition, in

[62] See Chart 8.

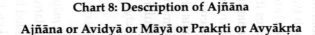

Chart 8: Description of Ajñāna

Ajñāna or Avidyā or Māyā or Prakṛti or Avyākṛta

Anirvacanīya (neither *sat* nor *asat* (*tuccham*)

Triguṇātmikā
→ *Sattva*
→ *Rajas*
→ *Tamas*

Jñāna-virodhinī (can be destroyed by *jñāna*) (*jñāna-virodhī*, not *jñāna-abhāva*)

Bhāvarūpa (is experienced, hence not unreal (*tuccham*)). Ontologically *vyāvahārika*

Power of Ajñāna/Avidyā/Māyā

→ *Āvaraṇa* (veiling power)
Covers the *jīva*'s real nature and causes bondage

→ *Vikṣepa* (power of projection)
Responsible for the creation/ manifestation starting from *ākāśa*

Types of Ajñāna/Avidyā/Māyā

→ *Samaṣṭi-ajñāna* (*māyā*)
Leads to appearance of *Īśvara, Hiraṇyagarbha* and *Virāṭ*

→ *Vyaṣṭi-ajñāna*
Leads to appearance of the *jīva* — *prājña, taijasa* and *viśva*

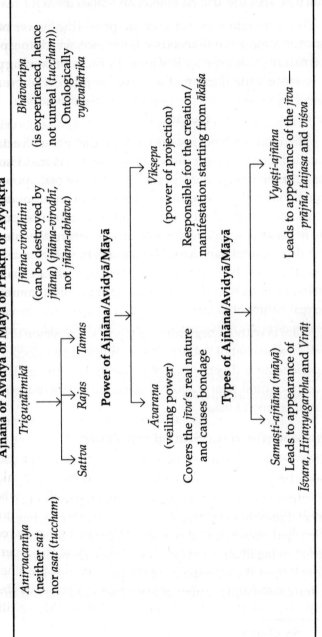

which he sees the dream-objects and takes them for real.

The concealing-power and the projecting-power of *māyā* function almost simultaneously. Ignorance, which conceals the real nature of the rope (or *Brahman*), by the very power inherent in it, creates the illusion of a snake (or *jagat*). The projecting power of *māyā* creates the entire universe (*brahmāṇḍa*) and all the objects dwelling therein.

Therefore, *Brahman* in association (as though) with *māyā* may be called the manifester (not creator) of the universe. However, this projection is only an appearance; it is not real. As has been stated above, *Brahman* cannot participate in an act of creation. When one sees the dual universe and seeks its cause, one finds it in *Brahman* associated with *māyā*. This is where Advaita differs with dualists and pantheists, as they take the creation to be real. According to Advaita, the universe is falsely super-imposed on *Brahman* through *māyā*; and the superimposition cannot affect the real nature of *Brahman*.

Māyā is without beginning; that is to say, a person under the spell of *māyā* cannot know its beginning; just as a sleeper while experiencing a dream, cannot know its beginning. The very concept of time, space, and causality, the pillars of the relative world, belong to *māyā*.

Two Modes of Māyā: Samaṣṭi and Vyaṣṭi[63]

Māyā appears to us in two different modes, or aspects, depending upon our way of looking at it. They are called the collective or cosmic (*samaṣṭi*) aspect, and the individual (*vyaṣṭi*) aspect. From the collective standpoint, *māyā* is one; but from the individual standpoint, it is many. Vedāntic philosophers give the following illustrations to explain the two modes of *māyā*. As a forest from the standpoint of the trees that compose it, may be designated as a number of trees, and as a reservoir from the

[63] See Chart 8.

Chart 9: Brahman & Its Aspects

Brahman
Pure Consciousness
Caitanya, Turīya

in association with *samaṣṭi-ajñāna*
Māyā

Īśvara,
Jagat-kāraṇa, possessing *sarvajñattvam,*
sarva-śaktimattvam,
sarva-vyāpakattvam

Mahat/Hiraṇyagarbha/Sūtrātmā/Prāṇa/Prajāpati/
Caturmukha Brahmā
(*samaṣṭi-sūkṣma-śarīra*, including my mind)

Virāṭ or *Vaiśvānara*
(*samaṣṭi-sthūla-śarīra*, including my physical body)

---

same point of view may be spoken of as bodies of water, so also ignorance when denoting separate units is spoken of as many.[64] This comparison is based on a Śruti statement, "Indra through *māyā* appears as many" (*ṚVS* VI.47.18).

Upādhi

Māyā, both in its cosmic and in its individual aspects, hides the true nature of *Brahman*. Thus, the infinite Absolute appears as a finite being, limited in time and space. In association with the cosmic *māyā*, as we shall see presently, *Brahman* appears as *Īśvara*, and in association with the individual *māyā* as the *jīva* (individual). Thus, *māyā* becomes the *upādhi* (limited adjunct) of *Brahman*. An *upādhi* seems to alter or limit the true nature of an object. However, this limitation is only apparent, not real. It is the association with the *upādhi*s or various physical bodies

---

64 *VeSā* 40.

that makes *Brahman* appear as *devatās*, *gandharvas*, *apsarās*, people, animals, birds, trees and the like. However, it must not be forgotten that an *upādhi* does not bring about any real change in *Brahman*. When an *upādhi* is discarded, the object regarded as finite by the ignorant is known as *Brahman*.

Īśvara as Defined by Śaṅkara

Ācārya Śaṅkara presents the one non-dual *Nirguṇa-Brahman* as the absolute. However, this *Nirguṇa-Brahman* with *upādhi*, becomes *Saguṇa*. This *Saguṇa-Brahman* is known as *Īśvara*.[65] *Īśvara* is omniscient and omnipotent, whereas *jīva* is with limited knowledge and power. Whereas both *Īśvara* and *jīva* possess qualities and are active, *Īśvara* does not suffer the way *jīva* suffers. Because of *adhyāsa*, *jīva* identifies with the physical body and mind, and experiences pains and pleasures. *Īśvara* is the creator of *jagat*, not *jīva*. *Jīva* is under the spell of *māyā*, whereas *Īśvara* wields *māyā*. Swāmī Vidyāraṇya, author of *Pañcadaśī* acknowledges the difference between *māyā* and *avidyā*, and explains:

> The omniscient *Īśvara* is the reflection of *Brahman* in *māyā*, and *jīva* is under the spell of *avidyā*. *Māyā* is dominated by *śuddha-sattva* whereas *avidyā* is dominated by *aśuddha-sattva*. *Māyā* is the *upādhi* – adjunct of *Īśvara*, whereas *avidyā* is the *upādhi* of *jīva*.[66]

One has to remember here that, even if *māyā* is the *upādhi* of *Īśvara*, He is not under its spell. Just as a magician is not under the spell of his magic, *Īśvara* is not affected by *māyā*; whereas, *jīva* with the *upādhi* of *avidyā* is under its spell. Pañcadaśīkāra therefore says "the other one (*jīva*) is under the control of *avidyā*

---

[65] See Chart 9.

[66] *sattvaśuddhi-aviśuddhibhyāṁ māyā 'vidye ca te mate* ।
māyābimbo vaśīkṛtya tāṁ syāt-sarvajña īśvaraḥ । – *Pañ* I.16

(impure *sattva*)".[67] As per Śaṅkara, *Īśvara* is to be worshipped. For any kind of worship, there has to be a difference between the worshipper and the worshipped. So long as *jīva* does not have *brahmajñāna*, he has a need to worship *Īśvara*, because he considers himself as the worshiper, and *Īśvara* as the worshipped. By worshipping *Īśvara*, the mind is purified and the path for *brahmajñāna* is opened. The only absolute reality is *Brahman*. Pañcadaśīkāra has described *Īśvara* and *jīva* as *māyika*. By a beautiful example, Vidyāraṇya Swāmī (fourteenth century) has explained Advaita Vedānta and fixed the place for *jīva* and *Īśvara*. He has compared *māyā* with *kāmadhenu*, and *Īśvara* and *jīva* as her two calves, meaning both *jīva* and *Īśvara* are effects of *māyā*. Through this allegory, one may drink as much duality from the *kāmadhenu*, meaning all the philosophies of duality is based on the *māyā*. However, the only absolute tenet is Advaita.

Jīva

The word *jīva* is derived from the root √*jīv*, which means "to continue breathing". The name gives prominence to one of the two aspects of life's activity, viz. the biological or unconscious activity such as breathing. *Brahman* or Consciousness, associated with individual ignorance, is called *jīva*. *Jīva* dwells in a body. That is why the mind, *buddhi*, the ego and the senses, which are products of ignorance and inert in nature, appear to be conscious. The individual *jīva* is unlike *Īśvara*, and is devoid of the power of lordship. For the same reason it is not omniscient like *Īśvara*.

Both *Īśvara* and *jīva* are associated with *māyā*; both are products of *māyā*. However, the difference between them lies in the fact that *māyā* is under the control of *Īśvara*, whereas *jīva* is under the control of *māyā*. The limitation imposed by *māyā* upon *jīva* makes it completely forget its real nature; but *Īśvara* cannot be affected by His *māyā*, just as a cobra cannot be injured by its

---

67 *avidyāvaśagaḥ-tu-anyaḥ-tad-vaicitryāt-anekadhā* । – *Pañ* I.17

poison. Both *Īśvara* and *jīva* are manifestations of *Brahman* on the relative plane; but *Īśvara* is free, like a spider that moves freely on its web, whereas *jīva* is entangled in the world like a silkworm imprisoned in its cocoon. *Īśvara* uses *māyā* as His instrument for the purpose of manifestation, preservation and dissolution of the universe; through *māyā* again, He exercises His lordship over it. However, *jīva* is a slave of *māyā*. It must never be forgotten from the standpoint of *Brahman*, that *māyā* is non-existent; therefore, both *īśvarattvam* and *jīvattvam* are non-existent from the standpoint of the Absolute. Both are appearances; on the relative plane, *jīva* is the worshipper, and *Īśvara*, the worshipped. *Īśvara* is the creator, *jīva*, the created being. However, *Īśvara*'s importance in the relative world is beyond all measure. He is omniscient and omnipotent. One cannot worship *Brahman*, since it cannot be an object of *jīva*'s thought or adoration, but one can worship *Īśvara*. In fact, *Īśvara* is the highest conception of the Infinite that can be formed by the finite mind.

Essential Nature of Ātmā

Now, we have to understand the essential nature of this *Ātmā*. As per Śaṅkara, based on the *avasthātraya prakriyā* in *Māṇḍūkya Upaniṣad*, our experience can be categorized into three types: (i) *jāgratāvasthā* (waking-state), (ii) *svapnāvasthā* (dream-state), (iii) *suṣupti-avasthā* (deep-sleep state). Śaṅkara explains that the one Consciousness that remains present in the waking, dream and deep-sleep state is *Ātmā*. *Turīya* is not a separate state like the waking, dream and deep sleep state. It is the un-negatable essential nature of *Ātmā*, and is always present in all the three states of waking, dream and deep sleep. To think, that such an *Ātmā* (Consciousness) does not exist, is not possible. Whatever is seen in dream state is negated by the waking state. The objects of the dream state have only *prātibhāsika* reality; available only during that dream state and to that individual dreamer alone. However, the objects of the waking world are not dependent on any particular person, it is the same for all. Therefore, in the waking state, the objects around have some kind of *vyāvahārika* (empirical) reality, that is not *prātibhāsika*, because it is possible to transact in the waking world; whereas, it is not possible to transact in the dream world of a person. In deep-sleep state, since both the experiences of the waking state and the dream state are negated, one has to understand these experiences as *asat* (unreal). However, the unreality of these two experiences is not *tuccham* (absolute non-existent), which can never be an object of cognition such *vandhyā-putra*, *ākāśa-kusuma* or *śaśa-śṛṅga*. Now, we see that since the cognition of the objects of dreams and waking state is negated in deep-sleep state, they are *asat* (unreal).

In deep-sleep state, it is not possible for the cognition of any object of experience of the waking state or dream state to remain. However, it is also not possible to state that Consciousness was not present during deep-sleep state; since on waking the person says: "I had a good sleep, I could not experience anything".[68] It becomes clear, therefore, that even without the cognition of any external object, *Ātmā* exists in the deep-sleep state as the cognition per se. It is not possible to state that this *Ātmā* of the nature of Consciousness is not there. The existence of everything else is dependent upon this *Ātmā*. Therefore, this *Ātmā* of the nature of Existence and Consciousness is always present in the deep-sleep state. This *Ātmā* is also of the nature of *Ānanda* (Infinite). If it were not of the nature of *Ānanda*, one would not experience that relative *ānanda* during deep-sleep state. (This is because the limitation of space and time and object does not remain during deep-sleep state.)

It is worth mentioning here that *sat*, *cit* and *ānanda* are not the attributes of *Ātmā*, rather they are its essential nature. The un-negatable Consciousness that remains undivided during the waking, dream and deep-sleep states is *cit* and *ānanda*. Since in deep-sleep state one recognizes the existence of cognition per se

---

68 *sukham aham asvāpsaṁ, na kiñcit avedिṣam* । – *BUB* IV.3.6

without the cognition of any object, as per Śaṅkara, it becomes evident that no object can exist without that existence per se. *Ātmā* is not an object of any cognition; it is self-evident, self-revealing. This *Ātmā* is one, without a second and is without any attribute. Therefore, in the Upaniṣad, it is presented by *neti neti.*[69] Śaṅkara established this unnegatable *Ātmā* as none other than *Brahman*. *Brahman* is presented as *satyaṁ–jñānam–anantam* in *Taittirīya Upaniṣad* II.1. Here, it will be incorrect to consider *satyam* and *jñānam* as the attributes of *Brahman*. In explaining the meaning of *satyam, jñānam* and *anantam* in his *Taittirīya-Upaniṣad-Bhāṣya*, Śaṅkara has said clearly: *satyaṁ-śabdena brahma lakṣyate, na tu ucyate* (by the three words *satyam, jñānam* and *anantam, Brahman* is defined), and not qualified as a big blue-fragrant lily is qualified by its bigness, blueness and fragrance. Thus, in defining *Brahman* as *satyaṁ–jñānam–anantam*, the attributeless feature of *Brahman* is not negatively affected, since *satyaṁ–jñānam–anantam* are not attributes of *Brahman*, rather they are definitions. One has to understand *Ātmā* or *Brahman* as being without any attribute. *Brahman* can also be understood by *neti neti* as not being *asatyam, ajñānam* or *śāntam*. Now let us analyse the doctrine of *mithyātvam* of *jagat* by Śaṅkara.

Brahman Is None other than Yourself: Ātmā

This presentation of *Brahman* by Śaṅkara can be understood by another point of view. As per Śaṅkara, there is no *Brahman* other than it being the *Ātmā*. This he has shown in *Brahmasūtra* – "*Brahman* is famous being the *Ātmā* of every being".[70] However, one has to analyse the essential nature of *Ātmā* and that is the only *satyam* (reality), with which Śaṅkara has established the unity and non-difference of *Brahman*.

To establish the difference between *sat* and *asat*, Śaṅkara has stated this criterion. The definition of *sat* and *asat* is presented in

---

69 *BṛUp* II.3.6, IV.4.22 and 5.15.

70 *sarvasya ātmātvāt ca brahmāstitva-prasiddhi* । – *BSSB*

Śaṅkara's *Bhagavadgītā-Śāṅkara-Bhāṣya* II.16: *yad viṣayā buddhiḥ na vyabhicarati, tat sat* । *yad viṣayā buddhiḥ vyabhicarati tat asat* ।[71] That about which the cognition does not change or is negated is *asat*.

To illustrate this definition Śaṅkara has continued in his *Gītā-Bhāṣyam*:

> if you say "the pot", it is possible to negate this statement, since the pot has no independent existence without the clay. The effect cannot exist without the cause. Before the creation of the pot and after its destruction, the existence of the effect such as the pot is not there. All these are the examples of the change of cognition of "pot-cognition". However, there is no change of cognition of the *sat-buddhi* (reality-cognition). This change or negation of the cognition of the *asat-vastu* establishes the unreal nature of the *vastu* (object). However, since there is no change in the cognition of the *sat-vastu*, with reference to the *sat-vastu*, one has to understand it as *sat*. When the pot is destroyed, the pot-cognition is negated is changed, but, the cognition of the *sat*, existence per se remains unchanged. The reality cognition goes to *paṭa-buddhi* (existence of the cloth). From this angle, the physical body is *asat* and the *Ātmā* or *Brahman* alone being unchanging and un-negatable is the only *sat* (Reality).

---

[71] *BGSB* II.16.

9

Mahāvākyavicāra in Taittirīya Upaniṣad

Oneness of the Jīva and Brahman

Śaṅkara is an Advaitin. According to Śaṅkara, Advaita-*Brahman* alone exists. By *jīva*, one has to understand the *antaḥkaraṇa-avacchinna* consciousness. He defines *jīva* as the owner of the body–mind-sense complex and the experiencer of results of one's past actions.[1] Therefore, *jīva* is indeed the complex of *Ātmā* and the physical body. However, the physical body is not real; it is *mithyā* ontologically. On self-knowledge, this identification of *Ātmā* with the physical body drops off. Based on Śruti-Pramāṇa, Śaṅkara presents *jīva* and *Brahman* as one and inseparable. It means, *Ātmā* is separated from the physical body, is not separate from *Brahman*. Therefore, in absolute sense, *jīva* and *Brahman* are one. This *Ātmā* appears as many *jīvas*. *Ātmā* or *Brahman* is absolute real, but *jīva* enjoys a *vyāvahārika* reality. *Jīva* is the doer and enjoyer. It has birth, death, reincarnation and bondage. However, all these are not the essential features of *jīva*. Actually, *jīva* and *Brahman* are one, but because of *avidyā* that is beginningless, *jīva* is endowed with the fear of death. Therefore, the real nature of *jīva* that is deathlessness and fearlessness is not exhibited.[2] When *avidyā* is removed by

---

1 *asti ātmā jīvākhyaḥ śarīrendriya-pañjarādhyakṣaḥ karmaphala-sambandhī* । – *BSSB* II.3.17

2 *yadyapi vijñānātmā paramātmāno 'ananya eva, tathāpyavidyā-kāma-karma-kṛtaṁ tasmin martyatvam-adhyāropitam, bhayaṁ ca iti, amṛtatva-abhayatve nopapadyete* । – *BSSB* I.2.17

Self-knowledge, the difference between *jīva* and *Brahman* goes away and one gets to know the essential non-difference. It now gets clear that, there is no absolute difference between the *jīva* and *Brahman*. Because of the *upādhi* of mind that is the result of *avidyā*, *Ātmā* appears as doer and enjoyer. Essentially *Ātmā* is non-different from *Brahman*.

Tātparya-Nirṇaya

The purport of Śāstra can be arrived at by taking into account six factors: (i) *upakrama* and *upasaṁhāra*, (ii) *abhyāsa*, (iii) *apūrvatā*, (iv) *phalam*, (v) *arthavāda*, and (vi) *upapatti*. It is expressed in a *śloka*:[3]

> *upakramopasaṁhārāvabhyāso'pūrvatāphalam* ।
> *arthavādopapattī ca liṅgaṁ tātparya-nirṇaye* ॥
>
> In ascertaining the purport, the characteristic signs are: (i) the introduction and the conclusion (*upakrama – upasaṁhārau*), (ii) repetition (*abhyāsa*), (iii) originality (*apūrvatā*), (iv) result (*phalam*), (v) eulogy (*arthavāda*), and (vi) demonstration (*upapatti*).

Now let us apply these characteristics to the text under discussion, i.e. *Taittirīyopaniṣad*.

(i) ***Upakrama-upasaṁhārau*** means presentation of the non-dual *Brahman* at the beginning and end of the text. In *Taittirīya Upaniṣad, satyam jñānam anantam brahma* is the *upakrama*. *Yato vaco nivartante* is the *upasaṁhāra* that establishes the *asaṅgattvam* of *Brahman*.

(ii) ***Abhyāsa*** or repetition is the frequent presentation of the subject matter, i.e. *Brahman* in a section. In *Taittirīya Upaniṣad, pañcakośa-viveka* that is presented in the Brahmānandavallī and repeated in the Bhṛguvallī is the *abhyāsa*.

---

3 Quoted in *Sarva-Darśana-Saṅgraha* and ascribed to *Bṛhat Saṁhitā*.

3. ***Apūrvatā*** means originality or exclusivity. The subject matter, i.e. *Brahman* of a section is not available through any other means of knowledge except Śruti. For instance, in *Taittirīya Upaniṣad, sa yaścāyaṁ puruṣe, yaścāsāvāditye*[4] is the *jīveśvara-abheda-vacanam*. For this statement, Śruti is the only *pramāṇa*.

4. ***Phalam*** or the result is the usefulness of the subject matter of a section, i.e. Self-knowledge. In *Taittirīya Upaniṣad, brahmavidāpnoti param* and *ānando brahmaṇo vidvān, na bibheti kutaścaneti* are the *phalam*.

5. ***Arthavāda*** (euology) is the praising of the subject matter, i.e. *Brahman* at different places. *Arthavāda* could as well be censuring the opposite, i.e. duality or difference. In the *Pañcakośa-vivaraṇa* – in *Taittirīya Upaniṣad brahma puchaṁ pratiṣṭhā* is *arthavāda* since by this statement *Brahman* becomes the *sarvapratiṣṭhā*. Also *asanneva sa bhavati, asat brahmeti veda cet*, and *udaram antaraṁ kurute, atha tasya bhayaṁ bhavati* are also *arthavāda* statements, since in these statements, the person who doubts the existence of *Brahman* is dismissed.

6. ***Upapatti*** (example) the oneness between *jīva* and *Brahman* is *upapatti in Taittirīya*. Establishing this oneness with reasoning with examples is adduced at different places. *Sa yaścāyaṁ puruṣe, yaścāsāvāditye* is the *jīveśvara-abheda-vacanam* as well as *ko hyevānyāt kaḥ prāṇyāt* are *upapattis*.

Mahāvākya-Vicāra

It becomes clear from the four *mahāvākyas* of the four Vedas, (i) *prajñānaṁ brahma* (*Ṛgveda – AiUp* III.1), (ii) *tattvamasi* (*Sāmaveda – ChāUp* V.8.7), (iii) *ayamātmā brahman* (*Atharvaveda – MāṇUp* I.2), and (iv) *ahaṁ brahmāsmi* (*Śukla-Yajurveda – BṛUp* I.4.10)[5] that essentially there is no difference between *jīva* and *Brahman*.

---

4 *TaiUp* II.8 and III.10.

5 See Chart 10.

In the statement *tat tvam asi* (You are That) the word *tvam* (you) is to be understood as *jīva*. The word *tat* (that) is to be understood as *Brahman*, which is Consciousness. So it is to be understood that the essential nature of *jīva* is Consciousness. From this aspect, there is no difference between *jīva* and *Brahman*. In the statement, *so 'yaṁ devadattaḥ* (This is that Devadatta) refers to one non-different person. The word "this" means the Devadatta that is being seen now and here, and "that" means Devadatta at a remote time and place. However, in understanding the statement, the associations regarding time and place are eliminated, and the person called Devadatta is accepted. Similarly, in the statement, *tat tvam asi* the two words *tat* and *tvam* both means one non-different Consciousness. A question may arise here – how can the *jīva* who is a body–mind-sense complex, is of limited knowledge and who is denoted by the word *tvam* be equated with omniscient, omnipotent *Brahman*, which is all-pervasive and is denoted by the word *tat* of the equation, since both are contradictory to each other? Therefore, as per Advaita Vedānta, to understand the meaning of the *mahāvākya* – *tat tvam asi* – one has to take the *lakṣaṇā* (intended meaning), and not the *abhidhā* or *vācyārtha* (direct meaning). Here it becomes necessary to explain the various *vṛtti*s used in the language to obtain the purport of any statement.

Chart 10: The Four Mahāvākyas

Ṛgveda	*Yajurveda*	*Sāmaveda*	*Atharvaveda*
prajñānaṁ brahma	*ahaṁ brahmāsmi*	*tat tvam asi*	*ayamātmā brahma*
(*AiUp* III.1.3)	(*BṛUp* I.4.10)	(*ChUp* VI.8.7)	(*MāṇUp* 2)

Types of Vṛttis

To ascertain the meaning of a *mahāvākya*, a thorough understanding of the method employed to know the purport is indispensable. When a sentence is used as a *pramāṇa*, its operation is effective, provided the meaning of the words therein and the sentence as a whole is properly understood.

The meaning of a given word or a sentence can be literal (*vācyārtha*), implied (*lakṣyārtha*) or figurative (*vyañjanā*), depending on the way it is employed. Words have an inherent capacity to yield appropriate meaning as per the context, which is called *vṛtti*. It indicates the relation (*sambandha*) between the word (*pada*) and its meaning (*padārtha*), resulting in an understanding of the word (*śābdabodha*). *Vṛtti* can also be defined as the power of the force of a word, by which it expresses, indicates or suggests the meaning of the given word. *Vṛtti*s are of three types.[6]

1. *Abhidhāvṛtti*

It gives the literal meaning (*vācyārtha* or *śaktyārtha*) of a word. It is also called *mukhyavṛtti*. For example, when you say, "this is a book", the direct meaning of the word "book" is immediately understood. Here, *abhidhāvṛtti* operates.

2. *Lakṣaṇāvṛtti*

When the literal meaning of a word or a sentence is incongruous, either the meaning must be wrong, or something else is indicated or implied thereby. If the sentence is not wrong, there may be a possibility of conveying some meaning other than the direct one. This is called *lakṣaṇāvṛtti* or *śakyasambandha*. It gives the *lakṣyārtha* (implied meaning). In this case, some aspects of the word or words may have to be discarded, some retained or added, or both, depending on the context. The three subdivisions of this *vṛtti* will be seen subsequently.

3. *Vyañjanāvṛtti*

This gives the figurative meaning. When the first two types of *vṛtti*s fail to convey suitably, one has to employ this *vṛtti*. This will not be applied in our topic.

---

[6] See Chart 11.

Chart 11: Meaning of Sentence

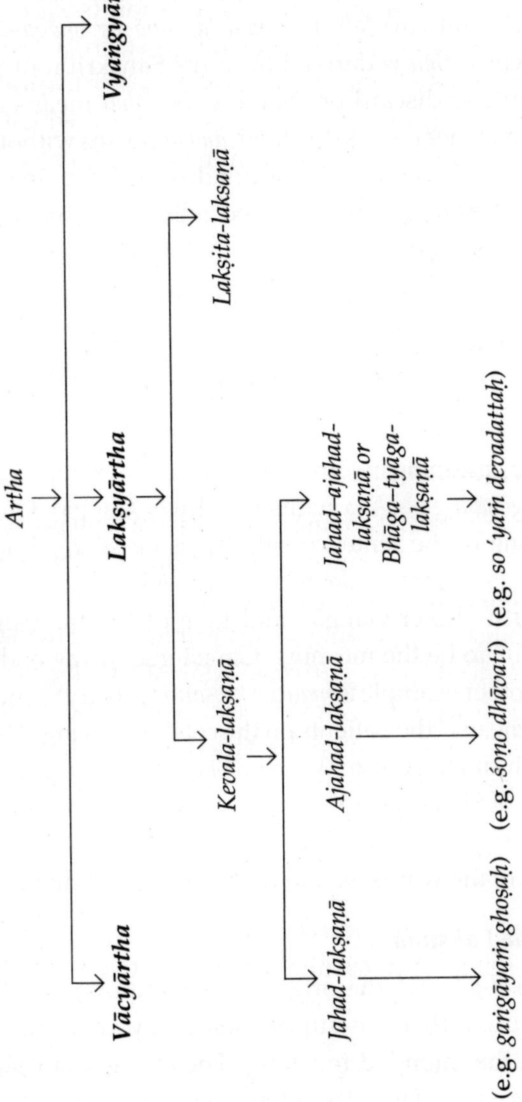

Types of Lakṣaṇāvṛtti

A *lakṣaṇāvṛtti* is applied when *vācya*, the immediate meaning of the sentence is incomplete or does not make sense. *Lakṣaṇāvṛtti* (implications) are of three types (i) *jahad–lakṣaṇā,* (ii) *ajahad–lakṣaṇā,* and (iii) *jahad–ajahad-laksaṇā* or *bhāga–tyāga lakṣaṇā.* The word *jahat* is derived from the Sanskrit root √*ohāk* = *tyāge,* meaning to discard or abandon. So *jahat* means to discard, so the direct meaning is dropped, *ajahat* means without discarding, hence the direct meaning is not dropped, but one more word is brought in to get the intended meaning. And *jahājahat* means part of the meaning is discarded and part of the meaning is retained to get the intended meaning.

Jahad-Lakṣaṇā

In *jahad-lakṣaṇā,* one has to discard the *vācyārtha* (primary meaning), yielding a different sense which is connected to the primary meaning in some way. The classic example of *jahad-lakṣanā* is *gaṅgāyāṁ ghoṣaḥ* (a hamlet on River Gaṅgā). One can get the meaning of the sentence only by using *jahad-lakṣaṇā.* Since it is impossible for a hamlet to be on River Gaṅgā, one has to discard the term "River Gaṅgā" and take *tīram* "the banks (of River Gaṅgā)" to be the meaning. Gaṅgā goes away and *tīram* comes in. Another example is *mañcāḥ krośanti* (cots cry). Since cots cannot cry, it means "the patients on the cots" are crying. This is found in English language also. "We read Shakespeare" means "we read the works of Shakespeare". However, this *lakṣaṇā* cannot be used to understand the *mahāvākya – tat tvam asi* – since the Consciousness aspect of the words *tat* and *tvam* is not being discarded.

Ajahad-Lakṣaṇā

In *ajahad-lakṣaṇā,* the original meaning of a word used is not given up, rather it is supplemented by an additional word to obtain the intended meaning. The classic example is *kākebhyo dadhi rakṣatām.* Here, the intended meaning is to protect the curd from all others, not only from the crows. The other example is *śoṇo dhāvati* (the red runs). Since the red (colour, being an adjective) cannot run by itself, it has to qualify a noun. Therefore it means "the red horse runs". We get the meaning of the sentence by associating a red horse with the red (colour). This method also cannot be used in deciphering *tat tvam asi*.

Jahad-Ajahad-Lakṣaṇā or Bhāga-Tyāga-Lakṣaṇā in deciphering Śrutivākya

In *jahad-ajahad-lakṣaṇā* or *bhāga-tyāga-lakṣaṇā*, one part of the apparent meaning (*vācyārtha*) of a sentence is given up and the other part is retained. The given-up meaning is contradictory and the retained meaning is adjustable. To understand *tat tvam asi*, both *jahallakṣaṇā* and *ajahallakṣaṇā* have to be used. *Jīva* or *tvam-pada* is endowed with *upādhi*s such as smallness, limited knowledge and limited pervasiveness, whereas *Īśvara* or *tat-pada* enjoys omniscience, omnipotent, all-pervasiveness status. However, if both the *upādhi*s are discarded, then what remains for both *tat* and *tvam* is the pure consciousness. This is the meaning of equation *tat tvam asi*. Here, by *jahad-lakṣaṇā* the contradictory nature of the *upādhi*s – remoteness and immediacy, omniscience and limited knowledge – are given up. By *ajahad-lakṣaṇā* the consciousness which is common to both *tat-pada* and *tvam-pada* is retained and the intended meaning of the equation *tat tvam asi* is understood. That is why it is known as *jahad-ajahad-lakṣaṇā*. As per Vidyāraṇya's (fourteenth century CE) *Pañcadaśī*, one has to understand the meaning of this *mahāvākya* not as *saṁsarga* or *viśiṣṭa*, rather as undifferentiated Consciousness.[7] The purport is the non-difference, which is the meaning of *mahāvākya*. Pañcadaśīkāra Vidyāraṇya has defined this method as *bhāga-lakṣaṇā*.[8]

---

7 *saṁsargo vā viśiṣṭo vā vākyārtho nātra sammataḥ* ।
akhaṇḍaikarasatvena vākyārtho viduṣāṁ mataḥ ॥ – *Pañ* VII.75

8 *tattvamasyādi-vākyeṣu lakṣaṇā bhāgalakṣaṇā* ।
so 'yam-ityādi-vākyastha-padayor-iva nāparā ॥ – *Pañ* VII.74

In *Taittirīya Upaniṣad, svarūpa-lakṣaṇam* is presented in Brahmānandavallī and *taṭastha-lakṣaṇam* in Bhṛguvallī. They work in almost the same way. In *satyam jñānam anantam brahma,* the *dhātus* retain their meaning – it is *svarūpa-lakṣaṇam.* There is *jahad–ajahd* because *satyam* does not mean just *asti.* There is *astitvasya kāla-avacchinnatvam.* Appreciation of existence includes a time-bound aspect. Usually "it exists" means "it exists in time". In the concept of existence, there is always a time element. In this *mahāvākya,* the time element is negated and existence is retained. The *dhātu* retains its meaning, at the same time there is a negation, because *astitvam* is not *anityam.*

Similarly, the *jñā dhātu* has no connotation of *jaḍatvam. Jñā dhātu* here means *ajaḍam.* In apposition with *anantam, jñānam* is *jñaptiḥ. Brahman* is not the knower, the known, or the knowing – it has to be all the three. That which is present in all the three, is itself not one of them. That is *caitanyam.* That is the meaning of *bhāva-sādhanam.* There again we have *bhāga-tyāga-lakṣaṇā,* part of the *svarūpa-lakṣaṇam.*

– Swami Dayananda Saraswati

Most of the criticisms cast at Advaita Vedānta are by those who are ignorant of the total context, or do not care to know it fully. This is the reason why one has to learn Vedānta from a competent teacher, who is able to unfold these statements. Śruti also emphasizes the importance of a right *guru.* Ācārya Śaṅkara while commenting on such an instruction given in *Muṇḍaka Upaniṣad*[9] advises that even a scholarly person should not independently enquire into the nature of *Brahman.* Elsewhere[10] Śaṅkara has been more strong – *asampradāyavit, mūrkhavat upekṣaṇīya* (a person not belonging to the tradition should be dismissed).

---

9 *śāstrajño 'pi svātantryeṇa brahmajñānānveṣaṇaṁ mā kuryāt* ।
– *MUSB* I.2.12

10 *BGSB* XII.2.

10

Śaṅkara's Refutation of Other Philosophical Systems

WITHIN the *āstika* (orthodox) Indian philosophical systems, there are different views on the reality of *ātmā*, as well as the reality of the world. All of them however talk about *mokṣa*. All of them say there is no return from *mokṣa*. Nevertheless, there are many contentions. Thus, within the *āstika* systems, when they quote Śruti and argue, one has to argue with them in terms of *śravaṇam*.

When the *nāstika* systems argue outside Śruti (Cārvākas, Bauddhas and Jainas), one has to argue logically. Then it becomes the realm of *mananam*. Śaṅkara in many places in the *bhāṣyam* has refuted other systems. Some of them are given below.

Refutation of Pūrva-Mīmāṁsā

There is no *Īśvara* in Pūrva-Mīmāṁsā, there are only only *devatās*.

Many believe that Buddhism ceased to have a large following in India because it came under the attack of Śaṅkara. This is not true. There are very few passages in *Śāṅkara-Bhāṣya* that are critical of Buddhism, which was opposed to the Vedas. Far more forcefully, he criticized the doctrines of Sāṁkhya and Mīmāṁsā that accept the Vedas.

While Śaṅkara acknowledges the interrelation and interdependence of Pūrva-Mīmāṁsā and Uttara-Mīmāṁsā, he spares no pains to point out the difference of contents and objectives of the two. Although Pūrva-Mīmāṁsā is not taken to be *paramata*, and hence is not taken into account in the Tarkapāda of *Brahmasūtra*, he differs with many of the Pūrva-Mīmāṁsā doctrines. He demolishes the Mīmāṁsaka's contention that *Īśvara* is not the creator of the *jagat*, and that He does not dispense the results of our actions. Śaṅkara maintains that there can be no *jagat* without *Īśvara*, and that it is wrong to conclude that our actions yield results of their own. He confines and limits the role and utility of Pūrva-Mīmāṁsā to the empirical realm. He makes it very clear that Pūrva-Mīmāṁsā is concerned only with *preyas*, whereas the objective of Vedānta is *niḥśreyas*. Hence, the former has to concentrate on *karma* and the latter on *jñāna*.

Refutation of Bhaṭṭa-Mīmāṁsā

In *Taittirīya Upaniṣad Bhāṣya* II.1, there is a view that – suppose we consider the same *Ātmā* as the knower and known. Śaṅkara replies,[1] "It is not possible since *Ātmā* is partless". The partless *Ātmā* cannot be both the knower and the object of knowledge at the same time. Further, if *Ātmā* can be an object of knowledge like pot, then teaching will become useless.

Refutation of Sāṁkhya

Some of the orthodox philosophies, the so-called *vaidika*s (Sāṁkhya, Yoga, Nyāya, Vaiśeṣika) use Śruti only as a support for what they have already concluded through *tarka* (reasoning). They quote Śruti to support what they have concluded by their own *yukti*.

For example, a Sāṁkhya places importance on Śruti, but in his contention, *tarka* predominates. In fact, Nirīśvara Sāṁkhya is a philosophy, since there is no God. Where there is no God, there is no theology. It must be acknowledged that unlike Western philosophy, Indian philosophy cannot be separated from theology.

---

1 *na yugapad-anaṁsatvāt* । *na hi nirvayavasya yugapaj-jñeya-jñātṛtva-upapattiḥ* । – *TUB* II.1

Sāṁkhya says that *jagat-kāranaṁ brahma na bhavati, jagat acetanaṁ, pradhānam eva kāraṇam*. He says that there is no connection between *puruṣa* and *pradhāna* (his equivalent of our *prakṛti*). When the *guṇa*s are in equilibrium, there is dissolution. When they are disturbed, creation starts. This is classical Nirīśvara-Sāṁkhya.

i. That there are many *ātmā*s, while there is one *pradhāna*. *Pradhāna* for uniformity is equivalent to *prakrti* or *māyā*.

ii. It says, between *ātmā* and *pradhāna* there is no connection. *Pradhāna* creates everything, and everything is *satyam*.

In *Taittirīya-Upaniṣad-Bhāṣya* II.6 Śaṅkara says, if we consider *Brahman* as the material cause of the *jagat*, just as clay is for the pot; then *Brahman* is inert. This is since Sāṁkhya considers *pradhāna* as the cause of the *jagat*. Śaṅkara defends stating this contention is not correct since Śruti states, "He desired".[2] Nobody in *jagat* who desires is inert. *Brahman* is omniscient. Hence, his desiring is tenable. Śaṅkara maintains the Vivartavāda or the doctrine that the world is a phenomenal appearance of *Brahman*. According to him, the belief to be refuted before Advaita is established was Sāṁkhya or Prakṛti-Pariṇāmavāda. Since *Brahmasūtra* on which he wrote commentary alludes so frequently to the Sāṁkhya, Śaṅkara considers it at length and shows how far Sāṁkhya is removed from the Upaniṣadic vision. His primary objective is to establish the Vivartavāda as against the Pariṇāmavāda of certain commentators on *Brahmasūtra*, especially Bhartṛprapañca who preceded him. Śaṅkara has another aim in his *Bhāṣya*. Owing to the seeming resemblance of his doctrine of *Nirguṇa-Brahman* to that of *śūnya* (void) of the Mādhyamika School of Buddhist nihilism, one might identify the two, and regard the Advaita as alien to the Upaniṣads. So he emphasizes now and again the fact that his teaching is not nihilistic. He does not expressly

---

[2] *so 'kāmayata* – *TaiUp* II.6.

mention this phase of Buddhism except in one place[3] and there he dismisses it summarily, but there is no doubt that he throughout tries to steer clear of these two doctrines opposed to his own, but yet so similar to it, viz., the Brahma-Pariṇāmavāda of some Vedāntins (i.e. Viśiṣṭādvaita) and the Śūnyavāda of the Mādhyamikas.

Śaṅkara has refuted theories of Sāṁkhya School more elaborately in *Brahmasūtra-Śāṅkara-Bhāṣya*. In *Brahmasūtra-Śāṅkara-Bhāṣya* starting from the fifth topic, i.e. Īkṣatyadhikaraṇam, commencing with *sūtra* I.1.5[4] Śaṅkara quotes elaborately in many places until the end of 54 topic, i.e. Racanānupapatti-adhikarṇam, ending with II.2.10, many a thesis carefully built by the Sāṁkhyas, even though he does not mention the names of the authors and works he is quoting from; and he refutes them all in his inimitable way. Śaṅkara is particularly critical of the Upaniṣadic interpretation offered by the Sāṁkhyas with a view to give a Vedic aroma and colour to their doctrine that the ultimate cause of *jagat* is the inert and ever fluctuating *pradhāna* (the Pradhāna-Kāraṇavāda). Śaṅkara spares no pain in exposing the hollowness and untenability of their way of interpretation. It may be noted that his effort in exploding the Sāṁkhya School alone seems to surpass his entire labour in refuting all other systems of philosophy. Again, more than once, he brands the Sāṁkhya alone as his chief and most powerful opponent (*pradhāna-malla*)[5] to fight out. Śaṅkara declared Sāṁkhya as the chief rival because of two reasons. First, it is very close to Vedānta and, therefore, was capable of misleading people easily. In the very beginning of the Tarkapāda[6] of *Brahmasūtra-*

---

3 *BSSB* II.2.31.

4 *īkṣaternāśabdam – BrSū* I.1.5

5 *ataḥ pradhānamalla-nirabahana-nyāyena atidiśati – BSSB* I.4.28 and II.1.12

6 *BrSū* II.2.

Śāṅkara-Bhāṣya, Śaṅkara speaks of the Sāṁkhya system as the one topping the list of philosophical schools that were enjoying great popularity in his days among the men of eminence.[7] He also describes the same as a system that is highly logical (*yuktigāḍha*). From Śaṅkara's own words, we know that the Sāṁkhya establishes the inert *pradhāna* as the ultimate material cause of *jagat*, primarily by inference, and then they turn to the Vedas next and twist the Vedic passages only to have a scriptural corroboration to their theory.[8]

Perhaps Śaṅkara thought that if Sāṁkhya views could be shown to be untenable, it would follow that other views that were remote could in no way be acceptable. He does not give this much of prominence to any other opponents, not even to the Vaiśeṣika or the Bauddha.

However, just as Śaṅkara accepted some of the Buddhist thoughts, with reference to Sāṁkhya, while he rejected the Pradhāna-Kāraṇavāda, he accepted its theory of evolution, and the theory of causation at the empirical level. Nevertheless, like Buddhism, he made Sāṁkhya redundant and superfluous, and that is why we do not find a continuity of Sāṁkhya tradition further.

Refutation of Nyāya

The Naiyāyika says *Īśvara* is the *kartā*, and without *Īśvara* there is no possibility of a creation, and continues to say, the atoms and so on have to be activated for *sṛṣṭi* to begin. *Īśvara* must be there as *nimitta-kāraṇa*. There is *nimitta-kāraṇa-apekṣā*, just as a potter is necessary for the creation of a pot. Through reasoning, the Naiyāyika establishes one *kartā* for creation and in that reasoning there is a fallacy. Why should there be one *kartā* and not many *kartā*s? *Jagat* consists of many things; there could be many *kartā*s.

---

7 *mahājana-parigṛhitāni mahanti saṁkhyādi-tantrāṇi* । – *BSSB* II.2.1

8 *sāṁkhyādayastu pradhānadini kāraṇāntarāṇi anumimānaḥ tatparatāyaiva vedānta-vākyāni yojayanti* । – *BSSB* I.1.5

One can argue that there are *aneka-kartā* for the creation of this *jagat*. It is just as reasonable. No school of thought should grant *prāmāṇya* to Śruti, and leave out its heart. Thus, the Naiyāyika ends up as a theology, with *Īśvara* sitting there, somewhere.

Refutation of Vaiśeṣika

The Vaiśeṣika is a theologian. The Vaiśeṣikas talk about various *paramāṇus* that obtained before creation.

In *Taittirīya-Upaniṣad-Bhāṣya* II.1 there is a contention that from the Śruti statement, *so 'kāmayata*, the agency of *Ātmā* is proved, hence it cannot be said that *Ātmā* is the root meaning of knowledge. Śaṅkara says, the effect that is *jagat* is an *upacāra* alone. Rather it is *vivarta*.

In *Brahmasūtra-Śāṅkara-Bhāṣya* also, after demolishing the independent status of Sāṁkhya and showing its reducibility to Vedānta, Śaṅkara proceeds to examine the Vaiśeṣika philosophy. First, he refutes Vaiśeṣika's charges against Brahmavāda and then advances his own arguments to disprove the Vaiśeṣika system. The Vaiśeṣika system traces *jagat* to primary atoms, posits *adṛṣṭa* as the unseen power responsible for bringing the atoms, together or separating them. However, Śaṅkara argues that, whether located in the atoms or in *jīvas*, *adṛṣṭa* being inert and unintelligent like atoms cannot move the atoms. Another serious fallacy in the Vaiśeṣika system is the theory that out of partless atoms, composite objects of *jagat* arise. Śaṅkara points out several other fallacies and brands this school as semi-nihilistic. He opines that this school is not to be relied upon as it is bolstered up by bad logic, goes against scriptures and is not accepted by worthy people.

However, unlike Sāṁkhya, Vaiśeṣika could survive. The main reason for this is the support provided to it by the Nyāya School, whose epistemology and logic were broadly acceptable to all. However, under the impact of Śaṅkara's examination, the Vaiśeṣika philosophy had to undergo a through revision.

Acceptance of *Īśvara*, recognition of *svarūpa-sambandha*, etc. are some of the examples of such a revision.

Refutation of Yoga

Yoga is also known as Sa-Īśvara Sāṁkhya. Yoga includes *Īśvara*. It is dualist. A Sāṁkhya who becomes a theologian is called a *yogī*. The *yogī*, Sa-Īśvara Sāṁkhya says, that there is an *Īśvara*, who disturbs the *guṇa*s.

As regards Yoga systems, it is both a philosophy and practice. Its philosophy is borrowed from the Sāṁkhya system, and is not acceptable to Śaṅkara. However, the practice of Yoga as a method of attainment of mental equipoise is not unacceptable to him. This means that he has an open mind about the Yoga system. Just as he accepts the Nyāya technique of logic, he also accepts the Yoga technique of meditation. Thus, like the Mīmāṁsā system, the Yoga system is neither accepted by him in full, nor is there the complete rejection of it.

Refutation of Śūnyavādī Buddhism

Buddhism is not a theology, because it has no place for God. It is a non-theistic ethical religion. The Mādhyamaka Buddhist says, there is *śūnya*. Yogācāra Buddhist says, there is *kṣaṇikavijñāna*.

In *Taittirīya-Upaniṣad-Bhāṣya* II.1, there is a contention, "since the words *satyam*", etc. are there to negate *anṛtādi* words, *satyam-jñānam-anantam* statement indeed means that *Brahman* is void like "mirage-water, etc." Śaṅkara refutes stating that the words *satyam*, etc. are to denote *Brahman*. Void cannot have adjectives. About Śūnyavāda, he argues that if partial nihilism is unacceptable, how can full nihilism be acceptable?

Refutation of Sarvāstivāda (Realism) Buddhism

Śaṅkara takes up the realistic school of Sarvāstivāda/Theravāda for examination. He questions the tenability of the theories of momentariness and non-substantiality of reality. If the real are momentary, how can the aggregation of the physical and mental entities take place? There is a procession of successive moments, but how can the moments be related? If there is no permanent *jīva*, how are memory and remembrance possible? If there is no permanent reality, how can existence come out of non-existence? These and many such questions remain unsolved in the realistic schools of Buddhism.

Refutation of Vijñānavādī Buddhism

Then Śaṅkara turns to the latter Buddhist School of Idealism. For the school of Vijñānavāda, there is no extra mental reality. What is real is a series of momentary ideas. The appearance of ideas is explained by residual impressions on the analogy of dreams. Śaṅkara argues that this view is also untenable.

As is well known, while Śaṅkara rejected most of the basic tenets of Buddhism and made that system redundant and superfluous in the face of Vedānta; he assimilated some of the good points of Buddhist thought. It would be incorrect to hold that he banished Buddhism from Indian soil and to label him as a pseudo-Buddhist would be unjust. He was basically a seeker of truth, and if he found some grains of truth in Buddhist thought, he did not hesitate in accepting the same. In the context of Buddhism, therefore, there is a need for reappraisal of Śaṅkara.

Decline of Buddhism

The next question naturally is: how did Buddhism cease to have a considerable following in the county of its origin? Well, it was due the Mīmāṁsakas and the Tārkikas. Those who are adept in the Tarka-Śāstra (logic) are called Tārkikas. Tarka is part of Nyāya. Kumārila Bhaṭṭa (eighth century CE), the famous Mīmāṁsaka, and Udayanācārya (tenth century CE), a Tārkika, opposed Buddhism for different reasons. The Mīmāṁsakas do not believe that *Īśvara* awards us the results of our actions, they believe that the Vedic rituals we perform yield their own results, and that the injunctions of the Dharmaśāstras must be carried out faithfully. They attacked Buddhism for its refusal to accept Vedic rituals. The Tārkikas severely criticized Buddhism for its denial of *Īśvara*. Kumārila Bhaṭṭa has written profusely in criticism of Buddhism. He and Udayanācārya were chiefly responsible for the failure of Buddhism to acquire a large following in India.

Refutation of Jainism

The Jainas say *ātmā dehaparimāṇaḥ* and that *ātmā* has to be made *śuddha*. There are varieties of theories, theologies and philosophies.

Coming to Jainism, Śaṅkara directs his polemic against the theory of *anekānta*. His main argument is that how can the same thing possess contradictory attributes? This apart, he also questions the acceptability of the theory of the increase and decrease of the size of *Ātmā*.

Unlike Buddhism, Jainism could continue because it is not only a school of philosophy, but also a mode of religion. As a system of philosophy, it could not regain its lost respectability. Its ethical tenets, which were not unacceptable to Śaṅkara, continued to be acceptable and remain in practice until today.

Refutation of Cārvākas

Though the materialist school of Cārvāka is not taken into account in the Tarkapāda of *Brahmasūtra*, Śaṅkara undertakes its examination in *Brahmasūtra-Śāṅkara-Bhāṣya* III.3.53-54. Refuting Dehātmavāda that identifies *Ātmā* with the body, Śaṅkara argues that if consciousness were an attribute of the body, why is it that a dead body is not conscious?

Various Theories about the Causality of the Universe

Then there are these various views about the causality of the universe. Some of them are:

1. That there is no cause for the world (*kāraṇaṁ nāsti*).

2. There are those who think that non-being (*abhāva*) or void (*śūnya*) is the cause of the world.
3. The Cārvākas explain the world in terms of naturalism (Svabhāvavāda).
4. Some others who subscribe to accidentalism (Yadṛcchāvāda) say that the existence of the world is an accident.
5. The Vaiśeṣika philosopher holds the view that the constituents of the natural world are composed of material atoms and that Lord (*Īśvara*) is the prime mover of these atoms.
6. According to Sāṁkhya, *pradhāna* is the cause of the world.
7. The Yoga holds the view that *Īśvara*, who is one of the *puruṣa*s, and who is not related to anything, brings about the connection of *prakṛti* and *puruṣa*, which is necessary for the evolution of the world from *prakṛti*.
8. The Mīmāṁsākas maintain that *karma* or *adṛṣṭa* is the cause of the world. Some schools of Vedānta hold that *Īśvara* is the efficient cause of the universe, and that *prakṛti* is the material cause.
9. Those who accept the reality of time, say that time (*kāla*) is the cause of the world.

None of these views is satisfactory.

i. If there is no cause for the world, one could argue by the same logic that even a pot comes into being without a cause. Hence, the view that the world exists without a cause cannot be accepted, as it goes against the evidence of perception.

ii. Non-being (*abhāva*) cannot be the cause of anything, only a positive entity can be the cause of some object. The view that a positive something comes out of non-being is contradicted by perception (*abhāvāt bhāvotpattir-iti pratyakṣa virodhaḥ*). And the view that void (*śūnya*) is the cause of the world is no more intelligible than the assertion that a plant comes into being without a seed. The variegated and the intelligently ordered universe cannot be an accident or a chance, nor can it be said that it comes into being of its own accord.

iii. If *Īśvara* were the only efficient cause to create the world out of some primordial matter (*prakṛti*), which is different from and external to him, he would be conditioned thereby. *Īśvara* who is one of the *puruṣa*s and not related to anything, cannot be the cause, which brings about the connection between *prakṛti* and *puruṣa*.

Neither the atoms, nor *prakṛti*, nor *karma*, nor *kāla*, nor anything else, can account for the universe, for they are all unintelligent.

Since it is not possible to account for the world in any way stated above, Advaita concludes that the world is an appearance of *Brahman* due to *māyā*.

11

Prakriyās in Taittirīya

THE vision of Advaita Vedānta is an equation of the identity between *jīva* and *Īśvara*. This vision of oneness (*aikyam*) is not available for perception or inference. Nor the oneness, that is unfolded by Vedānta, is contradicted by perception or inference. Therefore, oneness is purely in terms of understanding the equation. The entire teaching of Vedānta can be expressed in one sentence: *tat tvam asi* "You are That".[1] All other sentences in the Upaniṣads are meant to prove this equation.

In *Taittirīya*, this equation is in II.1, i.e. Brahmānandavallī. After defining *Brahman* as *Satyaṁ-Jñānam-Anantam*, the Upaniṣad states, *tasmāt* (from that *Brahman*) *etasmāt ātmanaḥ* (from this *Ātmā*) *ākāśa sambhūtaḥ*.[2] *Tasmāt* is equated with *etasmāt*, i.e. that *Brahman* is equated with this *Ātmā*. Then the model of creation starts. The *mahāvākya* here is the equation between *Brahman* and *Ātmā*.

To understand this equation in the teaching *paramparā*, there are a number of methodologies (*prakriyā*s) adopted by the Upaniṣads. In *Taittirīya*, three such methods are used. Vedānta is a *pramāṇa* only to reveal the oneness of *Ātmā* with *Īśvara*. One thing to be understood here is that Vedānta is not a *pramāṇa* to prove the existence of *Ātmā*, for *Ātmā* is self-evident and self-revealing. Vedānta is to reveal the nature of *Ātmā*.

---

1 *ChāUp* V.8.7, V.9.4, V.10.3, V.11.3, V.12.3, V.14.3, V.15.3, V.16.3.

2 *TaiUp* II.1.

Methodology of Teaching by Adhyāropa-Apavāda Nyāya

In Advaita Vedānta, to lead the student to the knowledge of *vastu*, the methodology of prior superimposition and subsequent negation is used. *Adhyāropa* assumes a false proposition for argument's sake and *apavāda* disproves it by eliminating bit by bit, the whole of that proposition as wrong. This is exactly what is known in Greek Philosophy as *reductio ad absurdum*.

The expression *adhyāropa* means "superimposition", "wrong imputation" or "attribution of a false characteristic". *Vedāntasāra* V.52 defines *adhyāropa* as "to project a snake on the rope, which in reality is not a snake at all".

The word *apavāda* means "negation" or "denial" of what has been imputed, attributed, assumed or superimposed (*adhyāropita*). This is born of knowledge of an object "as it is" (*vastutantra*). It is not the negation of the object, but of the particular attribute that is projected on it. Śaṅkara refers to this as a methodology:

> *tathā hi sampradayavidaṁ vacanam adhyāropa-apavādābhyāṁ niṣprapañcam iti* । – *BGSB* XIII.13
>
> For instance, there is a word of knowledge of tradition – "By superimposition and denial, that which is free from phenomena is made phenomenal".

This *jagat* was there before the creation. *Sat eva saumya idam agra āsīt* । (*ChāUp* VI.2.1). Also *īśā vāsyam idaṁ sarvaṁ yat kiñcit jagatyāṁ jagat* । (*ĪśāUp* 1).

When an object is recognized as something else other than what it is, this *nyāya* is used, e.g. rope–snake. It is used in the teaching methodology of Advaita Vedānta to reveal the object as what it is, and there is no more confusion about its identity.

When the Upaniṣad presents the creation, it is called *adhyāropa* (superimposition). However, the objective of the Upaniṣad is not to teach the cosmology (*sṛṣṭi-prakriyā*). The objective, in fact, is to explain the truth of *jagat* that it is *Brahman*.

The intention of the Upaniṣad is to shift our attention from the creation (i.e. the effect) to *Brahman* (i.e. the cause). As the vision is shifted, the effect is dismissed, since it does not exist separate from the cause. This dismissal is called *apavāda* (negation).

However, this shift cannot take place in one stroke. One cannot turn the attention from the grossest effect to the subtlest cause all of a sudden. Hence, the Upaniṣad takes us gradually through stages. This is known as *pañca-kośa-viveka*. The method used here by the Śruti is known as *śākhā-candra-nyāya*, which is pointed out by Śaṅkara in his *Bhāṣya*. One *kośa* has been spoken of as the self of the another only relatively, i.e. without reference to the absolute truth. In reality, all *kośa*s are apparent aspects of the one real Self.

Pañcakośa-Prakriyā: Analysis of the Five Levels of Experience of Oneself in Taittirīyopaniṣad

Pañcakośa-Prakriyā[3] is the analysis of the *pañca-kośa*. In *Taittirīya* we see this *prakriyā*. *Kośa* means a cover, a sheath, *kośa iva kośaḥ*. Five *kośa*s are presented as (though) the covers for *Ātmā*. If *Ātmā* is invariable in all situations, there cannot be any cover for *Ātmā*. So how do the *kośa*s cover? We have to understand that they are seeming covers (*kośavat ācchādakatvāt kośaḥ*). In the error born of self-ignorance, there are five universal erroneous notions. The physical body (*annamaya*) is one *kośa* inasmuch as it is taken to be oneself. I am mortal, tall, short, male, female, thin, fat – all these notions are imputed to *Ātmā* with reference to physical body. This being universal, the physical body becomes a *kośa*. Similarly, when I am hungry or thirsty, *Ātmā* is taken to be subject to hunger and thirst and *prāṇamaya* becomes a *kośa*. The notions that I am happy, sad, anxious are due to *manomaya*. The *vijñānamaya* is also a *kośa*, because of the sense of doership, which is its attribute, is taken to be belonging to *Ātmā* and the notion "I am the doer" is the outcome. *Ānandamaya* is a *kośa*

3 *TaiUp* II.2.5.

with reference to enjoyership. It is to be understood that while the presence of *Ātmā* is there in all the five *kośas*, *Ātmā* itself is, or I am free from all of them.

The methodology of teaching is to unfold *Ātmā,* following *sthūla-arundhati-nyāya*. Brahmānandavallī of *Taittirīyopaniṣad* presents this method by first introducing *annamaya* that is the *sthūla-śarīra* (gross physical body) as *Ātmā*. Then by saying that there is another *Ātmā,* it negates the previous notion. The process continues until the real *Ātmā* as *Brahman* is pointed out as the basis of *ānandamaya*.

It begins with the physical body, *annarasamaya,* which is like a cover, *kośa* (*kośa iva kośa*), because everyone mistakes it for *Ātmā*. It is born out of the essence of the food that is eaten, *annarasa*. The assimilated form of food is *annarasamaya*. The affix *mayaṭ* here means modification, *vikāra*, so *annarasamaya* is a modification of the essence of food.

annāt puruṣaḥ । *sa vā eṣa puruṣo 'nnarasamayaḥ* ।

We generally conclude (before exposure to Advaita Vedānta) that the body is *Ātmā*.

Therefore, Śruti points out that there is another *Ātmā*, which is more interior, subtler. That is *prāṇa*. Śruti then describes the physiological function (*prāṇamaya*).

tasmād-vā etasmād-annarasamayāt । *annyo 'ntara ātmā prāṇa-mayaḥ* । *tenaiṣa pūrṇaḥ* ।

Now when one thinks *prāṇamaya* is *Ātmā*, Śruti leads the person further to another (*anyo 'ntara*) *ātmā manomaya* (*bhoktā*).

tasmād vā etasmāt prāṇamayāt । *anyo 'ntara ātmā mano-mayaḥ*। *tenaiṣa pūrṇaḥ* ।

And from *manomaya* (*bhoktā*) to *vijñānamaya*, the doer (*kartā*);

tasmād-vā etsmān-manomayāt । *anyo 'ntara ātmā vijñāna-mayaḥ* । *tenaiṣa pūrṇaḥ* ।

Then from *vijñānamaya* (*kartā*) to *ānandamaya* (*bhoktā*'s *anubhava-ānanda*).

tasmād-vā etasmād-vijñānamayāt । *anyo 'ntara ātmānandamayaḥ* । *tenaiṣa pūrṇaḥ* ।

Contemplation of Ānandamaya

sa vā eṣā puruṣavidha eva । *tasya puruṣavidhatām* । *anvayaṁ puruṣavidhaḥ* । *tasya priyam-eva śiraḥ* । *modo dakṣiṇaḥ pakṣaḥ* । *pramoda uttaraḥ pakṣaḥ* । *ānanda ātmā* । *brahma pucchaṁ pratiṣṭhā* ।
(this *brahma* = *satyaṁ jñānam anantaṁ brahma*)

Anvaya-vyatireka Prakriyā

In *Taittirīya Upaniṣad*, Bhṛguvallī, Varuṇa advises Bhṛgu to arrive at *Brahman*, by *vicāra*. He says, *annaṁ prāṇaṁ cakṣuś-śrotraṁ mano vācam iti*. Bhṛgu has to understand what are the variables (*vyatireka*), and what is the invariable (*anvaya*). This is *anvaya-vyatireka*, which in fact is *vicāra*. The *vṛtti*s are negated by this method. Since one *vṛtti* negates the previous *vṛtti*; the *vṛtti*s are variable. Whether or not (the variable) *vṛtti*s are there, *anvaya* (the non-variable) is there. There is *anvaya* (non-variable) for *caitanyam*. *Caitanyam* is never gone. That which is invariably present in all the changing *vṛtti*s is indeed *pratyag-ātmā*, and that is *Brahman*. That is the recognition.

One *Vārttikaśloka* says that *tapaḥ* takes the form of *anvaya-vyatireka*. Using that method with *yato vā imāni bhūtāni jāyante*, *anna* becomes *Brahman*.

What about *prāṇa*? There is *anvaya* for *anna*, but *prāṇa* is *vyatireka*. *Prāṇa* is left out, and one has to include *prāṇa*. Since *anna* is *dṛśya* for *prāṇa*, *prāṇa* is *Brahman*.

Then what about *manas*? Since *prāṇa* is *dṛśya* for the mind; *prāṇa* cannot be *Brahman*, because mind is left out. So *bhoktṛ-svarūpa* is *Brahman*.

Then what about *vijñāna*? Since *manas* is *dṛśya* for the *vijñāna*;

manas cannot be *Brahman,* because *vijñāna* (*buddhi*) is left out. So *kartṛ-svarūpa* is *Brahman. Ānandasvarūpa* is *Brahman.* That *Svarūpa-ānanda* is *Brahman.* While none of these *dṛśya – anna, prāṇa, cakṣus* (sense), *śrotra* (sense), *manas, vācam, vijñāna* – is present in the *dṛk,* the *vastu,* i.e. *Nirguṇa-Brahman,* He is *anvita* in all. Bhṛgu comes to understand that *tapas* is *anvaya-vyatireka.*

However, one has to remember that *anvaya-vyatireka* is not *pramāṇa.* It is the *tapas,* the *vicāra. Vicāra* is not *pramāṇa. Vicāra* is meant for understanding the Śruti.

Śṛṣṭi-Prakriyā or Kāraṇa-Kārya-Prakriyā

Another important *prakriyā* is *kāraṇa-kārya-prakriyā. Brahman* is presented in Upaniṣads, especially here in *Taittirīya,* as the cause of everything. Bhṛguvallī states:

> *yato vā imāni bhūtāni jāyante* । *yena jātāni jīvanti* । *yat prayantyabhisaṁviśanti* । *tad vijijñāsasva* । *tad brahmeti* ।[4]
>
> From whom all these have come, having come by whom all these are sustained, to whom all these go back, understand that to be *Brahman.*

Brahman, the cause of the world, is earlier defined as *Satyam* in Brahmānandavallī.[5] The *jagat* presented in *Taittirīya* in the form of five basic elements is the effect (*kārya*) of that *Satyam* (the *kāraṇa*). The *jagat* being a *kārya* is *mithyā* as revealed by the famous *vacārambhaṇa-śruti* in *Chāndogya.*[6] Śruti presents *kārya* as neither *satyam,* that which is real, nor *tuccham,* that which is non-existent, but as *mithyā,* that has a dependent existence. The *jīva*'s physical body, mind and senses are all within the *kārya,* and are therefore *mithyā,* but *jīva* is not created and its *svarūpa* is *Satyaṁ-Jñānam-Anantam,* the infinite consciousness that is the reality of everything.

---

[4] *TaiUp* III.1.

[5] *TaiUp* II.1.

[6] *ChāUp* VI.1.4.

If the product, whether *jagat* or *jīva* is non-separate from the material cause, then the cause and effect are not two separate things. The effect is non-separate from the cause, and the cause being what it is, is independent of the effect. *Chāndogyopaniṣad*, therefore, makes a *pratijñā*,[7] an opening statement that, knowing one thing, everything else is known (as well). This *pratijñā* is established by proving that *kārya* is non-separate from *kāraṇa*, therefore *kārya* is essentially *kāraṇa*. One or more clay pots are but clay. While there can be plurality in *kārya*, there is only one clay from the standpoint of cause. If the elemental *jagat* that includes my body–mind–senses complex is from one non-dual *Brahman*, then the *jagat*, being an effect, is non-separate from one non-dual *Brahman*. *Brahman* is the uncreated *jīva* (you, me, the self) which is *Satyaṁ–Jñānam–Anantam*. The recognition of this fact that I am *Satyaṁ–Jñānam–Anantam Brahman* and this *jagat* is non-separate from me, while I am independent of the *jagat*, is the result of studying *Taittirīya*. Otherwise, it becomes a mere intellectual exercise. Praising such a person *Taittirīya* states, *sa yaścāyaṁ puruṣe, yaścāsāvāditye*[8] (That Being in the sun and this person are the same), because s/he is free from all sense of limitation.

The *kāraṇa-kārya-prakriyā* is used in the *sṛṣṭi-krama* in Brahmānandavallī, *ākāśādi kāryam* is *mithyā; kāraṇam* alone is *satyam*. Because, *kārya* is non-separate from *kāraṇam*. And logically if *kāryam* is *mithyā*, then *kāraṇatvam* for *Brahman* is also *mithyā*. *Kāraṇatvam* for *Brahman* does not exist. In the understanding of *Brahman*, there is neither *kāraṇatvam*, nor *kāryatvam*. Just as in the understanding of clay, there is no pot-ness, and there is no pot, similarly in the appreciation of *Brahman*, all that is there is *caitanyam* (consciousness). *Caitanyam* alone is *Brahman*. For that, *kārya* and *kāraṇatvam* must be *mithyā*.

---

7 *ChāUp* VI.1.3.

8 *TaiUp* II.8 and III.10.

First we say pot is an effect. Then we swallow the effect. Then cause alone is there. All *kārya* is *nāmarūpātmaka* (its all word and its meaning).

To bring about further clarity, if one looks closely, what Śruti says is that *dehādi-kāryam* is *mithyā*. *Kāraṇam* is *satyam*, but *kāraṇatvam* for *Brahman* is *mithyā*. The status of being a cause is *mithyā*. When we say that the pot is *mithyā*, the clay does not become *mithyā* – it is just that there is no *kāraṇatvam* for the clay. In terms of *vivakṣā* – of the intention of Śruti – of the vision of Śruti, the *mantra* that includes *guhānihitatvam* and *praveśa-śruti* are meant for *abheda-jñānam*. Thus, *pratyag-ātmā* is *Brahman*.

Kāraṇa-kārya-prakriyā is used in the Brahmānandavallī in the first to fifth *anuvākas*. This *prakriyā* is meant to point out that *kārya* is not *Ātmā*. The mistake is taking one *kārya* (whether *śarīra*, *prāṇa*, *manaḥ*, *buddhi*) to be the *ātmā*. In fact, *jīva* is *sarvasya kāraṇaṁ caitanyam*, *ekamevādvitīyaṁ brahma*, non-dual *Satyam*, and all *kārya* (whether *śarīra*, *prāṇa*, *manaḥ*, *buddhi*) is *mithyā*. The *śarīra*, *prāṇa*, *manaḥ*, *buddhi* – all are *upādhis* – and are ontologically *mithyā*. The *upahita-caitanyam*, *adhiṣṭhāna-caitanyam* alone is *Satyam*. Wherever *mithyā* is, *caitanya* continues to be there. What was there originally is also there now – *sad eva asti*. That *Satyam* is *pratyag-ātmā*. Therefore, *tat tvam asi*. You are that *Sat* alone. The whole *kāraṇa-kārya-prakriyā* is meant to point out *tat tvam asi*.

Like the (i) *sṛṣṭi-prakriyā* or *kāraṇa-kārya-prakriyā* (in *Taittirīya* and *Chāndogya*), there are other *prakriyās* such as (ii) *avasthā-traya-prakriyā* (in *Māṇḍūkya*), analysis of the three states of experience; and (iii) *pañcakośa-prakriyā* (again *Taittirīya*), analysis of the five levels of one's experience of oneself; and *dṛk-dṛśya-prakriyā*, subject–object analysis to distinguish *ātmā* from *anātmā* and later prove that *anātmā* is not separate from *ātmā*, because it is *mithyā*. The five-elemental model of this universe is a part of the creation or cause–effect *prakriyā*, *sṛṣṭi-prakriyā* or *kāraṇa-kārya-prakriyā*. We find this *sṛṣṭi-prakriyā* in many Upaniṣads.

Glossary of Vedāntic Words

THE definitions of many of the words cited in this glossary are drawn from *Vedāntasāra* of Sadānanda Yogīndra and *Vedānta-Paribhāṣā* of Dharmarāja Adhvarindra. Several secondary sources have also been referred. These include R.K. Mission's *A Dictionary of Advaita Vedānta*; L. Rāmamurty, *Encyclopaedia of Vedānta*; John Grimes, *A Concise Dictionary of Indian Philosophy*; and expositions of Swami Dayananda Saraswati of Arsha Vidya.

A

abādhita	Non-contradicted, unsublated. In the epistemology of Advaita Vedānta, *pramā* (valid knowledge) is that which cannot be contradicted.
abhidhā	Primary meaning, literal meaning – *vācyārtha*.
abhinna-nimitta-upādāna-kāraṇa	The intelligent/efficient and the material cause being the same. Advaita Vedānta posits that the intelligent/efficient and material cause of *jagat* (creation) is the same *vastu*, i.e. *Brahman*. Śruti-Pramāṇa being – *yathorṇanābhiḥ sṛjate gṛhṇate ca* – *MuṇUp* I.1.7. *Svapradhānena nimitta-kāraṇa, upādāna-pradhānena upādāna-kāraṇa*. Viśiṣṭādvaita also accepts this.
abhyāsaḥ	1. Continuous endeavour, practice (lit.). 2. Repetition, from the √*as* = to throw, + *abhi* = towards. One of the six *liṅga*s (characteristics) by which the purport of Vedāntic texts is determined. *upakrama-upasaṁhārau, abhyāsa-apūrvatā-phalam* । *arthavāda-upapatti ca, liṅgaṁ tātparyanirṇaye* ॥ – *Bṛhat Saṁhitā*

See also *ṣaḍliṅga*.

adṛṣṭa — Invisible (lit.), unseen potency, destiny, fate. Also called *apūrva*.

adhikārī — An eligible/qualified person. One of the four *anubandhas* (factors) of *anubandha-catuṣṭaya*. The other three are *viṣaya, prayojanam* and *sambandha*. A Vedānta *adhikārī* has to be *sādhana-catuṣṭaya-sampanna*, should possess (i) *viveka*, (ii) *vairāgya*, (iii) *śamādi-ṣaṭka-sampatti* (*śama, dama, uparati, śraddhā, samādhāna, titikṣā*), and (iv) *mumukṣuttvam*.

adhyāsaḥ — Superimposition. False attribution, wrong supposition. Śaṅkara defines this in his *Adhyāsa-Bhāṣya* as *atasmin tad buddhiḥ*. The superimposition of unreal on real and vice versa is called *adhyāsa*. The real is called *adhiṣṭhāna* in Advaita Vedānta. To explain *adhyāsa*, examples of rope–snake and nacre–silver are used in Advaita Vedānta, e.g. seeing a snake (*adhyāsa*) on the rope (*adhiṣṭhāna*), silver (*adhyāsa*) on mother-of-pearl (*adhiṣṭhāna*), *jagat* (*adhyāsa*) on *Brahman* (*adhiṣṭhāna*). *Adhyāsa* is derived from the root √*as* (to sit, to abide, to remain) with the particle *adhi* (down). Śaṅkara gives another definition in his *Adhyāsa-Bhāṣya* as *smṛtirūpaḥ paratra pūrvadṛṣṭa-avabhāsaḥ* (the apparent presentation, in the form of memory, to consciousness of something previously seen, in some other thing).

[*Note*: It is not a desirable method of teaching, since the example belong to *prātibhāsika* order of reality and *jagat* is a *vyāvahārika* reality (superimposed (*adhyastha*) on *Brahman*, who is the only *satyam* (*pāramārthika*). This methodology creates more confusion than facilitating the understanding. An otherwise intelligent student can be on the spin for years, since the examples are inappropriate. *Satyam–mithyā* model is the best model.]

Advaita — Non-dual, unchanging, absolute, ultimate, *Brahman*, identity of *jīva* with *Brahman*, Truth. The doctrine of Absolute Reality. It is also called Kevala-Advaita-Vāda, the doctrine that *Ātmā* that is *Brahman* is the only Reality. Śaṅkara Bhagavatpāda (CE 788–820) is the propounder of the doctrine of Advaita.

ahaṁkāra — I-ness, ego, one of the four aspects of the *antaḥkaraṇa* – *manas, buddhi, citta* and *ahaṁkāra*. See also *antaḥkaraṇa*.

aikyam — Oneness, identity, unity of the *jīva* with *Brahman*.

ajahad-lakṣaṇā — When the original/primary meaning of a sentence is not adequate to convey a coherent idea, then the implied/secondary meaning is resorted to. In this case, the primary meaning is not totally rejected, but is retained and added to the implied meaning. The entire original meaning is retained in total. In the expression *śoṇo dhāvati* (the red runs), means "the red (horse) runs". The original/primary meaning of "red" is retained and clarified by adding to it the implied meaning, namely "horse". See also *lakṣaṇā*.

ajātavāda/*ajātivāda* — 1. Non-origination, birthless. *Ajāti* is a term employed by the Śūnyavādin Mādhyamika School of Buddhism and Gauḍapāda to mean that nothing is born and nothing dies (though for different reasons). It says that *jagat* (the world), and the *jīva* (individuals) are not there, have not been born and will not die. Nothing is real from an ultimate standpoint.

2. The theory of non-origination. Principle of the unborn, uncreated *Ātmā, jīva*. It is the Advaita Vedānta theory, propounded by Gauḍapāda (around CE 700) which denies any causal change.

ādāvante ca yan-nāsti, vartamāne ca tat-tadā ।
– *MāṇKār* II.6

"That which is non-existent in the beginning, and non-existent in the end, is also non-existent in the middle."

ajñānam Ignorance. *Avidyā, māyā, avyakta, avyākṛta, prakṛti, ākāśa, akṣara.* In Advaita Vedānta, *ajñāna* is beginningless (*anādi*), existent (*bhāva-rūpa*), removable by right knowledge (*jñāna-nivartya*), having its locus in either in *Brahman* or *jīva*, having two powers – concealment (*āvaraṇa*) and projection (*vikṣepa*), of three types of attributes (*triguṇātmikā*), and categorically undefinable (*anirvacanīya*). It is not a negation of existence (not *jñāna-abhāva*), but is opposite to knowledge (*jñāna-virodhi*), *virodhārthe nañ.*

ajñānaṁ tu sad-asadbhyām-anirvacanīyaṁ, triguṇātmakaṁ, jñāna-virodhi, bhāvarūpaṁ yat kiñcit iti। – *VeSā* 34

amūrta Formless, incorporeal, e.g. *Brahman. Ākāśa* and *vāyu* are also treated as *amūrta*, relatively.

anādi Beginningless. According to Advaita Vedānta, six things are *anādi*. They are *Brahman, Īśvara, jīva, avidyā*, the difference between *Īśvara* and *jīva*, and relation between Consciousness and *avidyā*. Whereas *Brahman* that is *jīva* has no end, *avidyā* although *anādi*, has an end.

anirvacanīya *sat-asatbhyām anirvacanīya* – different from *sat* (real, *Brahman*) and *asat* {false, subjective reality, e.g. rope–snake or nacre–silver (but not *alīka/ tuccham* (i.e. non-existent), e.g. *śaśa-śṛṅga* – (horn of a hare)}, categorically indescribable. An ontological definition of *māyā*, ontologically *mithyā*.

ajñānaṁ tu sad-asadbhyām-anirvacanīyaṁ, triguṇātmakaṁ, jñāna-virodhi, bhāvarūpaṁ yat kiñcit iti । – *VeSā* 34

anirvacanīya-khyāti The categorical indefinability of the object. The theory of error in Advaita Vedānta, which holds that the object of error is neither real (*sat*), nor unreal (*asat* – false), nor non-existent (*tuccham*). As the object of error is sublatable, it is not absolute real (*Brahman*). And as the object of error is perceivable, it is not absolutely unreal (*tuccham* like *vandhyā-putra* or *śaśa-śṛṅga*). It cannot be both real and unreal, for that amounts to a violation of the law of contradiction. For perpetual error to take place, two main factors are necessary, there must exist a substratum (*adhiṣṭhāna*) on which the unreal is superimposed and there must be a *doṣa* called ignorance (*avidyā* / *ajñānam*). This ignorance projects the unreal object upon the substratum. One of the *khyāti*s (errors).

antaḥkaraṇa — The internal organ (lit.), the mind. Vidyāraṇya describes two aspects of *antaḥkaraṇa* – *manas* (thinking aspect) and *buddhi* (intellect). Sadānanda, however, describes four aspects of *antaḥkaraṇa* – *manas, buddhi, citta* and *ahaṁkāra*. He does not accept *citta* (memory or awareness) and *ahaṁkāra* ("I" sense) separately and adjusts them with *buddhi* and *manas* – *anayoreva citta-ahaṁkārayor-antarbhāvaḥ* (*VeSā* 13). These four aspects of the mind are accepted in Advaita Vedānta.

The Sāṁkhya School recognizes only the intellect, mind and ego as the aspects of *antaḥkaraṇa*.

Apara-Brahman — *Saguṇa-Brahman, Īśvara, Brahman* with *Māyā-śakti*. See also *Saguṇa-Brahman*.

apūrva — 1. That which did not exist before. Unseen consequence of a *karma* (action). Unseen potency. An imperceptible result produced by a *karma*, which is fruitful in this world, or the other world, which cannot be proved through any other *pramāṇa*s than Śruti. (*pramāṇāntara-aviṣayikaraṇam-apūrvatā* – *VeSā* 187)

2. As per Mīmāṁsā, *apūrva* is the force, which brings about the future effects of a *karma*. See also *adṛṣṭa*.

āropaḥ — Attributing properties of one thing on another, superimposition. *Śāligrame viṣṇuṁ dhyāyet* – meditating Lord Viṣṇu on *śāligrāma* is deliberate *āropa* sanctioned by Śāstra.

artha — 1. Purpose, objective. 2. One of the four objectives of human life, i.e. *dharma, artha, kāma* and *mokṣa*.

asat — 1. That which is contrary to *sat*. *Anṛta–Mithyā*. About which the understanding undergoes a change is *asat* (*yad viṣayā buddhiḥ na vyabhicarati tat sat* । *yad viṣayā buddhiḥ vyabhicarati, tat asat – BGSB* II.16).The objects of the world are *asat* (*vyāvahārika*, ontologically *mithyā*, being *adhiṣṭhāna-ananya*), meaning not non-existent (not *tuccham*) but not independently existent (like *Satyam*) because of their changeability.

2. Note – *asat* is also used in the Śāstra to represent non-existent (*alīka*), e.g. *asann-eva sa bhavati – TaiUp* II.6.

Asatkāryavāda — Theory of non-pre existent effect held by Nyāya-Vaiśeṣika School that posits that the cause is one thing, the effect is another. The effect is held to be non-existent before its production by the cause. Effect comes into being, on destruction of the cause. Also known as Ārambhavāda.

avaccheda — Boundary, limitation.

Avacchedavāda — Name of the School propounded by Vācaspati Miśra, the *bhāmatikāra*. According to this School, *Brahman*, due to *avidyā-upādhi* becomes *jīva*, as the space limited by a pot becomes *ghaṭākāśa* (*ghaṭākāśavad-antaḥkaraṇa-avacchinnaṁ caitayanaṁ jīvaḥ – SiLeSa* I.4.1). In Advaita Vedānta, this term has been used to prove non-duality between *Brahman*, *jīva* and *jagat*.

avidyā — Ignorance, *māyā*, the seed power for creation. What is *māyā* from objective side is *avidyā* from subjective viewpoint, hence Śaṅkara does not differentiate between *māyā* and *avidyā*, and uses the two terms in the same sense (*BSSB* I.4.3). However, later Advaitins find a distinction between the two. Prakāśātma Yati (twelfth century CE) in his *PañVi* says that when there is predominance of obscuring power, it is *māyā* and it predominates. According to Vidyāraṇya (fourteenth century CE), when pure *sattva* dominates, it is *māyā*, while when impure *sattva* dominates, it is *avidyā*.

Avidyā has twofold powers: (i) *āvaraṇa* – obscuring the real, and (ii) *vikṣepa* – projecting the unreal. *Vedāntasāra* 34 defines *ajñāna/avidyā* as a positive entity, which is neither real, nor unreal, undescribable, comprising three *guṇa*s and which is opposed to knowledge (*jñāna-virodhi*).

avyākṛta — Undifferentiated *avidyā*. *Akṣaram-avyākṛtaṁ nāmarūpa-bīja-śakti-rūpam* – *BSSB* I.4.3. Advaita Vedānta takes *avyākṛta* as the *upādāna-kāraṇa* and as the power of *Īśvara* that helps Him in the manifestation of the world. In Sāṁkhya, it is for *pradhāna*, the *mūla-prakṛti*.

The undifferentiated form of the world.

avyakta — Unmanifest. *avidyā*. The subtle, potential state of the differentiated world. *Mahataḥ param-avyaktam avyaktāt puruṣaḥ paraḥ* – *KaUp* I.3.11. In Sāṁkhya, *avyakta* is *mūla-prakṛti* – *vyaktāvyaktajña-vijñānam* – *SāKā* 2.

Ā

ābhāsaḥ — Unreal appearance, reflection.

Ābhāsavāda — The theory that the *jīva* is an appearance of *Brahman*, propounded by Sureśvarācārya. It posits that the *jīva* is a seeming appearance of *Brahman* – the Absolute. It maintains that all manifestations of name and form are unreal appearances because of *avidyā*. An unreal thing appears as real because of *avidyā*. It gives the analogy of the red crystal to explain the theory (in contrast to the analogy of a reflection in a mirror given by Padmapāda in his Bimba-Pratibimbavāda). It maintains that all manifestations of name and form are unreal appearances because of *avidyā*. It is because of *avidyā* that an unreal thing appears as real. It posits that *Brahman* is the locus of *avidyā*.

It must be remembered here that, though Ābhāsavāda, Avacchedavāda and Pratibimbavāda were propounded by Sureśvara, Vācaspati Miśra and Prakaśātma Yati respectively to support the Advaitic tenet, they have their clear base in the philosophy of Śaṅkara. The views of *ābhāsavādin*, *avacchedavādin* and *pratibimbavādin* were also elaborated by post-Śaṅkara *ācārya*s like Amalānanda (*Vedānta-Kalpataru* I.1.40), Vidyāraṇya (*Pañcadaśī*, Kūṭastha Dīpa 27), Appaya Dīkṣita (*SiLeSa*, p. 112, and *Parimala* 1.1.40).

Ābhāsavāda is the creation theory of the Śaiva and Śākta schools, as well as of Kashmiri Śaivism.

ācārya — An honorific title affixed to the names of learned spiritual teachers. From the root √*car* = to go + prefix *ā* = towards; hence to approach:

upanīya tu yaḥ śiṣyaṁ, vedam-adhyāpayed dvijaḥ ।
saṁkalpaṁ sa-rahasyaṁ ca tam-ācāryaṁ pracakṣate ॥
– *MaSm* II.140

A general term for a spiritual teacher; one who instructs the knowledge of *Brahman*.

ācaryavān puruṣo veda । *tasya tāvad evaṁ ciraṁ, yāvat na vimokṣye 'tha saṁpatsya iti* । – *ChāUp* VI.14.2

– Uddālaka-Śvetaketu-Saṁvāda, meaning "A person who has a teacher, knows".

ācinoti hi sāstrārthān-ācāre sthāpayatyapi ।

svayam-ācarate tasmād-ācāryas-tena kathyate ||
– *Āpastamba-Gṛhyasūtra*

The title *ācārya* is affixed to the names of learned persons, e.g. Śaṅkarācārya, Sureśvarācārya, Rāmānujācārya, Madhvācārya, Vallabhācārya, Durgācārya.

āśramaḥ — A stage or order of life. There are four stages (*āśramas*) of life – *brahmacarya, gārhasthya, vānaprastha* and *sannyāsa*. As per Appaya Dīkṣita, the brāhmaṇas, kṣatriyas and vaiśyas are entitled for the four *āśramas* – *brāhmaṇaḥ kṣatriyo vāpi vaiśyo vā pravrajed gṛhāt* | *trayāṇām api varṇānāṁ catvāra āśramaḥ* || – *SiLeSa* 2nd pariccheda. However, some of the scholars are of the opinion that only a brāhmaṇa is eligible for *sannyāsa* – *ucyate brāhmaṇasya eva sannyāso bahudhā śrutaḥ* – *VāSaṁMā* III.12. Śaṅkara opines that *āśrama* is not important for the eligibility of a *brahmajñānī* – *anāśramitvena vartamāno 'pi vidyāyām adhikriyate* – *BSSB* III.4.36.

ādeśa — Lesson. *Eṣa ādeśaḥ eṣa upadeśaḥ* – *TaiUp* I.11 – That (*Brahman*) which can be learnt only from the instructions of the scriptures through the teacher, or by which the teachings about *Brahman* are given. Also *ādeśa ātmā* – *TaiUp* III.3.

ādhāraḥ — Basis, support, that which sustains (not substratum), lends its existence. *Sattā-sphūrti-pradānena.*

ādhibhautika — Of inanimate objects, of elements, physical, extrinsic. One of the three types of afflictions according to Sāṁkhya. *Ādhibhautika-tāpa* means "afflictions caused by extrinsic natural influences inflicted by other individuals, animals, birds and inanimate objects", on whom one does not have immediate control.

mṛga-pakṣī-manuṣyādyaiḥ piśāca-uraga-rākṣasaiḥ |
sarīsṛpādyaiśca nṛṇāṁ jāyate cādhibhautikaḥ ||
– *ViPu* VI.5.7

ādhidaivika — Cosmic, supernatural, divine, relating to deities – *adhideva*. One of the three types of afflictions according to Sāṁkhya. *Ādhidaivika-tāpa* means "cosmic/supernatural afflictions" on which human have no control, e.g. earthquake, tsunami, heavy rains, sunshine, cold storm, etc.

śita-vātoṣṇa-varṣā-aṁbu-vaidyutādi-samudbhavaḥ ।
tāpau dvijavara śreṣṭhai kathyate cādhidaivikaḥ ॥
– *ViPu* VI.5.8

ādhyātmika — Relating to *ātmā*, the self/person/individual. One of the three types of afflictions according to Sāṁkhya. *Ādhyātmika-tāpa* means "afflictions relating to *ātmā*, the self/person/individual". Intrinsic physical or/and mental effects caused in the self, i.e. (strong) desire, anger, fear, conflict, greed, delusion, depression, sadness, jealousy, etc. are the *ādhyātmika* afflictions (could include indisposition of the body also, i.e. fever, etc. that result in the mind not being available for studies).

kāma-krodha-bhaya-dveṣa-lobha-moha-viṣādajaḥ ।
śoka-asūyā-avamāna-īrṣā-mātsaryādi-mayas-tathā ॥

mānaso 'pi dvija-śreṣṭha tāpo bhavati naikadhā ।
iti evam-ādibhir-bhedais-tāpohi-ādhyātmiko mataḥ ॥
– *ViPu* VI.5.5 and 6

ākāśa — Space. Also used for *Brahman* – *akāśas-talliṅgāt* – *BrSū* I.1.22; *ākāśo vai nāmarūpayor-nirvāhita te yadantara tad brahma* – *ChāUp* III.14.1. Also used for *avidyā* or *māyā* – *avidyātmikā hi bījaśaktir-avyakta-śabda-nirdeśyāt idam-avyākṛta, kvacid-ākāśa-śabda-nirdiṣṭam* – *BSSB* I.4.3.

ānandaḥ — Highest pleasure, spiritual delight – *rasaṁ hyevāyaṁ labdhvānandī bhavati* – *TaiUp* II.7. Further, *Taittirīya Upaniṣad* III.1 identifies *ānanda* with the essential nature of *Brahman*. Also means *Brahman* – *vijñānam-ānandaṁ brahma* – *BṛUp* III.9.28. Absolute happiness.

Ātmā — The Self, the *jīva*. In the vision of Advaita Vedānta, *Ātmā* is identical (non-separate from) with *Brahman* – 1. *ayamātmā brahma* – *MāṇUp*. 2. *tad brahma, sa ātmā* – *TaiUp* I.5.1.

āvaraṇa — Veiling, obscuring, concealing, one of the two powers of *ajñāna* – *āvaraṇa* and *vikṣepa* – *asya-ajñānasya āvaraṇa vikṣepa-nāmakam asti śaktidvayam* – *VeSā* 14.

Ī

Īśvara — Lord, Almighty, *Saguṇa-Brahman*. The Lord, the Creator and Ruler who is non-different from the Creation. He is *sarvajña, sarvaśaktimān* and *sarvavyāpī, abhinna-nimitta-upādāna-kāraṇa* of this *jagat*. Upaniṣads present Him as *yato vā imāni bhūtāni jāyante* – *TaiUp* III.1. In Advaita Vedānta *Brahman* with the adjunct *māyā* is known as *Īśvara*: *māyā-avacchinna-caitanya.*

Sāṁkhya as well as Mīmāṁsā do not accept *Īśvara*. Sāṁkhya posits *pradhāna* (inert) as the creator of *jagat*. Mīmāṁsā considers the Vedic *mantra*s to be potent enough to give the result of *karma*, without any intervention of a third party – *Īśvara*, whom Vedānta considers as *karmaphaladātā*.

U

upādāna-kāraṇam — Material cause. In the vision of Advaita Vedānta, *Brahman* is the efficient cause (*nimitta-kāraṇa*) as well as the material cause (*upādāna-kāraṇa*) of this *jagat*. Hence, He is also known as *abhinna-nimitta–upādāna-kāraṇa* | *yathorṇānabhi sṛjate gṛhṇate ca* – *MuṇUp* I.1.7

upādhi — Adjunct, limitation, condition. Any kind of adjunct, limitation, condition, frame or composition. When it is said – *māyā* is with *Brahman* – then *māyā* is *upādhi*. If we say *jīva* is with *Brahman*, then *jīva* is *upādhi*, with reference to the *śarīra* (body).

Buddhi is *upādhi, Caityanam* is *upahita.*

Nirupādhika Brahman means *Brahman* without *upādhi. Sopādhika Brahman* means *Brahman* with *māyā upādhi.* (*Brahman* and *māyā* are not parallel realities. *Māyā* is *brahmāśritā.*)

upakrama — Beginning, commencement. *Prakaraṇa-pratipādyasya arthasya tad-ādyantayor-upapādanam-upakrama-upasaṁhārau'* – *VeSā* 185.

Upaniṣad/ Upaniṣat — Knowledge regarding the Reality of *Brahman*, *brahma-vidyā. Vedanto nāma-upaniṣat-pramāṇam* – *VeSā* 3; *upaniṣadaṁ bho vruhi-iti, uktā ta upaniṣad brāhmī vāva ta upaniṣadam-abruma-iti* – *KeUp* IV.7. Secret knowledge, mystical knowledge.

The meaning of the word *upa-ni-ṣad* is explained elaborately by Ācārya Śaṅkara in his *Saṁbandha-Bhāṣyam* on *Kaṭhopaniṣad*. He defines the word *upa-ni-ṣad* on his introduction to this commentary as "leading to acquisition of the knowledge of *Brahman*". The word *upa-ni-ṣad* is derived from the root √*ṣadḷ* of first conjugation (*bhvādigaṇa*) as well as sixth conjugation (*tudādigaṇa*) in the text *Dhātupāṭha*. The meaning of the root √*ṣadḷ* however is same in both the places as – *viśaraṇa-gati-avasādaneṣu*. There are two prefixes *upa* and *ni*, before the root. *Viśaraṇa* means destruction, here destruction of ignorance (*avidyā*), the root cause of *saṁsāra*. *Avasāna* means putting an end to *avidyā-kāma-karma*.

The above two meanings are in the negative sense. The positive meaning is denoted by the word *gati*, meaning the knowledge it takes one to *Brahman*. Hence, the meaning is that knowledge which takes one to *Brahman*. The *kvip* affix, which is a zero affix, is added after the root, bringing in the meaning of the agent. Śaṅkara points out that the secondary sense of Upaniṣad is the text, the primary meaning being knowledge.

	Usually in Upaniṣad it is written: *ya evaṁ veda, iti upaniṣat* – *TaiUp* II.9, III.10; *MahUp* XXII.2
uparati	Ceasing, stopping, refraining from worldly duties. Formal renunciation of the prescribed duties. *Tad-vyatirikta-viṣayebhyaḥ uparamaṇam uparatiḥ* – *VeSā* 4.
upasaṁhāra	Conclusion. One of the six *liṅgas* in ascertaining the purport of the Śruti.
upodghāta	Introduction, Preface, e.g., *Śāṅkarabhāṣya-Upodghāta, Sāyaṇabhāṣya-Upodghāta.*

Ṛ

ṛtam — 1. Truth in general, righteousness, the Cosmic order, proper, right, fit, suitable, honest, law, rule (esp. in religion).

Ṛtam in *Ṛgveda* generally meant the order in the universe. *Yajurveda* gives that principle a practical form, the one that could be applied in the everyday world of people. It says, in heavens *ṛtam* could very well be the cosmic order, but on earth *ṛtam* means the social, ethical, religious and such other laws that govern him.

ṛtaṁ dakṣiṇaḥ pakṣaḥ । *satyam-uttaraḥ pakṣaḥ* ।
– *TaiUp* II.4

2. *Karmaphalam* is also known as *ṛtam* since all *karmas* have results (*avaśyambhāvitvāt*) – *ṛtaṁ pibantau sukṛtasya loke, guhāṁ praviṣṭau parame parārdhe* ।
– *KaUp* I.3.1

E

ekarasaḥ	Undifferentiated, *Paramātmā.*
Ekātmavāda	The theory of one Self. It is an Advaitic concept. According to this theory, there is only one *Ātmā*, which is real and all-pervading, and everything else is unreal, *mithyā.*

(Sāṁkhya subscribes to *aneka* (many) *ātmā* and still accepts Veda as *pramāṇa*).

ekatvam Non-duality. Oneness.

yasmin sarvāṇi bhūtāni-ātmā-eva-abhūd-vijānataḥ ।
tatra ko mohaḥ kaḥ śoka, ekatvam anupaśyataḥ ।
– *ĪśaUp* 7

O

oṁ The sacred sound symbol of *Para-Brahman* as well as *Apara-Brahman*. Also known as *Praṇava, Udgītha, Sphoṭa*. The linguistic aspect of *Oṁkāra* has been unfolded by Bhartṛhari, Bhartṛmitra and Patañjali, who explain its timelessness and being *sphoṭa*, it is the root of the meaning.

Ka

karma Any action, where there is a free will involved and which creates *adṛṣṭa* – *pāpa* or *puṇya* (not *calanātmakam karma* – since a train carriage also moves). Action, consequence of action. In Hindu philosophy, *karma* is the law of retributive action, which brings back the individual, in this or a future life, pleasant or unpleasant situations for acts (*puṇya* or *pāpa*) committed.

Kiṁ karma kimakarmeti kavayo 'pyatra mohitāḥ – *BhGi* IV.16. There are three types of *karma* – *prārabdha, sañcita* and *kriyamāṇa*. *Prārabdha karmas* are those that have already started fructifying. *Sañcita karmas* are kept in the account of the *jīva* and have not fructified. *Kriyamāṇa karmas* are those that have currently begun and will determine the future birth of the *jīva*. After *brahmajñāna*, the *sañcita* and *kriyamāṇa karmas* are nullified, however *prārabdha karmas* continue to manifest even in the life of a *jñānī*.

karma (types as per Śaṅkara)	Śaṅkara divided *karma* into four kinds: (i) *utpatti/utpādyam* – origination of a thing, (ii) *āpti/āpyam* – the attainment of a place/state (e.g. going to a village), (iii) *saṁskāra/saṁskṛtam* – purification (e.g. cleaning a copper vessel), and (iv) *vikāra/vikāryam* – modification of a thing (e.g. milk becoming curd). In the vision of Advaita, liberation can never be accomplished by *karma* – *nāsti akṛtaḥ kṛtena* – *MuṇUp* I.1.6. *Brahman na āpyaṁ, sarvagatatvāt; sarvātmatvat brahma na āpyam.*
karma (types as per Veda)	Ritual/s. In the *karma-kāṇḍa* portion of the Veda, various kinds of rituals are enumerated, (i) *vidhi* – injuncted rituals, e.g. Agnihotra, *svādhyāyo 'dhyetavyaḥ* – (one should study one's own *śākhā* of the Veda); (ii) *pratiṣiddha* – prohibited actions, e.g. *brāhmaṇo na hantavyaḥ, kalañjaṁ na bhakṣayet, surāṁ na peyā;* (iii) *kāmyakarma* is an optional rite, which is performed to fulfil any particular desire, e.g. *svargakāma yajeta*, Putrakāmeṣṭi, Kāriri, Somayāga, Vājapeya, Rājasūya, Aśvamedha; (iv) *nityakarma* – daily/regular obligatory rites, e.g. Agnihotra, Darśapūrṇamāsa; (v) *naimittika-karma* – occasional rites as and when due are also obligatory rites, e.g. *jātyeṣṭi, vivāha, antyeṣṭi;* and (vi) *prāyaścitta-karma* – rites for atonement of a wrong action, e.g. Cāndrāyaṇa.
Kāryakāraṇavāda or Vivartavāda	The theory of cause and effect or the theory of causation. According to Advaitic theory of causation, *Brahman* is the efficient cause and *māyā* is the material cause of this *jagat*, which is the effect. *Svapradhānatayā nimittaṁ sva-upādhi-pradhānatayā-upādānaṁ ca bhavati* – *VeSā* 9. This Advaitic theory of causation is also called Vivartavāda or the theory of manifestation.

kūṭastha Immutable, unchangeable, *kūṭavat tiṣṭhati iti kūṭastha,* i.e. *Brahman. Kūṭasthokṣara ucyate – BhGi* XV.16.

Kha

khyāti Theory of error, the doctrine of erroneous knowledge.

There are mainly three types of theory of error in Indian philosophy:

1. *Sat-khyāti* – Theories where the object of error is real. Under this are: *Anyathā-khyāti* (of Nyāya), *Ātmakhyāti* (of Vijñānavādin Yogācāra Buddhists), *Akhyāti* (Sāṁkhya and Prābhākara-Mīmāṁsā schools), *Viparīta-khyāti* (Bhāṭṭa-Mīmāṁsā School) and *Satkhyāti* (Viśiṣṭādvaita of Rāmānuja).

2. *Asat-khyāti* – Theories where the object of error is unreal. Under this are *Asatkhyāti* (of Śūnyavādin Mādhyamika Buddhists) and *Abhinava-anyathā-khyāti* (Dvaita of Madhva).

3. *Anirvacanīya-khyāti* – Theory where the object of error is neither real nor unreal (of Advaita Vedanta).

Ga

guṇa 1. Attribute, quality, particular modification, adjective.

2. Sāṁkhya and Yoga philosophies accept three types of *guṇas* – *sattva, raja*s and *tama*s.

3. Nyāya-Vaiśeṣika philosophy admits the *guṇa* as one of the seven *padārthas* – *dravya-guṇa-karma-sāmānya-viśeṣa-samavāya-abhāvaḥ sapta-padārthaḥ* | Again as per them, the number of *guṇa* is twenty four – *rūpa, rasa, gandha, sparśa, saṁkhyā, parimāṇa, pṛthaktva, saṁyoga, vibhāga, paratva, aparatva, buddhi, sukha, duḥkha, icchā, dveṣa, prayatna, gurutva, dravatva, sneha, saṁskāra, adṛṣṭa-dharma, adharma*

and *śabda*. (Few of these 24 are mentioned in *Bhagavadgītā* XIII.7) Kaṇāda, the author of *Vaiśeṣika-Sūtra*, indicates the first seventeen (*VaiSū* I.1.6) only; however, Praśastapāda (third-fourth century CE) mentions all the twenty-four *guṇas*.

4. One of the four meanings (*jāti, guṇa, kriyā, sambandha*) that a word can convey as per Patañjali *MaBh* I.8.

Ca

caitanyam — Consciousness, the essence of all beings. As per Advaita Vedānta, there are three types of *caitanya* – (i) *jīvacaitanya*, (ii) *sākṣīcaitanya* or *kūṭasthacaitanya*, and (iii) *tūriyācaitanya*. *Jīvacaitanya* is the experience, *sākṣīcaitanya* or *kūṭasthacaitanya* is the witness (*sākṣī*) and *tūriyācaitanya* is *Brahman*.

cetā — The *jīva*, the knower of the body, the *kṣetrajña*. *Sākṣī ceta kevalo nirguṇaśca* । – *ŚvUp* VI.11.

cetanā — Consciousnes. *Bhūtānam asmi cetanā* । – *BhGi* X.22.

cit — Consciousness. Śaṅkara deems *Sat* and *Satyam*, as well as *Cit* and *Jñānam* as equivalents.

cittam — *anusandhānātmikā-antaḥkaraṇa-vṛttiś-cittam*. One of the four aspects of *antaḥkaraṇaḥ*, i.e. – *manas* (mind), *buddhi*, *cittam*, and *ahaṁkāra*. See *antaḥkaraṇaḥ*.

mano-buddhyahaṁkāra-cittāni nāhaṁ,
na ca śrotra-jihve na ca ghrāṇa-netre । – *Nirvāṇaṣaṭkam*

2. *Cittam* includes the conscious, subconscious and unconscious, thus comprises known and unknown memory. – Swāmi Dayānanda Saraswati.

Cha

chandas — 1. The Vedas. 2. Discipline of prosody and metres. One of the six Vedāṅgas – Śikṣā, Kalpa, Vyākaraṇa, Nirukta, Chandas and Jyotiṣam. There are many metres used in *Ṛgveda*, list of which is given in *ṚV* X.130.4-5.

Ja

jagat — The empirical world. In Advaita Vedānta, *jagat* is visible in the shape of name and form – *vācārambhaṇaṁ vikāro nāmadheyam* – *ChāUp* VI.1.4-6, VI.4.1, VI.4.3, VI.4.4. Based on this, Śaṅkara has presented *jagat* as *mithyā* – *brahma satyaṁ jagat mithyā jīvo brahmaiva nāparaḥ*. Śaṅkara however attributes a *vyāvahārika* reality to this *jagat*. Ontologically *jagat* is *vyāvahārika mithyā* (*adhiṣṭhāna-ananyat* – not independently existent without *Satyam*).

jahad-ajahad-lakṣaṇā — A kind of secondary implication, in which part of the primary/original meaning of a word is given up, and a part is retained. In an identity statement – *so 'yaṁ devadattaḥ*, meaning "This is that Devadatta", the word "this" means Devadatta of present time and place, and "that" means Devadatta of past time and place. In this type of a sentence, the qualification of "present time and place" and "past time and place" is relinquished, and the person that is "Devadatta" is retained. This method is used by Advaita Vedāntins to explain the meaning of *mahāvākyas*, wherein the root meaning is retained (*ajahad*) and the apparent meaning is given up (*jahad*).

jahad-lakṣaṇā — *Jahāti* means to drop/abandon from the root √(o) *hāk* = *tyāge* (*juhotyādigaṇa*, third conjugation). *Jahad-lakṣaṇā* is where a word loses its primary meaning, but is used in some way connected to the completely given up (*jahad*) meaning; and the implied meaning is accepted which is "related" to the primary meaning. In the phrase *gaṅgāyāṁ ghoṣaḥ* (the hamlet on River Gaṅgā), the primary meaning of the word "River Gaṅgā" is given up, and the "bank" that is "related" to the "River Gaṅgā" is implied and accepted.

jīva — The individual Self that transmigrates until the identity with *Brahman* is known, when further transmigration ceases. – *VeSā* 73

Appaya Dīkṣita refers to two theories regarding *jiva* – Ekajīvavāda and Anekajīvavāda (*SiLeSaṁ* I.123). Ekajīvavāda is a theory in Advaita that posits that there is but one *jīva* and one material body. This one *jīva* (Hiraṇyagarbha) is a reflection of *Brahman* and all other individuals are mere semblances of individuals, and to these semblances belong bondage and liberation.

Jīvanmukti — Freedom in present life while living.
To know oneself as non-different from *Brahman* is *jīvanmukti*.

Jīvanmukti and *videhamukti* are two states of *mukti* that are not contradictory at all. A *jīvanmukta* continues his life, even after *brahmajñāna*, because of his *prārabdha karma*, after exhaustion of which, at the fall of the body, he attains *videhamukti*. *Jīvanmukti* is a concept in Advaita Vedānta, not accepted by others, i.e. the Vaiṣṇava Vedānta – Viśiṣṭādvaita, Dvaita, etc.

puram-ekādaśa-dvāram ajasyāvaktra-cetasaḥ ।
anuṣṭhāya na śocati, vimuktaśca vimucyate ॥
– *KaUp* II.2.1

and

yadā sarve pramucyante kāmā ye 'sya hṛdi śritāḥ ।
atha martyo 'mṛto bhavati, atra brahma samśnute ॥
– *KaUp* II.3.14

tathā puruṣa-prayatna-sādhya-vedānta-śravaṇādi-janita-samādhinā jīvanmuktyādilābho bhavati – *MukUp* II.1

are *pramāṇa vākyas* for the concept of *jīvanmukti* in Advaita.

jñānam — Knowledge (lit.) – *jñānaṁ jñeya parijñātā* – *BhGī* XVIII.18.

Also means Consciousness, one of the *lakṣaṇa* (indications) of *Brahman – satyaṁ-jñānam-anantaṁ brahma – TaiUp* II.1.

As per *Bṛhadāraṇyaka Upaniṣad* (II.4.5 and IV.5.6). *śravaṇa, manana, nididhyāsana* – listening (to Upaniṣads through a competent teacher), reflection, and deep and continuous contemplation on the Vedānta texts are the means to liberation. Therefore, the word *jñānam* is equated with the means to liberation.

Śaṅkara deems *Sat* and *Satyam* as well as *Cit* and *Jñānam* as equivalents.

jñeya The object of knowledge. *Brahman.*

jñeyaṁ yat tat pravakṣyāmi yaj jñātvā 'mṛtam aśnute ।
anādimat paraṁ brahma na sat tan nā 'sad ucyate ॥
– *BhGī* XIII.12

jyoti The Light. In Advaita Vedānta, *jyoti* although means light, however symbolizes *Brahman. Jyotiṣām api tad jyotis-tamasaḥ param-ucyate* । – *BhGī* XIII.17

Ta

taṭastha-lakṣaṇa Incidental attribute of *Brahman. Brahman* from the standpoint of *jagat* is the creator, sustainer and dissolver of *jagat*. This is presented in *Taittirīya Upaniṣad* III.1 as – *yato vā imāni bhūtāni jāyante, yena jātāni jīvanti, yat prayantyabhisaṁviśanti* (*TaiUp* III.1) "out of which everything has come, by which everything is sustained, unto which everything goes back". Also *yathorṇnābhiḥ sṛjate gṛhṇate ca – MuṇUp* I.1.7. Also *yatha sudiptāt pāvakād visphuliṅgāḥ – MuṇUp* II.1.1.

However, from its own standpoint there is no *jagat*. If we use the *anvaya vyatireka* method, we can say, *jagat* is, *Brahman* is, *jagat* is not, *Brahman* is. Hence, *Brahman* as the creator of *jagat* is its *taṭastha-lakṣaṇa*. *Taṭastha-lakṣaṇa* does not reveal the *svarūpa*. It is with reference to the *upādhi* only. Here *Brahman* is defined by attributes, which are extrinsic, rather than intrinsic to its essential nature.

Since *svarūpa-lakṣaṇa* of *Brahman* does not explain the existence of this overwhelming *jagat*, therefore *taṭasta-lakṣaṇa*. Also see *svarūpa-lakṣaṇa*.

tapas — Any spiritual penance. Religious austerity. In Advaita Vedānta *jñānam eva tapaḥ* (knowledge alone is the penance.)

tattva — Truth, fact, reality, essence. Knowledge of Reality.

Trayī — Threefold knowledge. The three Vedas – *Ṛgveda, Yajurveda* and *Sāmaveda* are Vedatrayī. The *trayī vidyā* is especially concerned with the Vedic rituals, which are conducted by the Hotā, Adhvaryu and Udgātā by employing selections from *Ṛgveda, Yajurveda* and *Sāmaveda* respectively.

Atharvaveda is considered to be of later origin. *Atharvaveda* has no *mantras* that can be used in a Vedic ritual.

Following are the Śruti-Pramāṇa for three Vedas only:

(i) *prajāpatirlokān-abhyatapat-tebhyo-abhitaptebhyas-trayī vidyā saṁprāsravattām-abhyatapat-tasyā abhitaptāyā etanyakṣarāṇi saṁprāsravanta bhūr-bhuvaḥ-svar-iti.* – *ChāUp* II.23.2

(ii) *tasmād-ṛcaḥ sāma yajūṁṣi* । – *MuṇUp* II.1.6

(iii) *trayo vedā eta eva vāg-evargve-ṛgvedo mano yajurvedaḥ prāṇaḥ sāmavedaḥ* ॥ – *BṛUp* I.5.5

(iv) *vedyaṁ pavitram oṁ-kāra ṛk-sāma-yajur-eva ca* । – *BhGi* IX.17

Maybe, by the time of Jaimini, *Atharvaveda* had not manifested. – Swami Dayananda Saraswati

However, the four Vedas find a place in an early Upaniṣad, i.e *Bṛhadāraṇyaka Upaniṣad* in

Yājñavalkya–Maitreyī-Saṁvāda).

(i) *yasya mahato bhūtasya niḥśvasitam etad-yad-ṛgvedo-yajurvedaḥ-sāmavedo 'thrvāṅgirasa* । – *BṛUp* II.4.10

Taittirīya also refers to four Vedas in Brahmānandavallī.

(ii) *tasya yajureva śiraḥ* । *ṛg dakṣiṇaḥ pakṣaḥ* ।
sāmottaraḥ pakṣaḥ । *ādeśa ātmā* ।
atharvāṅgirasaḥ puccham pratiṣṭhā । – *TaiUp* II.3

triguṇa — Consisting of three qualities – *sattva, rajas* and *tamas*. In Sāṁkhya, *pradhāna* consists of these three qualities. Śaṅkara has accepted/adapted this explanation/model in Advaita Vedānta, where *pradhāna* is known as *māyā*.

tripuṭī — The triad of *jñātā*, *jñānam* and *jñeyam*.
Jñātṛ-jñāna-jñeyarūpā tripuṭī pralaye hi no ॥ – *Pañ* XI.14

tuccham — In Advaita Vedānta it means non-existent. Examples of *tuccham* is very well presented by Śaṅkara in his *Taittirīya-Upaniṣad-Bhāṣyam*:

mṛgatṛṣṇāmbhasi snātaḥ, khapuṣpakṛta-śekharaḥ ।
eṣo-vandhyāputro yāti, śaśaśṛṅga-dhanurdharaḥ ॥

Look at this son of a barren-woman walking, who has bathed in the mirage-water, his hair adorned with sky-flower, holding a bow made out of rabbit-horn.

According to Advaita Vedanta, *māyā* is real to the ordinary individual, neither real nor unreal, i.e. *anirvacanīya* to the philosopher and *tuccham* (unreal) to the enlightened individual.

Da

duḥkham — Pain, afflictions, obstacles that come up in spiritual pursuit. Three types of afflictions are recognized in Sāṁkhya philosophy. See also *ādhidaivika*, *ādhibhautika* and *ādhyātmika*.

Pa

Pariṇāmavāda — Theory of transformation. It posits that the effect exists in a latent state in the cause, prior to its manifestation, and that the cause is continually transforming itself into its effects. This theory has two sub-schools: (i) Brahma-Pariṇāmavāda, held by Viśiṣṭādvaita School, according to which, *jagat* is a transformation of the Absolute (*Brahman*). (ii) Prakṛti-Pariṇāmavāda, held by Sāṁkhya and Śaiva Siddhānta schools, according to which, *jagat* is a transformation of primordial Nature (*prakṛti*).

Pratibimbavāda — Reflection Theory. It postulates that the individual (*jīva*) is an appearance of the Absolute (*Brahman*). The reflection is real as it is not distinct from *Brahman*, and it is due to *avidyā/ajñāna* that the reflection seems different from its disc (*bimba*). This theory is propounded by the Vivaraṇa School of Advaita Vedānta. Padmapāda gives an analogy of a reflection in a mirror in contrast to the analogy of the red-crystal that is given in Ābhāsavāda of Sureśvara.

Va

Vivartavāda — The theory of apparent change (not intrinsic change) or the theory of phenomenal appearance. The Advaita Vedānta theory of causation posits that *jagat* is an appearance superimposed by ignorance (*avidyā*) on the Absolute (*Brahman*). The definition of *vivarta* is *sva-svarūpa aparityāgena rupāntara āpattiḥ vivartta iti* ।

La

lakṣaṇā — Implied meaning of a word or sentence. When a primary meaning of a word does not fit in with the context, the word must be interpreted in a secondary sense. This is classified in two ways: (i) *kevala-lakṣaṇā* (bare implication), and (ii) *lakṣita-lakṣaṇā* (implication by the implied). Bare implication stands in direct relation to the expressed sense as in the expression, "the hamlet on the Gaṅgā". For the word *gaṅgā*, there is bare implication of the bank, which is in direct relation to Gaṅgā. Implied implication has no direct relation to the expressed sense, as in the example *māṇavakaḥ siṁhaḥ* (the boy is a lion); the *gauṇī* type of implied implication refers to his strength.

A second classification of *lakṣaṇā* (implication) is divided into three types: (i) *jahad-lakṣaṇā*, (ii) *ajahad-lakṣaṇā*, and (iii) *jahad–ajahad-lakṣaṇā*.

(i) *Jahad-lakṣaṇā* is where the original meaning is given up and a new meaning is acquired. A meaning is implied (other than the sense primarily implied) which is related to the primary meaning, while the primary meaning is totally rejected. In the phrase *gaṅgāyāṁ ghoṣah* (the hamlet on river Gaṅgā), the primary meaning of the word river Gaṅgā is rejected, and the bank which is related to it is implied.

(ii) *Ajahad-lakṣaṇā* cognizes another sense even while including the expressed sense. The entire original meaning is retained in total. In the expression *śoṇo dhāvati* (the red runs) means the red horse runs. The entire original meaning of "red" is retained, and the implied meaning "horse" is added to it.

(iii) *Jahad–ajahad-lakṣaṇā* preserves a part of the original meaning, and rejects the rest. In the phrase *so 'yaṁ devadattaḥ* (this is that Devadatta), "this" and "that" as they relate to Devadatta (the substance) are accepted, as they relate to time and place, they are relinquished.

Note: There are three essential conditions necessary in a *lakṣaṇā*: (i) in the context, the primary meaning must be inapplicable; (ii) there must exist some relation between the primary and actual referent of the word; and (iii) either popular usage must sanction the implied sense, or else there must be a definite motive justifying the transfer of meaning.

Ṣa

ṣaḍliṅga/ tātparyaliṅga — Six means used to determine the purport of the Veda, these include:

(i) *upakrama-upasaṁhārau* (the unity of the commencement and conclusion),

(ii) *abhyāsa* (repetition of them),

(iii) *apūrvatā* (uniqueness),

(iv) *phalam* (result, utility),

(v) *arthavāda* (eulogy, praise, commendation), and

(vi) *upapatti* (argument, intelligibility in the light of reasoning, explanation, evidence, illustration).

upakrama-upasaṁhārau, abhyāsa-apūrvatā-phalam ।
arthavāda-upapatti ca, liṅgaṁ tātparyanirṇaye ॥

This definition of *ṣaḍliṅga* is mentioned in *Bṛhat Saṁhitā*.

Sa

Saguṇa-Brahman — The Lord: the Creator and Ruler, who is non-different from the Creation. He is *sarvajña*, *sarvaśaktimān* and *sarvavyāpī*, *abhinna-nimitta-upādāna-kāraṇa* of this *jagat*. This is presented in *Taittirīya Upaniṣad* III.1 as – *yato vā imāni bhūtāni jāyante, yena jātāni jīvanti, yat prayantyabhisaṁviśanti* "out of which everything has come, by which everything is sustained, unto which everything goes back". In Advaita Vedānta *Brahman* with the adjunct *māyā* is known as *Īśvara* – *māyā-avacchinna-caitanya*.

Sāṁkhya as well as Mīmāṁsā do not accept *Īśvara*.

Satkāraṇavāda The theory that cause (*kāraṇa*) alone is real (*sat*) and is ever existent (*nityam*), and the effect (*kārya*) is unreal (*asat*). Strictly speaking, the Advaita Vedānta theory of causation should be called in this name.

Satkāryavāda This theory is held by Sāṁkhya School, which holds that this *jagat* is an effect of the Absolute. The theory of causation that, the effect exists prior to its manifestation in a latent state in the cause. According to this theory, the causal operation makes patent the latent effect. It is also called Pariṇāmavāda.

Svarūpa-lakṣaṇa Essential/intrinsic definition. *Satyaṁ jñānam anantaṁ brahman* (*Tai.Up.* II.1) is the *svarūpa-lakṣaṇa* of *Brahman* meaning "*Brahman* is Existence, Consciousness and Infinity".

In the *svarūpa-lakṣaṇa* one gets to know *Brahman* as neither the cause, nor the effect. It is presented in few other Upaniṣads also:

yat-tad-adreśyam-agrāhyam-agotram-avarṇam-acakṣuḥ-śrotraṁ tad-apāṇipādaṁ । *nityaṁ vibhuṁ sarvagataṁ susūkṣmaṁ tad-avyayaṁ yad-bhūtayoniṁ paripaśyanti dhīrāḥ* ॥ — *Mun.Up.* I.1.6

aśabdam-asparśam-arūpam-avyayaṁ, tathā 'rasaṁ nityam-agandhavac ca yat । *anādi-anantaṁ mahataḥ paraṁ dhruvaṁ, nicāyya tat mṛtyumukhāt pramucyate* ॥
— *Ka.Up.* I.3.15

Appendix A

List of 108 Upaniṣads

Ṛgveda (10)

1.	*Aitareya Upaniṣad*	Major Upaniṣad
2.	*Akṣamālikā Upaniṣad*	Śaiva Upaniṣad
3.	*Ātmabodha Upaniṣad*	Sāmānya Vedānta Upaniṣad
4.	*Bahvṛcā Upaniṣad*	Śākta Upaniṣad
5.	*Kauṣītaki-Brāhmaṇa Upaniṣad*	Sāmānya Vedānta Upaniṣad
6.	*Mudgala Upaniṣad*	Sāmānya Vedānta Upaniṣad
7.	*Nādabindu Upaniṣad*	Yoga Upaniṣad
8.	*Nirvāṇa Upaniṣad*	Sannyāsa Upaniṣad
9.	*Saubhāgya(lakṣmī) Upaniṣad*	Śākta Upaniṣad
10.	*Tripurā Upaniṣad*	Śākta Upaniṣad

Śukla-Yajurveda (19)

11.	*Adhyātma Upaniṣad*	Sāmānya Vedānta Upaniṣad
12.	*Advaya-Tāraka Upaniṣad*	Yoga Upaniṣad
13.	*Bhikṣuka Upaniṣad*	Sannyāsa Upaniṣad
14.	*Bṛhadāraṇyaka Upaniṣad*	Major Upaniṣad
15.	*Haṁsa Upaniṣad*	Yoga Upaniṣad
16.	*Īśāvāsya Upaniṣad*	Major Upaniṣad

17. *Jābāla Upaniṣad*[1]	Sannyāsa Upaniṣad
18. *Maṇḍala-Brāhmaṇa Upaniṣad*	Yoga Upaniṣad
19. *Mantrikā Upaniṣad*	Sāmānya Vedānta Upaniṣad
20. *Muktikā Upaniṣad*	Sāmānya Vedānta Upaniṣad
21. *Nirālamba Upaniṣad*	Sāmānya Vedānta Upaniṣad
22. *Paiṅgala Upaniṣad*	Sāmānya Vedānta Upaniṣad
23. *Paramahaṁsa Upaniṣad*	Sannyāsa Upaniṣad
24. *Śāṭyāyanīya Upaniṣad*	Sannyāsa Upaniṣad
25. *Subāla Upaniṣad*	Sāmānya Vedānta Upaniṣad
26. *Tārasāra Upaniṣad*	Vaiṣṇava Upaniṣad
27. *Triśikhi-Brāhmaṇa Upaniṣad*	Yoga Upaniṣad
28. *Turyātītāvadhūta Upaniṣad*	Sannyāsa Upaniṣad
29. *Yājñavalkya Upaniṣad*	Sannyāsa Upaniṣad

Kṛṣṇa-Yajurveda (32)

30. *Akṣi Upaniṣad*	Sāmānya Vedānta Upaniṣad
31. *Amṛtabindu Upaniṣad*	Yoga Upaniṣad
32. *Amṛtanāda Upaniṣad*	Yoga Upaniṣad
33. *Avadhūta Upaniṣad*	Sannyāsa Upaniṣad
34. *Brahmavidyā Upaniṣad*	Yoga Upaniṣad
35. *Brahma Upaniṣad*	Sannyāsa Upaniṣad
36. *Dakṣiṇāmūrti Upaniṣad*	Śaiva Upaniṣad
37. *Dhyānabindu Upaniṣad*	Yoga Upaniṣad
38. *Ekākṣara Upaniṣad*	Sāmānya Vedānta Upaniṣad
39. *Garbha Upaniṣad*	Sāmānya Vedānta Upaniṣad
40. *Kaivalya Upaniṣad*	Śaiva Upaniṣad
41. *Kālāgni-Rudra Upaniṣad*	Śaiva Upaniṣad

[1] Not to be confused with *Jābāli Upaniṣad* of *Sāmaveda*.

42. *Kalisanataraṇa Upaniṣad*	Vaiṣṇava Upaniṣad
43. *Kaṭha Upaniṣad*	Major Upaniṣad
44. *Kaṭharudra Upaniṣad*	Sannyāsa Upaniṣad
45. *Kṣurikā Upaniṣad*	Yoga Upaniṣad
46. *Nārāyaṇa/Yājñikī Upaniṣad*[2]	Vaiṣṇava Upaniṣad
47. *Pañcabrahma Upaniṣad*	Śaiva Upaniṣad
48. *Prāṇāgnihotra Upaniṣad*	Sāmānya Vedānta Upaniṣad
49. *Rudra-hṛdaya Upaniṣad*	Śaiva Upaniṣad
50. *Sarasvatī-rahasya Upaniṣad*	Śākta Upaniṣad
51. *Śārīraka Upaniṣad*	Sāmānya Vedānta Upaniṣad
52. *Sarvasāra Upaniṣad*	Sāmānya Vedānta Upaniṣad
53. *Skanda Upaniṣad*	Sāmānya Vedānta Upaniṣad
54. *Śukarahasya Upaniṣad*	Sāmānya Vedānta Upaniṣad
55. *Śvetāśvatara Upaniṣad*	Śaiva Upaniṣad
56. *Taittirīya Upaniṣad*	Major Upaniṣad
57. *Tejobindu Upaniṣad*	Yoga Upaniṣad
58. *Varāha Upaniṣad*	Yoga Upaniṣad
59. *Yoga-kuṇḍali Upaniṣad*	Yoga Upaniṣad
60. *Yogaśikhā Upaniṣad*	Yoga Upaniṣad
61. *Yogatattva Upaniṣad*	Yoga Upaniṣad

Sāmaveda (16)

62. *Avyakta Upaniṣad*	Vaiṣṇava Upaniṣad
63. *Āruṇi Upaniṣad*	Sannyāsa Upaniṣad
64. *Chāndogya Upaniṣad*	Major Upaniṣad
65. *Darśana Upaniṣad*	Yoga Upaniṣad

[2] Popularly known as *Mahā-Nārāyaṇa Upaniṣad*. It is the tenth and concluding chapter (prapāṭhaka) of *Taittirīya Āraṇyaka* of *Kṛṣṇa-Yajurveda*. It comes immediately after *Taittirīya Upaniṣad*.

66. *Jābāli Upaniṣad*[3]	Śaiva Upaniṣad
67. *Kena Upaniṣad*	Major Upaniṣad
68. *Kuṇḍikā Upaniṣad*	Sannyāsa Upaniṣad
69. *Mahā Upaniṣad*	Sāmānya Vedānta Upaniṣad
70. *Maitrāyaṇī Upaniṣad*	Sāmānya Vedānta Upaniṣad
71. *Maitreya Upaniṣad*	Sannyāsa Upaniṣad
72. *Rudrākṣa Jābāla Upaniṣad*	Śaiva Upaniṣad
73. *Sannyāsa Upaniṣad*	Sannyāsa Upaniṣad
74. *Sāvitrī Upaniṣad*	Sāmānya Vedānta Upaniṣad
75. *Vajrasūcikā Upaniṣad*	Sāmānya Vedānta Upaniṣad
76. *Vāsudeva Upaniṣad*	Vaiṣṇava Upaniṣad
77. *Yoga-cūḍāmaṇi Upaniṣad*	Yoga Upaniṣad

Atharvaveda (31)

78. *Annapūrṇā Upaniṣad*	Sāmānya Vedānta Upaniṣad
79. *Atharvaśikhā Upaniṣad*	Śaiva Upaniṣad
80. *Atharvaśīrṣa Upaniṣad*[4]	Śaiva Upaniṣad
81. *Ātmā Upaniṣad*	Sāmānya Vedānta Upaniṣad
82. *Bhasma-Jābāla Upaniṣad*	Śaiva Upaniṣad
83. *Bhāvanā Upaniṣad*	Śākta Upaniṣad
84. *Bṛhad-Jābāla Upaniṣad*	Śaiva Upaniṣad
85. *Dattātreya Upaniṣad*	Vaiṣṇava Upaniṣad
86. *Devī Upaniṣad*	Śākta Upaniṣad
87. *Gaṇapati Upaniṣad*[5]	Śaiva Upaniṣad
88. *Gāruḍa Upaniṣad*	Vaiṣṇava Upaniṣad

---

[3] Not to be confused with *Jābāla Upaniṣad* of *Śukla-Yajurveda*.

[4] Not to be confused with the popular *Gaṇapati-Atharvaśirṣa Upaniṣad*. The content is totally different.

[5] This is popularly known as *Gaṇapati-Atharvaśirṣa Upaniṣad*.

89.	*Gopāla-tāpanī Upaniṣad* (Pūrva and Uttara)	Vaiṣṇava Upaniṣad
90.	*Hayagrīva Upaniṣad*	Vaiṣṇava Upaniṣad
91.	*Kṛṣṇa Upaniṣad*	Vaiṣṇava Upaniṣad
92.	*Tripādvibhūti-Mahānārāyaṇa Upaniṣad*[6]	Vaiṣṇava Upaniṣad
93.	*Mahāvākya Upaniṣad*	Yoga Upaniṣad
94.	*Māṇḍūkya Upaniṣad*	Major Upaniṣad
95.	*Muṇḍaka Upaniṣad*	Major Upaniṣad
96.	*Nārada-Parivrājaka Upaniṣad*	Sannyāsa Upaniṣad
97.	*Nṛsiṁha-Tāpanī Upaniṣad* (Pūrva and Uttara)	Vaiṣṇava Upaniṣad
98.	*Parabrahma Upaniṣad*	Sannyāsa Upaniṣad
99.	*Paramahaṁsa-Parivrājaka Upaniṣad*	Sannyāsa Upaniṣad
100.	*Pāśupatabrahma Upaniṣad*	Yoga Upaniṣad
101.	*Praśna Upaniṣad*	Major Upaniṣad
102.	*Rāma-rahasya Upaniṣad*	Vaiṣṇava Upaniṣad
103.	*Rāma-tāpanī Upaniṣad* (Pūrva and Uttara)	Vaiṣṇava Upaniṣad
104.	*Śāṇḍilya Upaniṣad*	Yoga Upaniṣad
105.	*Śarabha Upaniṣad*	Śaiva Upaniṣad
106.	*Sītā Upaniṣad*	Śākta Upaniṣad
107.	*Sūrya Upaniṣad*	Sāmānya Vedānta Upaniṣad
108.	*Tripurā-tāpanī Upaniṣad*	Śākta Upaniṣad

[6] Not to be confused with (*Mahā*) *Nārāyaṇa Upaniṣad* of *Taittirīya Āraṇyaka* of *Kṛṣṇa-Yajurveda*.

Appendix B

षद्लृँ विशरणगत्यवसादनेषु

In धातुपाठ, a book of roots authored by पाणिनि, there is a root "षद्लृ" in the sense of to destroy (विशरण), to go (गति), to put to an end (अवसाद).

षद्	लृँ is defined as an indicatory letter by 1.3.2 उपदेशेऽजनुनासिक इत्।
	The indicatory letter is elided by 1.3.9 तस्य लोपः।
सद्	ष् at the beginning of धातु is substituted by स् by 6.1.64 धात्वादेः षः सः।
उप + नि + सद्	In front of the root, two verbal prefixes, *upa* and *ni* are added.
उप + नि + सद् + क्विँप्	To the root, a suffix *kvip* is enjoined by 3.2.61 सत्सूद्विषद्रुहदुहयुजविदभिदच्छिद-जिनीराजामुपसर्गेऽपि क्विप्।
	By 3.1.93 कृदतिङ्।, *kvip* is defined as a कृत् type of suffix.
	The meaning of the suffix is "the agent" of the action indicated by the root. This is understood by 3.4.67 कर्तरि कृत् ।
उप + नि + सद	प् is defined as an indicatory letter by 1.3.3 हलन्त्यम्।

	क् is defined as an indicatory letter by 1.3.8 लशक्वतद्धिते।
	इँ is defined as an indicatory letter by 1.3.2 उपदेशेऽजनुनासिक इत्।
	The indicatory letters are elided by 1.3.9 तस्य लोपः।
	The remaining व् is also elided by 6.1.67 वेरपृक्तस्य।
उप + नि + षद्	The स् of the root is substituted by a cerebral sound, ष् by 8.3.66 सदिरप्रतेः।
उपनिषद्	Being the one which ends with a कृत् suffix, उपनिषद् is a nominal base by 1.2.46 कृत्तद्धितसमासाश्च।

Workout of Upaniṣad

ṣad	*l̥m̐* is defined as an indicatory letter by 1.3.2 *upadeśe 'janunāsika it* । The indicatory letter is elided by 1.3.9 *tasya lopaḥ* ।
sad	*ṣ* at the beginning of *dhātu* is substituted by *s* by 6.1.64 *dhātvādeḥ ṣaḥ ṣaḥ* ।
upa + ni + sad	In front of the root, two verbal prefixes, *upa* and *ni* are added.
upa + ni + sad + kvim̐p	To the root, a suffix *kvip* is enjoined by 3.2.61 *satsūdviṣadruhaduhayujavidabhidacchidajinīrājāmupasarge 'pi kvip* । By 3.1.93 *kr̥datiṅ* ।, *kvip* is defined as a *kr̥t* type of suffix. The meaning of the suffix is "the agent" of the action indicated by the root. This is understood by 3.4.67 *kartari kr̥t* ।
upa + ni + sad	*p* is defined as an indicatory letter by 1.3.3 *halantyam* । *k* is defined as an indicatory letter by 1.3.8 *laśakvataddhite* । *im̐* is defined as an indicatory letter by 1.3.2 *upadeśe 'ijanunāsika it* ।

	The indicatory letters are elided by 1.3.9 *tasya lopaḥ* ।
	The remaining *v* is also elided by 6.1.67 *verapr̥ktasya* ।
upa + ni + ṣad	The *s* of the root is substituted by a cerebral sound, *ṣ* by 8.3.66 *sadirapratेḥ* ।
upaniṣad	Being the one which ends with a *kr̥t* suffix, *upaniṣad* is a nominal base by 1.2.46 *kr̥ttaddhitasamāsāśca* ।

Bibliography

Primary Sources

Aṣṭādhyāyī, ed. Gopala Sastri, Varanasi: Chaukhamba Surabharati Prakasana, 1997.

Aṣṭādhyāyī-Sūtrapāṭha, ed. Medha Michika, Anaikatti: Arsha Vidya Gurukulam, 2014.

Arthasaṁgraha of *Śrī Laugākṣi Bhāskara with Kaumudī Vyākhyā*, ed. Sri Tatambari Svami, Varanasi: Chowkhamba Sanskrit Series Office, 1979.

Arthasaṁgrahah, ed. Narayanaram Acarya, Varanasi: Krishnadas Academy, repr., 1999.

Bhagavadgītā with Commentary of Śaṅkarācārya, tr. Swāmī Gambhirānanda, Calcutta: Advaita Ashrama, 1984.

Brahmasūtra-Bhāṣya of Śrī Śaṅkarācārya, tr. Swāmī Gambhirānanda, Calcutta: Advaita Ashrama, 1977.

Brahmasūtra-Śāṅkara-Bhāṣya (with the Commentary, *Bhāṣya-Ratnaprabhā* of Govindānanda, *Bhāmatī* of Vācaspati Mishra and *Nyāya-Nirṇaya* of Ānanda Giri), ed. Jagadish L. Śāstrī, Delhi: Motilal Banarsidass, 1980.

Brahmasūtram-Catussūtrī with Śāṅkara-Bhāṣya, Ratnaprabhā of Govindānanda, *Ṭippaṇī* of Swāmī Viṣṇudevānanda Giri, ed. Swāmī Vidyānanda Giri, Rishikesh: Sri Kailash Vidya Prakasanam, 1996.

Chāndogya Upaniṣad with Commentary of Śaṅkarācārya, tr. Swāmī Gambhirānanda, Calcutta: Advaita Ashrama, 1984.

Complete Works of Śrī Śaṅkarācārya, Chennai: Samata Books, 1999.

Daśa-Śāntayaḥ, Swāmī Maheśānanda Giri, Varanasi: Mahesh Research Institute, 1982.

Dhātukośaḥ, Medha Michika, Anaikatti: Arsha Vidya Gurukulam, 2014.

Dhātupāṭhaḥ, ed. J.L. Shastri, Delhi: Motilal Banarsidass, 1984.

Eight Upaniṣads with the Commentary of Śaṅkarācārya, vols. I-II, tr. Swāmī Gambhirānanda, Kolkata: Advaita Ashrama, sixth impression, 1977.

Manusmṛti, Surendranath Saxena, Delhi: Manoj Publications, 2000.

Mīmāṁsā-Sūtras of Jaimini, Mohanlal Sandal, Delhi: Motilal Banarsidass, 1st edn., 1993, repr., 1999.

Pāṇinīyaśikṣā, Commentary by Shivaraja Acharya Kaundinnyayana, Varanasi: Chaukhamba Vidyabhavan, 1998.

Pañcadaśī of Śrī Vidyāraṇya Swāmi, tr. Swāmī Swāhānanda, Madras: Sri Ramakrishna Math, 1st edn., 1967, repr. 2001.

Patañjali-Yoga-Darśana with Simple Hindi translation, Harikrishnadas Goyandka, Gorakhpur: Gita Press.

Sāṁkhya-Kārikā with Gauḍapāda-bhāṣya, ed. and tr. Jagannath Sastri, Varanasi: Motilal Banarsidass, 5th edn., 1982, repr. Delhi, 2003.

Taittirīyopaniṣad with commentary of Śaṅkara, sub-commentary of Ānandagiri and *Ṭippaṇī* of Viṣṇudevānanda Giri, ed. Umeshananda Shastri and Svarnalal Tuli, Rishikesh: Kailash Ashram, 2nd edn., 1999.

Taittirīyopaniṣad, tr. Swāmi Sarvānanda, Madras: Sri Ramakrishna Math, 6th edn., 1995.

Tarka-Saṁgraha, Sesharaj Sharma, Varanasi: Chaukhamba Surbharati Prakashan, repr., 2000.

The Taittirīya Upaniṣad with the Commentaries of Śrī Śaṅkarācārya, Śrī Sureśvarācārya and Śrī Vidyāraṇya, tr. Alladi Mahadeva Sastri, Chennai: Samata Books, 2007.

The Taittirīya Upaniṣad with the Commentary of Śaṅkarācārya, tr. Swāmī Gambhirānanda, Calcutta: Advaita Ashrama, 3rd edn., 1995.

Upadeśasāhasrī of Śaṅkarācārya, tr. Swāmī Jagadānanda, Madras: Sri Ramakrishna Math, 13th edn., 2006.

Upaniṣads in Śaṅkara's Own Words, vols. I-II, tr. Panoli V., Calicut: Mathrubhumi Printing & Publishing, vol. I (1st edn.), 1991, vol. II (rev. 2nd edn.) 1996.

Vaiyāsika-Nyāyamāla of Śrī Bhārati Tīrtha Muni, ed. Swāmī Vidyānanda Giri, Rishikesh: Kailash Ashram, 2000.

Vanamālā: A Commentary on Taittirīya Upaniṣad Bhāṣya, Śrī Acyutakṛṣṇānanda Tīrtha, Madras: Chinmaya Foundation of Education & Culture, 1981.

Vyākaraṇa-Mahābhāṣyam-Paspaśāhnikam, ed. Jayasankaralal Tripathy, Varanasi: Krishnadas Academy, 1989.

Works of Śaṅkarācārya (vol. I): *Ten Principal Upaniṣads with Śaṅkarācārya*, Delhi: Motilal Banarsidass, 1978.

Works of Śaṅkarācārya (vol. II): *Bhagavadgītā with Śāṅkarabhāṣya*, Delhi: Motilal Banarsidass, 1978.

Yoga-Darśana, Gorakhpur: Gita Press.

Secondary Sources

Avasthi, Vinay Kumar, 2002, *Upaniṣad: Ek Rahasya*, Lucknow: Lucknow Kitabghar.

Balasubramaniam, R., 1976, *Advaita Vedānta*, Madras: Centre for Advanced Study in Philosophy, University of Madras.

Basham, A.L. (ed.), 2003, *The Wonder that Was India*, New Delhi: Rupa & Co., 3rd rev. edn.

Bhargav, Dayananda, 2003, *Tarkasaṁgraha*, repr., Delhi: Motilal Banarsidass, 1st edn., 1971.

Buhler, Georg, Sacred Books of the East, vol. 25: *The Laws of Manu*, Delhi: Motilal Banarsidass.

Commans, Michael, 2000, *The Method of Early Advaita Vedānta*, Delhi: Motilal Banarsidass, 1st edn.

Cowel, E.B. and A.E. Gough (trs.), 2007, *Sarva-Darśana-Saṅgraha* (*or Review of the Different Systems of the Hindu Philosophy*) *of Mādhvācārya*, repr. Delhi: Motilal Banarsidass, 1st Indian edn., 1996.

Deussen, Paul, 1906, *The Philosophy of Upaniṣads* (*die Phlosophic der Upaniṣads*), 1899 in German, tr. A.S. Geden, Delhi: Motilal Banarsidass.

Deussen, Paul, 2010, *Sixty Upanisads of the Veda*, vols. I-II, tr. V.M. Bedekar and G.B. Palsule, Delhi: Motilal Banarsidass, repr.

Grimes, John, 1990, *Seven Great Untenables* (*Saptavidha Anupapatti*), Delhi: Motilal Banarsidass, 1st edn.

Hirakawa Akira, Paul Groner (tr.), 2007, *A History of Indian Buddhism*, Delhi: Motilal Banarsidass, repr.

Jacob, G.A. (ed.), 1971, *Concordance to the Principal Upaniṣads and Bhagavadgītā*, Delhi: Motilal Banarsidass, repr.

Kalupahana, David J., 2006, *Mūlamadhyamaka-Kārikā of Nāgārjuna*, Delhi: Motilal Banarsidass, repr.

Keith, A.B., 2007, *Religion and Philosophy of the Veda and Upaniṣads*, Delhi: Motilal Banarsidass, repr.

Keith, A.B. (tr.) 1967, *The Veda of Black Yajus School* (*English Translation of Taittirīya Saṁhitā*), Delhi: Motilal Banarsidass, repr.

Macdonald, A .A., 1994, *Bṛhaddevatā* (*Attributed to Śaunaka*), Delhi: Motilalal Banarsidass, repr.

Macdonald, A.A., 2006, *A Vedic Reader for Students*, repr. Delhi: Motilal Banarsidass, first published in England, 1917.

Mādhavānanda, Swāmi, 1997, *Vedānta-Paribhāṣā* (*of Dharmarāja Adhvarīndra*), Calcutta: Advaita Ashrama, 7th edn.

Mādhavānanda, Swāmi, 2006, *Mīmāṁsā Paribhāṣā*, Kolkata: Advaita Ashrama, fifth impression.

Max Müller, F., 2006, *India: What Can It Teach Us*, New Delhi: Vishv Books, reprint.

Max Müller, F., 1879, Sacred Books of the East, vol. 1: *The Upanishads — Part I*, Oxford: Oxford University Press; Delhi: Motilal Banarsidass.

Max Müller, F., 1884, Sacred Books of the East, vol. 1: *The Upanishads — Part II*, Oxford: Oxford University Press; Delhi: Motilal Banarsidass.

Menon, Y. Keshava, 1989, *The Mind of Shankaracharya*, Bombay: Jaico Publishing House, third impression.

Nayak, Gauranga Charan, 1995, *Bhāratīya Darśana*, Bhubaneswar: Orissa State Bureau of Text Books.

Nikhilānanda, Swami, 1978, *Ātmabodha*: *Self-Knowledge of Śrī Śaṅkarācārya*, Madras: Śri Ramakrishna Math.

Nikhilānanda, Swāmi, 1995, *Dṛg-Dṛśya-Viveka*, Calcutta: Advaita Ashram, seventh impression.

Nikhilānanda, Swāmi, 1997, *Vedāntasāra*, Calcutta: Advaita Ashram, tenth impression.

Oldenberg, Hermann, 1997, *The Doctrine of The Upanisads and the Early Buddhism*, tr. Shridhar B. Shrotri, repr. Delhi: Motilal Banarsidass, 1st edn. 1991.

Prabhavānanda, Swāmi, 2011, *Patanjali Yoga Sutras*, Chennai: Sri Ramakrishna Math.

Prajnānānanda, Swāmi, 1973, *Schools of Indian Philosophical Thought*, Calcutta: Firma K.L. Mukhopadhyaya.

Radhakrishnan, R. Balasubramaniam (ed. & tr.), 1984, *The Taittirīyopaniṣad-Bhāṣya-Vārttikā of Sureśvara*, Madras: Institute for Advanced Study in Philosophy, University of Madras (2nd rev. edn.).

Rajadhyaksha, N.D., 1986, *The Six Systems of Indian Philosophy*, New Delhi: Bharatiya Book Corporation.

Rambachan, Anantanand, 1991, *Accomplishing the Accomplished: The Vedas as a Source of Valid Knowledge in Śaṅkara*, Monographs of the Society for Asian and Comparative Philosophy, no. 10, Honolulu: University of Hawaii Press.

Rambachan, Anantanand, 1994, *The Limits of Scripture: Vivekananda's Reinterpretation of the Vedas*, Honolulu: University of Hawaii Press.

Saraswatī, Ātmaprajñānanda Swāminī, 2008, *Daśaśānti*, Bhubaneswar: Arsha Vidya Vikas Kendra.

Saraswatī, Ātmaprajñānanda Swāminī, 2008, *Rūpasiddhi*, Bhubaneswar: Arsha Vidya Vikas Kendra.

Saraswatī, Ātmaprajñānanda Swāminī, 2012, *Nomenclature of the Vedas*, New Delhi: D.K. Printworld.

Saraswatī, Ātmaprajñānanda Swāminī, 2013, *Ṛṣikās of the Ṛgveda*, New Delhi: D.K. Printworld.

Saraswatī, Ātmaprajñānanda Swāminī, 2014, *Oṁ: The Sound Symbol*, Delhi: Munshiram Manoharlal.

Saraswatī, Dayānanda Swāmī, 1997, *Vivekacūḍāmaṇi, Talks on 108 Selected Verses*, Rishikesh: Sri Gangadharesvar Trust.

Saraswatī, Dayānanda Swāmī, 2008, *Kenopanishad*, Chennai: Arsha Vidya Centre Research Publication Trust, 1st edn.

Saraswatī, Dayānanda Swāmī, 2011, *Bhagavadgita Home Study Course*, 4th edn., Chennai: Arsha Vidya Research and Publication Trust.

Saraswatī, Dayānanda Swāmī, 2011, *Mundakopanishad — I and II*, Chennai: Arsha Vidya Centre Research and Publication Trust.

Saraswatī, Dayānanda Swāmī, *Taittiriyopanishad*, Transcription of Talks.

Shastri, Jagannath, 2003, *Sāṁkhya-Kārikā*, Varanasi: Motilal Banarsidass, 5th edn., 1982, repr.

Shastri, S. Subramanya, 1997, *Prakaraṇa Aṣṭakam*, Varanasi: Mahesh Research Institute.

Singh, Jaidev, 1968, *Introduction to Madhyamaka Philosophy*, Varanasi: Bharatiya Vidya Prakashan, 1st edn.

Swahananda, Swami, 1996, *Chandogya Upanishad*, Chennai: Sri Ramakrishna Math, eighth impression.

Swarup, Lakshman, 2002, The *Nighaṇṭu & the Nirukta, The Oldest Indian Treatise on Etymology, Philology and Semantics*, repr., Delhi: Motilal Banarsidass, 1st Indian edn., 1920-27.

Tachikawa Musashi, 1997, *An Introduction to the Philosophy of Nagarjuna*, Delhi: Motilal Banarsidass, 1st edn.

Telang, K.T., 1882, Sacred Books of the East, vol. 8: *The Bhagavadgita*, Delhi: Motilal Banarsidass.

Thibaut, G., 1896, Sacred Books of the East, vol. 34: *The Vedanta Sutras*, Part I, Delhi: Motilal Banarsidass.

Thibaut, G., 1896, Sacred Books of the East, vol. 38: *The Vedanta Sutras*, Part II, Delhi: Motilal Banarsidass.

Thibaut, G., 1904, Sacred Books of the East, vol. 48: *The Vedanta Sutras*, Part III, Delhi: Motilal Banarsidass.

Thrasher, Allen Wright, 1993, *The Advaita Vedānta of Brahmasiddhi*, Delhi: Motilal Banarsidass, 1st edn.

Venkatachalam V., 2003, *Śaṅkarācārya: The Ship of Enlightenment*, repr., New Delhi: Sahitya Akademi, 1st edn., 1997.

Vimuktānanda, Swāmi, 2001, *Aparokṣa Anubhūti*, Kolkata: Advaita Ashrama, eleventh impresion.

Virupākshānanda, Swāmi, 1994, *Tarka-Sangraha with the Dipika of Annambhatta and Notes*, Madras: Sri Ramakrishna Math.

Virupākshānanda, Swāmi, 1995, *Sāṁkhyakārikā of Īśvara Kṛṣṇa with*

Tattvakaumudī of Śrī Vācaspati Miśra, Chennai: Sri Ramakrishna Math, 1st edn.

Winternitz, Maurice, 1991, *History of Indian Literature*, Delhi: Munshiram Manoharlal.

Dictionaries and Encyclopaedias

Bartley, Christopher, *Indian Philosophy A-Z*, New Age Books.

Bloomfield, Maurice, *A Vedic Concordance*.

Chakraborty, Nirod Baran, 2003 *A Dictionary of Advaita Vedanta*, Kolkata: The Ramakrishna Mission Institute of Culture, 3rd print 2010.

Grimes, John, 1996, *A Concise Dictionary of Indian Philosophy*, Albany: State University of New York Press.

Harṣānanda, Swāmi, 1995, *A Dictionary of Advaita Vedānta*, Madras: Ramakrishna Math.

Murty, Ram, *Encyclopaedia of Vedānta*.

Potter, Karl H., 1998, *Encyclopedia of Indian Philosophies*, vol. III: *Advaita Vedanta up to Saṁkara and His Pupils*, Delhi: Motilal Banarsidass, repr.

Yogakanti Swami, 2007, *Sanskrit Glossary Terms*, Munger: Yoga Publications Trust.

Index